Relationships Among
Asian American Women

PSYCHOLOGY OF WOMEN
BOOK SERIES

CHERYL BROWN TRAVIS, Series Editor

Bringing Cultural Diversity to Feminist Psychology: Theory, Research, and Practice, Hope Landrine, Editor

The New Civil War: The Psychology, Culture, and Politics of Abortion, Linda J. Beckman and S. Marie Harvey, Editors

Shaping the Future of Feminist Psychology: Education, Research, and Practice, Judith Worell and Norine G. Johnson, Editors

Sexuality, Society, and Feminism, Cheryl Brown Travis and Jacquelyn W. White, Editors

Relationships Among Asian American Women, Jean Lau Chin, Editor

Relationships Among Asian American Women

Edited by Jean Lau Chin

American Psychological Association
Washington, DC

Published by
American Psychological Association
750 First Street, NE
Washington, DC 20002

Copies may be ordered from
APA Order Department
P.O. Box 92984
Washington, DC 20090-2984

In the U.K., Europe, Africa, and the Middle East, copies may be ordered from
American Psychological Association
3 Henrietta Street
Covent Garden, London
WC2E 8LU England

Typeset in Goudy by EPS Group Inc., Easton, MD

Printer: Hamilton Printing, New York, NY
Cover Designer: NiDesign, Baltimore, MD
Technical/Production Editor: Eleanor Inskip

The opinions and statements published are the responsibility of the authors, and such opinions and statements do not necessarily represent the policies of the APA.

Library of Congress Cataloging-in-Publication Data
Relationships among Asian American women / edited by Jean Lau Chin.
        p. cm.—(Psychology of women)
     Includes bibliographical references and index.
     ISBN 1-55798-680-0
     1. Asian American women—Psychology.   2. Asian American women—Social conditions.   3. Asian American women—Family relationships.   4. Interpersonal relations—United States.   I. Chin, Jean Lau.   II. Psychology of women book series.

E184.O6 R454 2000
305.48'895073—dc21

                                                                         00-027411

British Library Cataloguing-in-Publication Data
A CIP record is available from the British Library.

Printed in the United States of America
First Edition

CONTENTS

CONTRIBUTORS

Alice F. Chang, PhD, private practice, Tucson, Arizona

Christine M. Chao, PhD, private practice, Denver, Colorado

Jean Lau Chin, EdD, CEO Service, Newton, MA

Kunya Des Jardins, PhD, private practice, Somerville, MA

Diane C. Fujino, PhD, assistant professor, University of California, Santa Barbara

Carolee GiaoUyenTran, PhD, private practice, Davis, CA

Divya Kakaiya, PhD, private practice, San Diego, California

Hyoun K. Kim, doctoral candidate, Ohio State University, Columbus

S. Cathy Louie, PhD, private practice, San Diego, CA

Kem B. Louie, RN, PhD, professor, College of Mount St. Vincent, New York

Donna K. Nagata, PhD, associate professor, University of Michigan, Ann Arbor

Felicisima C. Serafica, PhD, associate professor, Ohio State University, Columbus

Liang Tien, PhD, private practice, Seattle, Washington

Reiko Homma True, PhD, assistant professor, University of California, San Francisco

Alice Weng, doctoral candidate, Ohio State University, Columbus

FOREWORD

I am very excited that a book dedicated to the subject of Asian American women is being published. I applaud the editor, Jean Lau Chin, EdD, for her effort in gathering together an excellent team of contributors to speak on behalf of Asian American women and share their rich and diverse experiences.

The women's movement in the United States has encouraged the accumulation of significant knowledge and literature about American women in general. However, most of that literature and knowledge is based on the experiences of White American women. Although some attention is beginning to be focused on women of color, discussion of the experiences of Asian American women, if included at all, has been cursory at best. Asian American women have too long been ignored as an insignificant minority; yet, their stories are diverse and meaningful.

The popular images among the general American public are the old-world Asian stereotypes of the Asian American woman as meek and subservient or as an exploited sex object as portrayed in such stories as *The World of Suzie Wong* and *Miss Saigon*. However, Asian American women are not a homogeneous racial ethnic group at all; they represent more than 34 different ethnic groups. Some Asian American women are leaders in diverse professions, some are struggling in urban ghettos as refugees, and some are living in isolated rural communities as so-called "war brides." Some are fourth- and fifth-generation Americans, whereas others are more recent immigrants or refugees, often struggling with multiple day-to-day survival needs.

I am pleased that this book attempts to discuss the diverse experiences of Asian American women and their multiple social, familial, and interpersonal relationships. As a woman who emigrated from Japan 40 years ago, I have experienced many of the struggles discussed in the book; some were truly enriching, but others were devastating, including racial and sexual discrimination. I also had the good fortune to meet many Asian American women who forged their own paths through adversity. Meanwhile, there are others who are not so fortunate who are struggling in difficult circumstances. This book attempts to portray a sense of this diversity.

This book is useful not only for women's studies scholars, social scientists, and human services practitioners, but also for the general public. It will broaden their understanding of Asian American women. It provides a rich picture of the diversity of the Asian American women's ethnic and cultural roots and experiences. In addition, it should be a source for Asian American women themselves to better understand their own diversity, to enrich their experiences, and to become personally and socially empowered.

I

DIVERSITY: VOICES OF ASIAN AMERICAN WOMEN

Little has been written or researched on Asian American women. We are left with the stereotypes that influence how we view, objectify, and disempower Asian American women. This book grew out of the work of the Asian American Women Task Force of the Society for the Psychology of Women (Division 35) of the American Psychological Association. The gap in writing and research on the psychological issues involved in the formation of relationships among Asian American women fueled the enthusiasm for this work. We felt that the psychological and feminist literature needed to include different voices.

Much of the work on Asian American women has come from sociology, ethnic studies, and Asian American studies; but few have addressed feminist theory and the issues unique to Asian American women. As we grappled with the issues of power and connections, inclusiveness, and equality, all common to a feminist perspective, many felt that the existing views of women did not include the experiences of Asian American women. The diversity of experiences and the different voices of the Asian American women have not been heard before.

We were not interested in the typical approach of recounting the history of Asian Americans. Rather it was our desire to view these histories as contexts for how the experiences influenced the formation of relationships. Significant to this process was the emphasis on resiliency, as opposed to risk factors, models that are empowering for women. Therefore, the book looks at how Asian American women have been successful in adapting, and authentic in maintaining their identities. This authenticity comes about by dint of an interactive dualism between multiple individuals and cultural identities across generations. They serve to bond groups and families together.

Also we emphasized using a different lens for viewing the psychological issues of Asian American women. The need to narrow one's lens to bring into focus different issues was viewed as essential to a feminist process that acknowledges and values diversity and difference. The voices of Asian American need to be heard if we are to transform feminist theory to be truly inclusive. We need to be heard in different ways and our diverse modes of transmission are reflected in the writing of this book. Some *talk story* to communicate concepts without rich empirical studies, others use anecdotal accounts, and others use empirical data; all enrich each another as valid methods for capturing the different voices of Asian American women.

Finally, the book speaks to the evolving roles of Asian American women living within a bicultural environment in the United States. The sociocultural contexts of looking at the dynamics of relationships will and have changed. The diverse voices of Asian American women across time and space, through the generations, and across ethnic groups contributed to the richness of our contributions.

1

ASIAN AMERICAN WOMEN: MANY VOICES, DIFFERENT SOUNDS

JEAN LAU CHIN

Relationships have been the defining aspect of people, the families of which they are a part, and the cultures and societies that they form. Throughout his or her lifetime, an individual typically engages in many types of relationships. For women, these include those of mother–daughter, husband–wife, friend, and coworker. As Miller (1986) indicated, one central trait of women "is that women stay with, build on, and develop in a context of connections with others. Indeed, women's sense of self becomes very much organized around being able to make and then to maintain affiliations and relationships" (p. 83; see also Deutsch, 1973). Relationships inevitably involve two or more people, consist of both positive and negative emotions, and are based on interactions including love, nurturing, power, and connections. Communication is the foundation of relationships, and the absence of it often is the basis for their dissolution. With the burgeoning interest in women's issues over the past decades, the literature has mushroomed with attempts to define and reconceptualize women's development; these have included theoretical formulations and empirical studies (Deutsch, 1973; Gilligan, 1982; Horney, 1967; Miller, 1986; Worell & Johnson, 1997), controversies and debates about differences between men and women (Bly, 1991; Forward, 1986; Gray, 1992; Tannen, 1991), and how-to books on understanding ourselves and improving relations between the sexes (Bassoff, 1992; Sanford & Donovan, 1985). The essence has been the simple fact that women are different from men and that these differences have been omitted from the theoretical and empirical literature.

The literature has had much to say about the relationships that we form. Recently, these relationships have been distinguished along gender lines. Men, it is said, often form and sustain relationships that are more aggressive and competitive in nature and based on power, whereas women form relationships that are based on connectedness and cooperation. Men use communication styles that are more confrontative or solution focused, whereas women use styles that emphasize feelings and empathy. Gray imaginatively described these differences in romantic relationships in the title of his 1992 book, *Men Are From Mars, Women Are From Venus*. Bly and Tannen (1992) focused on the misunderstandings that occur in male–female communication because of gender-based differences.

Relationships have also been distinguished in the literature along cultural and ethnic lines. Cultures have been defined as cooperative versus competitive and aggressive versus passive. These conceptualizations, however, when driven from a majority perspective, have led to the unfortunate consequence of devaluing, discriminating against, and disempowering those from ethnic minority groups; it is only with appreciation of and value for diversity that culturally competent and relevant models can be developed. (Chin, De La Cancela, & Jenkins, 1993). As concepts of cultural competence become incorporated into the psychological literature and gain acceptance as defining criteria of empirical study, academic training, and service delivery systems, it will be possible to move from simple dichotomous and value-driven definitions toward more complex and diverse conceptualizations of cultural and gender differences.

INTERACTION OF GENDER AND ETHNICITY

Although gender and ethnic studies exist, exploration of the interactive effects of gender and ethnic differences is scarce. Little is known about the lives and relationships of Asian American women and the characteristics that promote or impede their growth and development. Despite recent emphasis on differences and diversity, little has been researched and written on Asian American women and the factors that contribute to their formation of relationships. White, middle-class women have been overrepresented among researchers, theoreticians, and sample populations (Brown, 1990; Reid & Comas-Diaz, 1990; Yoder & Kahn, 1993). Consequently, myths continue to perpetuate a mystique about Asian American women, and stereotypes that objectify and disempower them remain.

From the work of the Asian American Women's Task Force of Division 35 of the American Psychological Association, which met between 1992 and 1997, there evolved a growing interest in examining the relationships of Asian American women. Task force members sought to reflect the differences of Asian American women from the existing women's literature. They sought to define the diversity among Asian American women and to juxtapose gender and ethnicity in exploring the relationships formed by Asian American women within multiple social, familial, and interpersonal contexts.

IMAGES OF ASIAN AMERICAN WOMEN

It became clear that sociopolitical and historical contexts inevitably shape and influence the nature of these relationships. Often, these are evident in the images and stereotypes of Asian American women. The most prominent images of Asian American women promulgated through the media and popular literature have been of Japanese war brides, geishas, china dolls, and prostitutes. Although viewed as beautiful, modest, and exotic, Asian American women have been portrayed negatively, as self-effacing, unworthy, and subservient to men (i.e., as transitional sex objects).

Asian women are rarely depicted positively in the media. As in *Sayonara*, a post–World War II movie, the relationships of Asian women have commonly been portrayed as self-sacrificing, self-denigrating, and blindly innocent. Additionally, Asian women frequently are cast as prostitutes. In a typical scenario, when an Asian woman forms a relationship with a White man, she generally loses him to a White woman; in the end, she is abandoned by her lover or husband when he returns home after the war, is pitied, and often commits suicide. This image was recently resurrected in the popular play *Miss Saigon*, which was modified from a Japanese context to an updated 1990s Vietnamese one. The persistence of this theme illustrates the prominence of these negative stereotypes. It is only very recently that these images have been balanced by more favorable and diverse images of Asian American women, such as in Maxine Hong Kingston's book *The Woman Warrior* and in Amy Tan's *The Joy Luck Club*. These books capture the diversity of experience and richness of character among Asian American women and their relationships.

Historical accounts in the Asian American studies and sociological literature have emphasized the plight of Asian men (i.e., "coolies," sojourners; Takaki, 1989) and the impact of immigration and labor laws that influenced the formation of their relationships and the establishment of their lives in the United States. Early accounts of Chinese Americans described their living situation as *bachelor societies*. The psychological literature has focused on the cohesiveness of Asian American families, the influence of Confucian philosophy, and the underlying cultural values of filial piety (Shon & Ja, 1982; Sue & Morishima, 1982) as organizing factors of Asian American life. Hsu (1971) pointed to the importance of the family in satisfying the important affective needs of individuals and believed that Chinese American families satisfy the basic need for interpersonal intimacy and provide social support better than the Western nuclear family. DeVos (1982) pointed to the integrity of Japanese American family roles and structure as defending against stress. However, with few exceptions, the Asian American literature has been relatively neutral or silent regarding the experiences and roles of Asian American women.

DIVERSITY AND DIFFERENCE

Fujitomi and Wong (1973) were among the earliest to write about Asian American women. At that time, they observed that the average Asian American woman was modally represented by a Sansei (third-generation Japanese American) or immigrant or second-generation Chinese American. However, the diversity among Asian American women has increased significantly since then. Bradshaw (1994), in reviewing the cultural imperatives of Asian American women and their relevance to mental health treatment, underscored the impact of immigration, its laws, and the oppressive forces of racism in the United States while, at the same time, recognizing the influence of the cultural variables of Confucian philosophy, Buddhism, and family values. Espiritu (1997) used a sociological perspective in looking at the relationship between Asian American men and women in the home, community, fields, factories, offices, and government. Using gender as an organizing principle, Espiritu examined immigration policy, labor laws, and ideological racism over several historical periods and how these shaped gender relations and the relative positions of power among Asian American women in the United States. The role of relationships among Asian American women from a psychological perspective is the focus of this book.

Activism and advocacy within the women's movement now emphasize empowerment and women taking charge of themselves, their health, their work, and their lives. In the psychological literature, feminist psychology has come of age as a field, with models for the examination of psychological phenomena within teaching, research, and service. Basic to these tenets have been principles of empowerment, diversity, and the value of including all voices (Worell & Johnson, 1997).

This book, therefore, is women centered and brings together many voices of Asian American women who will speak to the psychological issues of cultural and gender role identity and stereotypes as they influence and are influenced by the relationships formed by Asian American women. It will address thematic issues inherent in relationships, including attachment and communication styles, power and trust, and stage-of-life issues as they manifest both the unique and universal qualities of Asian American women. The influence of the women's movement in the United States has manifested itself in fashion (i.e., the power suit), in work (i.e., the power lunch, women's management styles), and in social and family relationships (i.e., networking, caregivers). How these differ for Asian American women needs to be heard and is the concern of this book.

THE MANY VOICES OF ASIAN AMERICAN WOMEN

The many voices of Asian American women are only partially captured in this volume. It opens in the foreword with the pioneering voice of Reiko Homma True as a feminist advocate. As discussed in Part 1, it is only but a start to represent the different contexts and experiences that give rise to these voices. Voices of women can be heard through advocacy scholarship and experiences; they are both defined by and defining of the context. Part 2, "Adaptive Relationships: Resilience in the Midst of Sociopolitical Change," addresses race and racism as they influence the nature of relationships among Asian American women (i.e., what they did). These include barriers faced by Asian American women and their resilience in adapting to racially discriminatory policies and practices. Sociocultural contexts and adapting to stressors of acculturation contribute to adaptive and maladaptive modes of adjustment and reflect issues of power on the formation of relationships. Part 3, "Biculturalism: Interactive Dualism in Relationships," considers cultural and ethnic factors as they influence the nature of relationships among Asian American women (i.e., how they experienced). These include familial and social relationships. More important, however, this part addresses the interaction and juxtaposition of cultures and includes issues of connectedness in the formation of relationships. Finally, Part 4, "Paradigms: From Whose Lens?" considers the different and multiple perspectives offered by Asian American women. The chapters describe two theoretical models and paradigms relevant to the study of relationships among Asian American women. It concludes with a commentary on the paradigms of power and connectedness for Asian American women and the perspectives needed to consider when describing these relationships. This challenges the reader to reconsider the color and shape of the lens used to view the world.

The ethnic backgrounds of the chapter authors include Chinese, Japanese, Vietnamese, Korean, Filipino, biracial, and Indian American. The chapter authors, although diverse in their experiences and histories, could not reflect the voices of all 30-plus different ethnic groups within Asian

American communities and the complexity of generations in the United States, immigration history, country of origin, ethnic origin, age, and so forth. However, their unique and diverse chapters reflect a shared agenda in promoting the value of diversity, the significance of empowerment, and the importance of cultural competence. Key elements of this perspective were articulated by Greene and Sanchez-Hucles (1997), who defined *diversity* as

- "openness to differences among and between people;
- the cultivation, appreciation, and nurturance of different perspectives;
- receptiveness to and respect for others;
- valuing difference;
- a noun and a verb in which which we are all subject and object." p. 185

The methodology for this book draws on historical contexts, empirical studies, case examples, and experiential data to provide the materials through which theoretical formulations can be made about the factors influencing Asian American women in relationships. The importance of empirical and objective data must be balanced against the value of ethnographic and qualitative methods. Storytelling, although viewed as subjective, has been a means for transmitting culture through the generations and forms the basis for connectedness. Consequently, the richness of this volume is in the variety of its approaches, which serve to validate and illustrate the diversity of issues and differences among Asian American women, many of which have been overlooked by both researchers and people in general. For example, Lui (1997) questioned why although Asians knew of the benefits of gingko nuts for 2,000 years, gingko is valid as a method of healing now only when a Western researcher can show its effectiveness through an empirical study.

Although the emphasis on relational contexts is consistent with a feminist perspective, the focus on sociopolitical and familial contexts is consistent with an ethnic perspective. In this book, the authors challenge the disenfranchising and disempowering stereotypes of Asian American women. They celebrate the strengths of Asian American women. They address the evolving roles of Asian American women living within a bicultural environment. Ultimately, they challenge the paradigms used to define and view Asian American women as monolithic; they choose to view relationships among Asian American women from a different lens. The goal in doing so is to define theory and direct study and research beyond unidimensional and narrow definitions. It is time to go beyond describing Asian Americans and Asian American studies simply from the vantage point of filial piety and strong family values. To achieve a greater understanding of relationships among Asian American women and to instruct practice and public policy toward improving the health, mental health, and overall well-being of Asian American women, their many voices and different sounds must be heard and acknowledged; the different lenses must be used to view the world.

REFERENCES

Bassoff, E. S. (1992). *Mothering ourselves: Help and healing for adult daughters*. New York: Plume.

Bly, R. (1991). *Iron John: A book about men*. New York: Vintage.

Bly, R., & Tannen, D. (1992, January/February). *Where are women and men today? New Age Journal*, 28–33, 92–97.

Bradshaw, C. (1994). Asian and Asian American women: Historical and political considerations in psychotherapy. In L. Comas-Diaz & B. Greene (Eds.), *Women of color: Integrating ethnic and gender identities in psychotherapy* (pp. 72–113). New York: Guilford Press.

Brown, L. (1990). The meaning of a multicultural perspective for theory building in feminist psychotherapy. *Women and Therapy, 9(1/2)*, 1–23.

Chin, J. L., De La Cancela, V., & Jenkins, Y. (1993). *Diversity in psychotherapy: The politics of race, ethnicity, and gender*. Westport, CT: Praeger.

Deutsch, H. (1973). *The psychology of women*. New York: Bantam.

DeVos, G. (1982). Adaptive strategies in U.S. minorities. In E. Jones & S. Korchin (Eds.), *Minority mental health* (pp. 74–117). New York: Praeger.

Espiritu, Y. L. (1997). *Asian American women and men: Labor, laws, and love*. Thousand Oaks, CA: Sage.

Forward, S. (1986). *Men who hate women and the women who love them*. New York: Bantam.

Fujitomi, I., & Wong, D. (1973). The new Asian American woman. In S. Sue & N. N. Wagner (Eds.), *Asian Americans: Psychological perspectives* (pp. 252–263). Palo Alto, CA: Science & Behavior Books.

Gilligan, C. (1982). *In a different voice*. Cambridge, MA: Harvard University Press.

Gray, J. (1992). *Men are from Mars, women are from Venus*. New York: Harper-Collins.

Greene, B., & Sanchez-Hucles, J. (1997). Diversity: Advancing an inclusive feminist psychology. In J. Worell & N. G. Johnson (Eds.), *Shaping the future of feminist psychology* (pp. 173–202). Washington, DC: American Psychological Association.

Horney, K. (1967). *Feminine psychology*. New York: Norton.

Hsu, F. L. K. (1971). Psychosocial homeostasis and Jen: Conceptual tools for advancing psychological anthropology. *American Anthropologist, 73*, 23–44.

Lui, M. (1997). Taking charge as an informed consumer. Panel presentation at Conference on *Women Taking Charge: A Healthy Challenge*, Boston.

Miller, J. B. (1986). *Toward a new psychology of women*. Boston: Beacon Press.

Reid, P. T., & Comas-Diaz, L. (1990). Gender and ethnicity: Perspectives on dual status. *Sex Roles, 22,* 397–408.

Sanford, L. T., & Donovan, M. E. (1985). *Women and self-esteem: Understanding and improving the way we think and feel about ourselves*. New York: Penguin.

Shon, S., & Ja, D. (1982). Asian families. In M. McGoldrick, J. K. Pearce, & J. Grordano (Eds.), *Ethnicity and family therapy* (pp. 208–228). New York: Guilford Press.

Sue, S., & Morishima, J. K. (1982). *The mental health of Asian Americans: Contemporary issues in identifying and treating mental problems*. San Francisco: Jossey-Bass.

Takaki, R. (1989). *Strangers from a different shore*. New York: Penguin.

Tannen, D. (1991). *You just don't understand: Women and men in conversation*. New York: Ballantine.

Worell, J., & Johnson, N. G. (1997). *Shaping the future of feminist psychology*. Washington, DC: American Psychological Association.

Yoder, J. D., & Kahn, A. S. (1993). Working toward an inclusive psychology of women. *American Psychologist, 48,* 846–850.

2

ASIAN AMERICAN WOMEN AND SOCIAL ADVOCACY

KEM B. LOUIE

This chapter examines the role of social justice and advocacy among Asian American women. Social advocacy among Asian American women has not been studied, often because of the misperception that Asian American women are passive and apolitical. Stereotypical images of Asian American women as demure and obedient and as sex objects persist in the media and literature. Nevertheless, there are Asian American women who are committed to alleviating society's problems and to achieving social justice for those who are discriminated against and disenfranchised. These Asian American women have played activist roles in their communities, yet they have rarely been profiled in the media and are often unknown within the larger society. In fact, women have led several of the national organizations that specifically address the health and human service and civic concerns of Asian Americans.

For example, there are several Asian American women worthy of note for their roles in the community mental health movement. Jean Lau Chin and Reiko Homma True began their activism in the late 1960s. In 1969 Jean Lau Chin became the first female Asian psychologist and the first Asian clinical psychologist in Massachusetts. Her career has combined both

13

health and mental health administration and the clinical practice of psychotherapy. Although she enjoys clinical work, she felt that she could effect greater social change through her administrative roles within the care delivery system to diverse communities. She continues her social activism in numerous Asian and non-Asian organizations (J. L. Chin, personal communication, 1998).

In 1972 Reiko Homma True was one of the founders of the Asian American Psychological Association. She also was the Director of Mental Health, Substance Abuse and Forensic Services for the City of San Francisco in the early 1970s, where she developed many programs specifically for Asian Americans and other underserved populations in San Francisco County. Among her many activities, which include disaster recovery for earthquake victims in Japan, she served as president of the Asian American Psychological Association in 1999.

National Asian advocacy organizations that have been led by women include the Asian Pacific Islander American Health Forum, the Asian American Pacific Community Health Organizations, the National Asian Pacific American Families Against Substance Abuse, the Japanese American Citizens League, and the Organization of Chinese Americans. In these leadership roles, Asian American women were instrumental in defining issues, formulating policy, and influencing social change. The more recent emergence of the National Asian Women's Health Organization demonstrates the outgrowth of such advocacy and the passion reflective of feminist values and changing times.

According to feminist perspectives, the experiences of women activists are shaped by the contradictions and inequalities of the larger social world in which they live (Crosby, Todd, & Worell, 1996). Others have noted that activism is often the result of hardships or, at least, being at odds with the established society (Lalonds & Cameron, 1994). Chin (personal communication, 1998) noted that sociopolitical issues such as immigration, acculturation, trauma, and biculturalism contribute to the values and beliefs that in turn influence social advocacy among Asian American women. Until this book, however, how these premises relate to Asian American women activists had not been studied.

ASIAN AMERICAN WOMEN AS SOCIAL ADVOCATES

To study these premises, questions were developed to explore the varied experiences of Asian American women as social advocates and to understand the role of social advocacy in the lives of Asian American women. It was believed that a qualitative survey of some prominent Asian American women activists would lend insight to the values and experiences shaping their commitment to social advocacy. Questions addressed the following:

- activities that constitute social advocacy among Asian American women
- facilitating factors supporting their advocacy work
- barriers posed in exercising these roles
- factors sustaining their continued commitment to social advocacy
- how advocacy may or may not be integral to their identity as Asian American women.

First, a definition of *social advocacy* was needed. A definition of assisting with achieving or pleading for another's well-being and working to bring about social and systems change was established. In this chapter, the concept of social advocacy will be confined to assisting Asian American groups or communities in the United States toward achieving political, social, or economic equality.

METHOD

Asian American women prominent in social advocacy within their communities were identified through national Asian American advocacy groups. Twelve women identified by their peers as social advocates were invited to participate in a qualitative survey.

Prospective participants were sent a letter of introduction and asked to participate in a survey consisting of six questions. Instructions were provided to mail the answers to the author. The women who agreed to participate in the study were asked to return their responses by the deadline date.

The six questions were open ended, and participants were free to respond in any format. Although this makes for greater coding difficulties, it allows for fuller answers. The questions were as follows:

1. What experiences led you to dedicate yourself to social change, advocacy, and activism?
2. What factors facilitated or presented barriers to you in your role as an advocate?
3. How do you sustain your commitment to social advocacy?
4. To what extent do you, as an Asian American woman, envision advocacy as an integral part of your identity?
5. How has your advocacy influenced the formation of your social or professional relationships?
6. In what advocacy activities are you involved?

SURVEY SAMPLE

Of the 12 women asked to participate, 8 responded. The 12 women invited represented several Asian American subgroups (i.e., Chinese, Japanese, Filipino, Thai, and Vietnamese). However, of those who responded, 6 were Chinese American, 1 was Filipino, and 1 was Thai. Four respondents were first generation born in the United States, and 4 were immigrants. Their professional backgrounds included physician, nurse, psychologist, minister, administrator, and educator. They lived in Washington, California, New Jersey, and Massachusetts.

QUESTIONNAIRE RESPONSES

Because this was a qualitative study, the responses to each question were analyzed to identify and highlight themes of social advocacy in the lives of these women. Additionally, specific quotes from the survey responses are included to illustrate the passion of their commitment to social advocacy.

Question 1: Experiences That Influenced Commitment to Social Advocacy

All of the respondents mentioned some aspect of injustice and oppression, often related to race, in their lives or observed in the lives of others that precipitated their dedication to the pursuit of social change. These experiences contributed to their involvement in seeking justice or "doing the right thing" for other Asian Americans and oppressed groups.

One woman wrote poignantly about how she was influenced:

> I was born right after World War II. My earliest childhood memories were of other children calling me names and hitting me because I was Chinese. This did not make any sense to me because my father was drafted into W.W.II when he didn't even speak English.

The contradiction between the patriotism expected of Asian Americans versus the pervasive racism during this time is reflected in the difficulties experienced by this woman growing up as a young Asian American girl after World War II.

A respondent born in the United States stated:

> My parents have always been involved with nonprofit organizations. When I traveled overseas, I was struck by the poverty and class difference that was so rampant in Asia. [Only then did I] realize how fortunate I was in the U.S. In college, I was with other Asian American students for the first time, and learned about the struggles of the [Asian

Americans as a group that I] began to take a leadership role to increase visibility of Asian Pacific Americans.

This vignette illustrates how many Asian American women were shielded from the racism and disenfranchisement of racial and ethnic groups in the United States.

A respondent who immigrated to the United States in her teens described her experience:

> I grew up witnessing the tremendous impact of social, political, and economic upheaval in Thailand, specifically towards those with less power such as the uneducated, poor, women, and children. My mother, [on the other hand], graduated from the first school established by women that realized self-empowerment and enrolled me in that school at the age of four. I come from three generations of adventurous spirits open to learning. It was during my college experiences in California that I encountered firsthand the many prejudices against ethnic minorities in the U.S. during the mid-sixties.

It is ironic that this woman's experience occurred during the height of the civil rights movement in the United States. Moreover, this account supports the strength and facilitating force of powerful maternal figures in the lives of many Asian American women.

Another woman wrote,

> My parents always instilled in me the value of helping others; my advocacy work is an opportunity to act on this value. When I came to the U.S. at seven years old, I realized then the poverty back in Hong Kong.

Common themes in the statements of many were the importance of cultural and family values and the contrasts made apparent by the immigration experience.

Question 2. Factors That Facilitated or Presented Barriers to Social Advocacy

All of the women identified various barriers that continue to persist. Four mentioned the glass ceiling, sexism, and racism. One mentioned the lack of financial and personal resources, whereas 2 felt that Asian American women role models were lacking.

One woman wrote, "I have found the subtle undermining effects of the glass ceiling to be quite wearing. Being the *Invisible Asian Person* and stereotyped have been barriers." Another woman stated, "The barriers [for me] have been a lack of Asian American women role models and mentors. Even when there [was] an Asian American woman role model, she was usually too busy [to mentor me] because of the demands of being a woman and Asian American." This vignette illustrates the burden and demands experienced by many Asian American women by virtue of their ethnic and gender minority status.

Themes of gender oppression and racism were more prevalent among women in male-dominated professions, whereas racism was the more common theme among women in female-dominated professions such as nursing.

Five of the women identified strong collegial and organizational supports as facilitating their commitment to social advocacy. One woman wrote, "The most important factor facilitating many aspects of my life has been collegial support, both offering and receiving, specifically organizations such as within the [APA]." Another woman stated, "I have also benefited from the guidance of older Asian American women advocates. Non-Asian women of color have also been a great source of personal and professional support."

Women who are active in advocacy organizations and hold volunteer positions value the support of the collegial networks. These women meet their affiliative needs in these organizations with like-minded people.

Support from family and friends was also a common theme. Two women responded that other Asian American women have mentored them in their work, whereas 1 spoke of "being spiritually grounded." One woman wrote, "My Asian American peers and peers from diverse cultural backgrounds who are social advocates. . . . Some of these people have been informal mentors and role models."

Two women identified their family as facilitating their role as social advocates. "My family and friends allow me to give up the time with them to pursue my goal." Although specific family background information was not obtained in the study, many respondents voluntarily mentioned that their families encouraged or allowed them to develop as independent women given their strong beliefs in social justice and the work ethic.

Nevertheless, 2 lamented that "there is a lack of unity among Asian Americans in the community. It is hard to get them to participate in various activities." As reflected in this last comment, even Asian American women who are passionate about their causes believe that Asian Americans are monolithic. The idea that everyone should do the right thing can be very frustrating.

Question 3. Means of Sustaining Commitment to Social Advocacy

The answers given to this question were similar to those to Question 2. Two of the women identified being spiritually grounded, 3 mentioned their family and friends, and 2 identified networking with others as factors that sustain their commitment to social advocacy.

The passion of these women is reflected in some of their comments. "It is my passion and vision for the future that sustains my commitment to advocacy." One stated, "Being spiritually grounded is very important to me. I go on meditation retreats and daily meditation practice." Another said, "Mindfulness training in the Buddhist tradition has played a major part in strengthening my commitment." The themes of justice and social change and the ability to "see the bigger picture" were common factors attributed to having transformed these women's lives.

Social networks also appeared to be a significant factor, as reflected in the following comments: "Being with my family and friends helps me realize that I am only but one person, and the changes, however small, will help others. They support and encourage me in my work ... I find collegial interactions, both mentoring and being mentored, enormously sustaining."

Question 4. Extent to Which Social Advocacy Is Integral to Identity

Six of the women believed that, for them, advocacy was an integral part of their identity as an Asian American woman, whereas 2 felt that being a social advocate was a role, "not who I am."

One woman stated, "I see myself as a problem-solving person and someone who gets things accomplished through what I am doing. I sometimes have trouble seeing advocacy as part of my identity ... but it must be." Another commented, "Advocacy is an integral part of the responsibilities of any women of color in a leadership role." These comments reflect the fact that the formation of one's identity is an ongoing and active process.

Question 5. Extent to Which Social Advocacy Has Influenced Formation of Social or Professional Relationships

All of the women derived a sense of self-satisfaction from their advocacy activities. It is clear from many of the comments that they felt that their social advocacy had expanded their horizons and had been a sustaining source of social and professional relationships. One stated, "My work with others in social advocacy has enriched my life. I have learned, through others, their struggles and strengths." Another wrote that "participation in advocacy efforts has certainly expanded my circle of social and professional contacts [beyond] geographical and cultural perspectives." One interesting comment was the following: "When I get tired and frustrated in my work for others, I think of all my colleagues who are doing the same thing and I feel less isolated." Another woman commented, "Some of my colleagues have become part of my inner core of friends who share my passion."

Each of the women in the study developed an individual commitment for social change and, as a result, their collegial network and friendships formed their support system. The commitment that began on an individual basis is now shared. These relationships have been empowering as well as sustaining for these women.

Question 6. Advocacy Activities Involved in by Asian American Women

The advocacy activities in which these Asian American women were involved are diverse and span a broad range from policy to practice, academic to community, federal to local, and public health to cultural activities. Activities listed by respondents included the following:

- providing counseling services to abused women
- providing cultural diversity training to students, community groups, and corporations
- shaping and influencing legislative policies
- serving in leadership roles in professional, ethnic, social, and political organizations
- providing social services to Asian refugees and immigrants
- developing research, presentations, and publications on social and cultural issues
- serving on national, state, and private boards and foundations
- working in grassroots organizing and lobbying for social change
- fund-raising for social causes.

Six of the 8 respondents reported being active in national advocacy activities, 1 was currently active internationally, and 1 described statewide activities. The activities in which the women were engaged generally focused on promoting political, legislative, economic, and social equality for Asian Americans. Many felt that social advocacy was part of their employment and jobs; at the same time, however, many of the activities went beyond their professional employment positions into their larger ethnic communities.

DISCUSSION

The purpose of this survey was to explore the role of social advocacy among Asian American women. Although the limitations of the small sample and the qualitative nature of the survey are inherent, the results still reveal some meaningful patterns. Analysis of the results shows that the respondents defy the typical stereotypes of Asian American women. The issues of empowerment and connectedness underlie the motivating factors for many of these socially and politically active women. They reported that there was a need as an individual. They sought to remedy the problem. They did not join or go through committees but forged ahead alone seeking support for their ideas.

Many of the women attributed their social advocacy activities to their strong family values and experiences of social inequities. Many began their work alone and were pioneers in their social advocacy activities. Some of the women's experiences were sudden and intense, whereas others were gradual. The women's survey responses showed determination as well as perseverance toward a goal. All of the women who responded to the survey were educated and in professional careers. It is likely that they felt that they had to excel and accomplish probably more than their peers, both male and female. This determination is due to the belief in hard work that is typical among many Asian families.

There are several themes evident from this study. The first is that most of the respondents experienced or witnessed injustices as Asian American women. They responded by committing themselves to doing the right thing. The second theme centers on their acute awareness of social injustices, particularly among Asian Americans groups. Despite continued sexism and racism in the United States, these women have continued to advocate and care for both those who are different from the majority and those who are less fortunate than themselves. The third theme addresses the collegial relationships developed in the course of the advocacy activities that have sustained these women's commitment to social advocacy. These supports are from both Asian Americans and non-Asian Americans, from family and spiritual foundations, and from professional and personal connections. Most clearly evident is the passion and responsibility felt by these women to confront the social injustices existent in today's society.

The results show that, unfortunately, no systematic avenues currently exist to promote developing and nurturing Asian American women as leaders in social advocacy. Most of the women described an internal locus of control against which they evaluated and gauged their notions of justice and oppression. Although family support was an influential factor for at least half of the women (i.e., parents), racism and injustices experienced during childhood was a common motivator. In particular, leadership development was notably lacking for these women, although 2 did identify support and opportunities for leadership development from professional organizations (i.e., the APA and the American Nurses' Association).

A majority of the women mentioned the lack of Asian American women role models. In addition, they noted that when present, potential role models or mentors often were too busy to offer support or mentoring because of the demands placed on them as Asian American women. Non-Asian women and men have served as role models for this group; however, it is clear that future leadership development to promote social advocacy among Asian American women is essential for the next generation. Given the importance of ethnic identity and biculturalism in the lives of these women and the importance of Asian elders as role models for the younger generation, it is particularly essential that there be some way to foster leadership by Asian American role models.

The results of the study also show that Asian American women in leadership positions both feel, and should share, a responsibility for social advocacy. What was not addressed in this study is how social advocacy can and should be taught. Are there cognitive skills such as organizing and political influence that can and should be taught? Once these skills are identified, what would contribute to the internalization of core values associated with these skills? All of the women in this study committed themselves to social advocacy in their work and voluntary activities because of an articulated vision for vulnerable and disenfranchised populations. Their focus on furthering an Asian American agenda was integral to their identities as Asian American women.

Rewards of social advocacy were clear and sustaining for these women although not measurable in monetary terms. Meeting others who hold similar attitudes and values increased their sense of affiliation and self-worth. Opportunities to share with others through peer recognition, invited presentations, and scholarly publications was validating for many of the women.

Although the sample of women in this study was small, the range of social advocacy activities in which these women participated varied widely and was diverse. Activities ranged from providing direct services to providing legislative testimony. Given the small sample of women surveyed, it is not feasible to generalize to a larger group of first-generation Asian American versus foreign-born Asian women or to specific Asian ethnic subgroups.

CONCLUSION

Despite the misperception that Asian American women are passive or apolitical, there are those who are active and committed to social advocacy. These women find social advocacy both rewarding and fulfilling, and they find support for their activities from both their families and their colleagues. They feel empowered and energized by their participation in activities that have value for improving the status of oppressed and disenfranchised groups. Striking, however, is the lack of organized support and leadership development for nurturing these activities and roles among Asian American women.

There are several challenges suggested by the findings of this study. How do we capture the energy, enthusiasm, and vision of this small group of pioneering Asian American women? There needs to be published a directory or monograph identifying the contributions of these and other

Asian American women. What collective efforts can be proposed to teach future generations of Asian American women to care for others and to commit to social justice and change? What specific models or strategies that combine the feminist perspectives of support and connectedness and the psychosocial perspectives of women of color will facilitate in orienting Asian American women toward social advocacy? Further research is needed in this area to answer these important questions.

REFERENCES

Crosby, F. J., Todd, J., & Worell, J. (1996). Have feminists abandoned social activism? Voices from the academy. In L. Montada & J. Lerner (Eds.), *Current societal concerns about justice* (pp. 85–102). New York: Plenum Press.

Lalonds, R. N., & Cameron, J. E. (1994). Behavioral responses to discrimination: A focus on action. In M. P. Zanna & J. M. Olson (Eds.), *The psychology of prejudice: The Ontario symposium* (vol. 7, pp. 257–288). Hillsdale, NJ: Laurence Erlbaum.

II

ADAPTIVE RELATIONSHIPS: RESILIENCE IN THE MIDST OF SOCIOPOLITICAL CONTEXTS

Although an emphasis on connectedness and relational contexts characterizes a feminist perspective, an emphasis on sociopolitical contexts characterizes an ethnic perspective. For Asian Americans, sociopolitical issues related to immigration, acculturation, trauma, and biculturalism contribute significantly to the lives of Asian American women and the adaptations they make in forming relationships. The consideration of these issues is necessary in valuing the diversity among these women; more important, however, these issues can be viewed from a positive perspective to illustrate the strength and resiliency of Asian American women. Too often, however, these differences have been characterized from a deficit perspective that encourages weakness rather than strengths (Espin & Gawelek, 1992).

Whereas feminist theory puts forth a general analysis of societal inequities that is based on gender oppression, Greene and Sanchez-Hucles (1997) noted that racial oppression must be emphasized if feminist psychology is to be inclusive and reflect the diversity of women's experiences. In this section, for example, evolution and developmental issues are considered from a social and historical perspective in chapters discussing the attitudes toward women of Asian ancestry reflected in U.S. legislation (chapter 3) and the World War II internment experiences of Japanese American women (chapter 4). Underlying this sociopolitical context is the racial oppression that has affected the promulgation of policies and practices toward Asian Americans in the United States. Such policies and priorities have been carried over into the relationships formed by Asian American women and have posed barriers and promulgated stereotypes that have defined rules and expectations of Asian American women both within Asian American communities and the United States in general.

The chapter on domestic violence in Vietnamese refugee and Korean immigrant communities (chapter 4) examines the stressors that precipitate these dysfunctional behaviors and patterns of coping among Asian American women. The chapter identifies the effects of immigration, war, and trauma on coping patterns and adaptive behaviors. What is significant is how these sociopolitical contexts are pervasive and persistent through generations in affecting women's lives and the relationships they form.

Particularly noteworthy is that the three chapters in this part reveal the influence of power that men often have over the lives and well-being of women. It is in the relationships women have with men and the power of physical strength, psychological attachment, or military terror that perpetuate these positions of inequality. Even when the oppressive forces themselves no longer exist, the psychological sequelae often are lifelong and affect subsequent relationships. Nevertheless, the resilience and strengths of Asian American women have been demonstrated by their ability to overcome such adversities.

REFERENCES

Espin, O., & Gawelek, M. (1992). Women's diversity: Ethnicity, race, class, and gender in theories of feminist psychology. In L. Brown & M. Ballou (Eds.), *Personality and psychopathology: Feminist reappraisals* (pp. 88–107). New York: Guilford Press.

Greene, B., & Sanchez-Hucles, J. (1997). Diversity: Advancing an inclusive feminist psychology. In J. Worell & N. G. Johnson (Eds.), *Shaping the future of feminist psychology* (pp. 173–202). Washington, DC: American Psychological Association.

3

U.S. ATTITUDES TOWARD WOMEN OF ASIAN ANCESTRY: LEGISLATIVE AND MEDIA PERSPECTIVES

LIANG TIEN

The image of women of Asian ancestry as erotic and sexual objects dominated the U.S. entertainment industry for decades. The "exotic Oriental" and her sexual objectification haunted the portrayals of Asian women, from Ah-Choi (the Chinese madam) of the 1880s to the Chinese prostitute in the movie *The World of Suzie Wong* (Mason & Patrick, 1960) and the sultry Indian princess in the movie *Far Pavilions* (Bond, 1984). To what extent does this erotic image of Asian American women portrayed in the media reflect the image and sentiment of the American people?

One method of determining a country's sentiment is to examine its national laws. In a representative government like that of the United States, the process of passing legislation must have popular support, or at least no great opposition. For a bill to become law, there must be a majority of favorable votes in the House of Representatives, the Senate, and acceptance by a president's administration. Legislation both influences and is influenced by the values and attitudes of the American people. To the extent that legislators are elected to represent their constituencies, the laws that they pass can be viewed as an indicator of the sentiment of the majority of the people. To the extent that Americans look to laws for guidance, bills that become law often shape the values and attitudes of the American people. The complex process of lawmaking and the infrequency with which laws are changed result in a relatively stable ideology that can be identified through an examination of U.S. statutes on a particular subject.

To ascertain U.S. sentiment toward women of Asian ancestry, federal legislation on the topic introduced during the past 100-plus years was reviewed. Immigration legislation is one area that has systematically and specifically addressed women of Asian ancestry. Immigration laws govern the admission and exclusion of particular groups of people to the United States. Immigration legislation defines the groups that the United States wishes to include in its citizenry through the granting of and eligibility for immigrant visas. Conversely, immigration legislation also defines those groups that the United States wishes to exclude. Historically, the United States has excluded and kept undesired groups outside of its borders through the denial of legal entry and citizenship and restriction of immigrant status. Consequently, U.S. ideology regarding women of Asian ancestry can be determined through study of its immigration legislation.

This chapter examines federal immigration legislation regarding women of Asian ancestry. Examining U.S. immigration legislation revealed that there have been significant laws addressing Asian women in relationships with U.S. servicemen that defined whether, when, and under what conditions they and their children were allowed to enter the United States.

This review of immigration legislation revealed a continued history of prohibitions against the entry of Asian women, specifically, Asian women who are fiancées or wives of U.S. servicemen stationed overseas and have borne Amerasian (i.e., mixed-race) children. Regardless of the feeling, intent, or wishes of individual servicemen toward the Asian women with whom they became romantically involved, federal legislation established the parameters regarding how they were to behave toward Asian women, and it failed to recognize or legitimatize U.S. servicemen's romantic relationships with women of Asian ancestry. Such exclusionary legislation suggests an American sentiment that Asian women are not acceptable for marriage to U.S. servicemen or that Amerasian children are not American citizens. U.S. laws bar the entry of Asian women and Amerasian children resulting in overseas-duty U.S. servicemen returning to the United States without the product (i.e., fiancée or wife and child or children) of their romantic liaisons with Asian women.

BEFORE WORLD WAR II: A LEGACY OF EXCLUSION

The United States entered World War II with legislative prohibitions against the entry of people of Asian ancestry. Three immigration laws firmly established the exclusion of people of Asian ancestry: (a) the Chinese Exclusion Act of 1882, (b) the Immigration Act of 1917, and (c) the National Origins Act of 1924.

The Chinese Exclusion Act of 1882 prohibited immigration of any person from China and barred from naturalization those Chinese immigrants who were already in the United States. Given the tendency of Chinese men to immigrate first, this in effect excluded the immigration of Chinese women to the United States. The 1800s were a time of widespread prostitution in the American West due to the paucity of women. Prostitutes of every nationality were abundant in California. However, the Chinese, as a group, were singled out as depraved "Orientals," and Chinese women were characterized as sexually subservient. The newspapers of the day described Chinese women as "reared to a life of shame from infancy and that not one virtuous China woman had been brought to this country. They were also accused of disseminating vile disease capable of destroying the very morals, the manhood and the health of our people" (Yung, 1995, p. 32).

The Immigration Act of 1917 perpetuated this image by naming all people from Asia *inadmissible aliens*. It created the "barred zone of the Asia-Pacific triangle" (U.S. Immigration and Naturalization Service, 1996, p. A-1-5). This legislation barred all Asians from immigration from 1917 until World War II. At that time, this legislation primarily affected the Japanese, given the hostile relations between the United States and Japan. After the earlier U.S. exclusion of Chinese immigrants, there was an influx of Japanese immigrants to the West Coast. Beginning in 1885, Japan permitted laborers to emigrate to the United States. The Japanese from drought ridden Japan could find a place and the United States received much needed workers. Japanese women immigrated some years after the peak years of the immigration of Japanese men. The majority of the Japanese women came as "picture brides," that is, women married in Japan by proxy to Japanese men in the United States through family arrangement. The practice of arranged marriages and marriage ceremonies by proxy with a photograph of the spouse was antithetical to the European practice of romantic marriage. Those who opposed Japanese immigration considered the practice of picture marriage as immoral (Glenn, 1986). Picture brides reinforced the existing image of Asian women as subservient, immoral, and depraved.

The National Origins Act of 1924 established an annual quota for each nation based on the percentage of people from that nation already residing in the United States as of 1920 and specified that aliens ineligible for citizenship could not enter as immigrants. The National Origins Act also specified that natives of Western Hemisphere countries were nonquota persons (U.S. Immigration and Naturalization Service [INS], 1996). This was racially discriminatory in that any people from Europe could immigrate to the United States at will, whereas no one from Asia and the Pacific

Islands could immigrate and all others had to wait for visas based on country-specific annual quotas.

These three federal acts effectively prohibited Asians already in the United States from becoming U.S. citizens, barred further immigration of people of Asian ancestry, and prohibited Asian wives from joining their husbands who were already in the United States. Asian American men found themselves permanently separated from their wives and relegated to "bachelor communities." To remedy this situation, legislation was introduced in 1935 to allow for the entry of Asian wives. The intent of the Alien Wife Bill was to "extend that privilege [immigration] to alien wives of other races ineligible for citizenship." This legislation died in committee. It was reintroduced in 1937 and again in 1939, with the same result—reflecting the unwillingness of Americans to accept Asian women.

These three pieces of immigration legislation, together with the defeat of the Alien Wife Bill, ensured that the Asian American community existing in the United States would not expand and that no new Asian American communities could be established. No other group of immigrants was ever targeted as such for exclusion. The anti-Asian sentiment of the United States reflected in these pieces of legislation, including women of Asian ancestry, was clear. The United States considered any person of Asian ancestry not only unfit for U.S. citizenship, but also unacceptable for entry into the United States.

America entered the World War II era with a firmly established tradition of exclusionary immigration legislation against people of Asian ancestry. Immigration legislation regarding women of Asian ancestry was set within the historical context of the exclusion of all Asians.

WORLD WAR II: SPLITTING ASIAN AMERICANS

On December 7, 1941, Japan attacked the U.S. naval base at Pearl Harbor, Hawaii, provoking a U.S. declaration of war against Japan the following day. On December 11, 1941, Germany and Italy declared war on the United States. World War II forced the entry of the United States into the global arena, leading to its evolution as a global superpower. Both during and since World War II, substantial numbers of U.S. military personnel were dispatched around the world, including various countries on the Pacific Basin and Asian continent.

During World War II, U.S. servicemen were stationed in Europe, China, and several countries in the Pacific. There were approximately 1 million World War II war brides, that is, women of various nationalities who married U.S. servicemen stationed abroad. Between 1944 and 1950, 150,000 to 200,000 couples married in Europe, and 50,000 to 100,000 couples married in Asia (Shukert, 1988). No legislation was enacted to exclude women of European ancestry from entering the United States to join their husbands. The differential treatment of European and Asian women illustrates the discriminatory image in the United States of women of Asian ancestry.

China as an Allied Country

The first legislation to address the immigration of Asian women was the repeal of the Chinese Exclusion Act of 1882 in 1943 (Immigration Act of December 17, 1943). During World War II, the enemy on the European front was Germany. On the Asian front, the enemy was Japan, whereas China became an allied nation in 1941. The repeal of the Chinese Exclusion Act, passed in the context of a nation at war, had the effect of splitting Asian groups.

Within the United States, Americans of Japanese ancestry were labeled a potential threat to domestic security and evacuated from the West Coast and imprisoned at alternate locations. This was not done with Americans of German ancestry. Instead of accepting the possibility that security forces were lax on the naval base in Hawaii, the blame for Pearl Harbor was placed on the "otherness" of Asians. Editorial comments like the following expressed the otherness view of Asians held by White Americans:

> We thought he [the Japanese] was bound by certain Western standards
> of international conduct. . . . They are not of the West, and have noth-
> ing to do with what we think is right. So Secretary Hull cried bitterly
> of "infamy" but the attack was not infamous. It was the Japanese acting
> according to their code. What earthly reason ever existed for expecting
> them to act according to our code? None. . . . The Pacific enemy will
> not change his nature. (Brier, 1994, p. 9)

Chinese immigrants, on the other hand, were not imprisoned but hailed as the good Asian. They were cast in a positive light by the newspapers of the day. Appearing daily on the front pages of U.S. newspapers were reports like the following: "*American and Chinese airmen of the United States* [italics added] fourteenth Air Force aided in the victory" (*New York Times*, 1943, p. 5). "Brig. Gen. Edgar Flenn, Chief of Staff of the United States Fourteenth United States Air Force, said . . . *American planes* [italics added] were striking from dawn to dusk *to support the Chinese* [italics added]" (*New York Times*, 1943, p. 5). The Chinese were considered brave soldiers worthy of American support.

Throughout the war, U.S. servicemen traveled to and were stationed in China. Concurrently, Chinese units were traveling to the United States for military training. With the friendly interchange, it became unseemly to exclude the immigration of Chinese people. Two years into the alliance with China, the United States passed the Magnuson Act of December 17,

1943 (Immigration Act of December 17, 1943). The Magnuson Act granted eligibility for naturalization to people of Chinese descent; it effectively repealed the Chinese Exclusion Act of 1882. Chinese people were no longer excluded from immigration by their ineligibility for citizenship. Although the act allowed for the immigration of Chinese people, it set an annual quota of only 105 immigrants. Chinese women who were wives or fiancées of U.S. servicemen stationed in China during the war were included as part of this numerical quota; this very low quota made the immigration of Chinese women negligible. In contrast, England, another allied nation, was allowed more than 40% of the annual quota for all countries. This made it possible for the English to migrate without waiting as the quota was so large. This quota system continued the United States's basic policy of excluding Asian women (Kim, 1992).

Continued Exclusion of Other Asians and Pacific Islanders

During World War II, U.S. servicemen were also stationed in the Philippines and other island countries in the Pacific Ocean. Although the Magnuson Act repealed the exclusion of Chinese immigrants, it let stand the Immigration Act of 1917, that continued to exclude Pacific Islanders and people from other Asian countries from entry into the United States. The romantic relationships that ensued between U.S. servicemen stationed in the Pacific and the women there are depicted in the movie *South Pacific* (Hammerstein & Osborn, 1958). Americans' unwillingness to accept mixed-race relationships legitimized through marriage is well articulated. Despite the large number of U.S. servicemen stationed in the Pacific, no waivers were introduced or passed to allow for the immigration of Pacific Islanders or other Asian women who became involved with U.S. servicemen.

AFTER WORLD WAR II: DIFFERENTIAL TREATMENT

On May 8, 1945, Germany unconditionally surrendered to the Allies. On September 2, 1945, Japan also surrendered unconditionally. The victorious Allies included Great Britain and the Commonwealth, France, the United States, the Soviet Union, and China. The U.S. military withdrawal from Europe began in August 1945. Troop withdrawal from Europe and the Far East continued through the end of the year. Immediately following the U.S. troop withdrawal the immigration of the women from various nations who married U.S. servicemen began.

After World War II, U.S. military personnel entered Germany and Japan. The United States participated in the postwar occupation of Germany by stationing U.S. military personnel there. Additionally, the United

States, the sole occupying power of Japan, stationed a sizable number of military personnel there.

The War Brides Act and the G.I. Fiancées Act: Preference for European Women

The next piece of legislation reflecting U.S. attitudes toward Asian women was the War Brides Act of 1945. The war in Europe ended in August of 1945. During the fall and winter of 1945, U.S. troops stationed in Europe began returning home. Every day, long lists of servicemen due to land in various ports around the country were published. Newspapers throughout the country published daily a "Schedule of the Arrival of Troops" derived from information provided by Army ports of embarkation in various cities. The schedules appeared as follows:

> New York—arrivals, due today, due tomorrow, due Sunday, due Monday, due Tuesday. Newport News, VA, arrived, due today. Boston, arrived, due today. San Francisco, due yesterday, due today. Portland, due yesterday. Tacoma, WA due yesterday. Seattle, WA due yesterday. San Diego, CA due yesterday. Los Angeles, due yesterday. (*New York Times*, 1945, p. 26)

At the same time, news of European wives trying to join their American husbands were also being reported in the newspapers. The December 10, 1945, *New York Times* ran the following stories:

> Since Herbert John Lamoureaux, 22-year-old former American soldier, could not swim to his wife, she is determined to sail to him. So said Mrs. Veronica Lamoureaux, attractive brunette English girl, today.... "It would have given him great happiness if we could all have been united this Christmas," the former GI's 23-year-old wife said. She added, however, that she was confident she could book passage to the United States. (p. 26)

> Mrs. Yvonne Goppert, 21-year-old Briton, was reunited with her American husband yesterday for the first time in seven months. They were married on May 11 and on May 18 Lieutenant Goppert received orders to go to France on a glider towed by a C-46. Mrs. Goppert hid on the plane in a box eighteen inches high, two feet wide and four and a half feet long. The couple spent two weeks honeymooning. (p. 26)

These reports systematically excluded women of Asian ancestry.

Beside the columns reporting the daily arrival of troops were announcements about the arrival of their wives. *The New York Times* reported the following on December 27, 1945:

> War brides of the United States soldiers from the Atlantic area will begin to follow their redeployed husbands in January, according to an official Army announcement today. The brides will embark through

Southampton, England, it said. Quotas have not yet been set, but once the movement of brides is started, it will continue until all brides have reached the United States, the War Department orders state. The ship on which brides will sail will be used for this purpose only. (p. 2)

The next day, December 28, 1945, before the first war veterans were barely home from Europe, the United States passed, without committee hearing or floor debate, the War Brides Act. The purpose of the Act was "to expedite the admission to the United States, of alien spouses and alien minor children of citizen members of the United States armed forces . . . provided they are admissible under the immigration laws." The act waived visa requirements and exclusion based on physical or mental defects for women who had married members of the American armed forces. Within months of U.S. servicemen returning to the United States, their British, European, New Zealander, and Australian wives were able to join them, at the expense of U.S. taxpayers. The War Brides Act was passed while European war brides were on their way to the United States.

One year after passage of the War Brides Act, the G.I. Fiancées Act of 1946 was enacted. Like the War Brides Act, this act was passed without committee hearings or floor debate. The purpose of the Fiancées Act was to "facilitate the admission into the US of the alien fiancées of members of the armed forces of the US . . . provided that the alien is not subject to exclusion from the United States under the immigration laws." With the passage of these two acts, all British, European, New Zealander, and Australian wives and fiancées of U.S. servicemen were allowed to enter the United States.

The image of and attitudes toward women from English-speaking and European countries had to have been positive for these two pieces of legislation to go forth with such speed and so little opposition. The policy of inclusion for women of European ancestry is repeated in both the War Brides Act and the Fiancée Act.

This was in marked contrast to the treatment of wives of Asian ancestry. Missing from the newspaper accounts were the stories of U.S. servicemen's wives from the Pacific Islands and China. Also missing were the wives themselves. Typical is the following story of a Chinese woman who married a U.S. serviceman:

> When she married Sam in China forty years ago, she had to keep the marriage secret at first. If the military found out, they would have shipped Sam out and the couple would have been separated. He could even have been court martialed and dishonorably discharged. The U.S. government discouraged its soldiers from taking war brides in foreign countries and did everything to prevent such marriages. Since Kun-yi lived with Sam, though married in fact, she was called a foreign prostitute. (Sung, 1990, p. 92)

The War Brides Act and the Fiancées Act let stand the exclusion of Asians. This allowed for the Kun-yi situation and thus continued the policy of excluding Asians, including Asian wives and fiancées.

Limited Inclusion of Chinese Women: China as an Ally

After World War II, the U.S. withdrew its servicemen from China. Chinese women were still restricted from immigration under the limited 105 persons per year quota. To facilitate the immigration of Asian wives, the Alien Wife Bill was reintroduced, for the third time, in 1939. After the start of World War II, when China became an ally, the same bill was again introduced in 1941, then in 1942. In total, this bill was introduced five times without passage. A restricted version of the bill was finally en-acted after the end of World War II. The Immigration Act of August 9, 1946 granted Chinese wives of U.S. citizens nonquota status. The effect of this legislation was the long-awaited entry to the United States of those Chinese women married to U.S. servicemen and civilians stationed in China.

This legislation had limited impact because it affected only the Chi-nese community. The Immigration Act of 1946 only allowed for American men who served in the armed forces during World War II to return to China, marry a Chinese woman, and bring her back to the United States. The men who took advantage of this were predominantly Chinese Amer-icans. This situation was depicted in the movie *Eat a Bowl of Tea* (Cha & Roscoe, 1989). By providing only for nonquota status for Chinese wives, the bill continued the exclusion of all other wives of Asian ancestry.

Limited Inclusion of Japanese Women: Occupation of Japan

Between 1944 and 1950, 50,000 to 100,000 couples were married in Asia (Shukert, 1988). Unlike British, European, New Zealander, and Aus-tralian women, Asian women married to U.S. servicemen were still barred from entry into the United States. During World War II, U.S. servicemen were stationed in large numbers in the Pacific Islands and later in Japan during the occupation. Both the War Brides Act and the Fiancées Act barred women of Asian ancestry from joining their servicemen husbands and fiancées in the United States. The War Brides Act provided that alien wives of U.S. citizens who were serving in the U.S. armed forces and were "admissible under the immigration laws, be admitted to the United States." Likewise, the Fiancées Act also included exclusionary language. It provided for the admission of "alien fiancées of members of the armed forces of the US . . . provided that the alien is not subject to exclusion from the United States under the immigration laws."

U.S. forces have been stationed on Japanese soil since 1945. Not surprisingly, a number of men developed romantic relationships with Japanese women. However, Japanese women, regardless of whether or not they were married to U.S. servicemen, could not immigrate to the United States. In an attempt to address the issue of U.S. servicemen in romantic relationships with Japanese women, the initial Alien Wife Bill was reintroduced in 1947 for the sixth time. In 1947, the bill passed as the Soldier Brides Act. It reflected minimal attempts to counteract exclusion based on race. The Act stipulated that an "alien spouse of an American citizen by marriage occurring before 30 days after the enactment of this Act (July 22, 1947), shall not be considered as inadmissible because of race." These time limitations were later extended, then finally removed.

In contrast to the War Brides Act, no exceptions were made to expedite the speedy immigration of these Japanese wives. Instead, placement of tight time restrictions made immigration almost impossible. Although the time restrictions were later extended, the restrictions echoed the earlier exclusion of women of Asian ancestry.

Differential Treatment and Racial Preference

The differential treatment of women of Asian ancestry compared to women of European ancestry in post–World War II legislation reflected a clear racial preference. The European wives of U.S. servicemen were welcomed and quickly reunited with their husbands in the United States. In contrast, wives of Asian ancestry were initially barred, then later tightly restricted from following their husbands to the United States. The exclusion of women from Asian and Pacific Islander countries resulted in a situation in which servicemen could engage in romantic relationships, even legitimize those relationships with local marriage ceremonies, and still return to the United States without their Asian wives or fiancées. The legislative message about Asian women was that it was acceptable and even expected for servicemen to fraternize with Asian women but not to make them legitimate wives. The legislation protected the overseas servicemen by enabling them to return home unencumbered by their Asian women. This implied that Asian women were acceptable as sexual partners but unacceptable as U.S. citizens or members of U.S. families.

The restrictive legislation regarding women of Asian ancestry perpetuated the myth of the erotic Oriental. The legislation reflected the image of the Asian seductress portrayed in the press and popular media. It relegated Asian women to the images of An-Choi, the Chinese madam of the 1880s; Suzie Wong, the Chinese prostitute in the movie *The World of Suzie Wong* (Mason & Patrick, 1960); and the geisha in the movie *Sayonara* (Mitchner & Osborn, 1957) and the play *The Story of Miss Saigon* (Behr & Steyn, 1989).

THE COLD WAR YEARS

Elimination of Race-Based Exclusions from Naturalization

With the end of the World War II and the spread of Communism from the Soviet Union to China, the United States was into the Cold War years. The nation's security interest was focused on containment of Communism abroad and eradication of Communist influences within the United States. Internationally, the United States was assuming increasing leadership of the Western nations against the perceived expansionist intentions of its former ally, the Soviet Union. As the Cold War heated up, it brought the United States into a military confrontation with Communist forces in Korea and Vietnam.

Within the United States's new role as a world superpower protecting the world from Communism, the 1952 Immigration and Nationality Act, commonly referred to as the McCarran–Walter Act, was passed on June 27, 1952. The McCarran–Walter Act eliminated race as a bar to naturalization. This allowed those people of Asian ancestry who were residing in the United States to become citizens. The act eliminated previous restrictive legislation that barred immigration based on a person's inability to become a U.S. citizen. The Asian wives of U.S. servicemen were no longer subject to exclusion based on race. In response to the elimination of race-based exclusion from naturalization, Japanese women married to U.S. servicemen were able to immigrate. As a result, 85.9% of the immigrants from Japan between 1952 and 1960 were women (Daniels, 1990).

Although it eliminated race-based naturalization discrimination, the McCarran–Walter Act continued the race-based national quota immigration system. The quotas continued the policy of race-based discrimination. For example, "Ireland had a quota of 17,756 and Germany had a quota of 25,814, while quotas for ... China (105), Japan (185), the Philippines (100), and the Pacific Islands (100) were negligible" (Kim, 1992, p. 1110).

Elimination of Race-Based Immigration: The Immigration and Nationality Act

Racial equality was in the national spotlight during the 1950s and 1960s. The 1954 U.S. Supreme Court ruling in the case of *Brown v. Board of Education* on the issue of segregation signaled a change in U.S. race relations. Out of this increased focus on civil rights, Congress passed the Immigration and Nationality Act Amendments on October 3, 1965. The 1965 Immigration and Nationality Act eliminated the race-based quotas. For the first time in the history of regulated immigration, each Asian country received the same quota as European countries. Each country received an annual quota of 20,000 immigrant visas, with a ceiling of 170,000 for the Eastern Hemisphere. In addition, immediate relatives of U.S. citizens were not subject to quota restrictions.

With the passage of this Act, there were no longer any legislative restrictions against the immigration of people from Asia, including Asian women. The barriers to Asians established by the Immigration Act of 1917 that created the "barred zone of the Asia-Pacific triangle" were eliminated (Yung, 1995). With the elimination of race-based barriers to naturalization in 1952 and immigration in 1965, Asian wives of U.S. servicemen could not be categorically excluded from immigration into the United States. However, despite the liberal changes in immigration legislation just described, the exclusion of women of Asian ancestry continued in the legislative treatment of wives of U.S. servicemen in the Korean and Vietnam Wars.

Return to Exclusionary Policies for Amerasians: The Korean and Vietnam Wars

The next immigration legislation to address women of Asian ancestry came in response to the Korean and Vietnam Wars. The Immigration Act of 1982, commonly referred to as the Amerasian Act, excluded women of Asian ancestry in their status as mothers of Amerasians. The idea that Asian women were not acceptable as legitimate spouses for U.S. citizens was thereby continued. *Amerasian* is a term first used by Pearl S. Buck in 1966 to refer to individuals of mixed American and Asian parentage, specifically children fathered by American servicemen stationed in Asia. However, the servicemen, by definition, cannot be U.S. citizens of Asian ancestry because U.S. officials "consider the physical appearance" (Pub. L. No. 97-359, § 1698(3)(B)) to determine parentage. Without mixed-race appearance, American lineage is not established for children of Asian women and Asian American servicemen.

On June 27, 1950, President Truman committed U.S. military forces to aid South Korea against a Communist-backed North Korean invasion. Three years later, on July 27, 1953, an armistice was signed that signaled the end to the shooting part of the war. The conflict ended in a military stalemate, not an end to the war. The United States continues to station military personnel in South Korea to protect it from communist North Korea. Large numbers of U.S. troops have been stationed in South Korea since 1950.

Simultaneously, the United States was involved in armed conflict in the southern tip of the Asian continent. In Vietnam, fighting erupted between France and the Communist-backed Viet Minh in 1947. The United States, in its role as the world defender of democratic freedom against Communism, supported the French. By 1953, the United States was providing 80% of the cost of France's war effort. After the French defeat in

1954, the United States assumed responsibility for the fight in Vietnam. Between 1954 and the U.S. withdrawal in 1975, increasing numbers of military personnel were deployed to Vietnam and the former French Indochina countries in Southeast Asia.

With the large number of U.S. military personnel stationed in Korea and Indochina, romantic relationships between U.S. servicemen and Korean and Vietnamese women inevitably developed. Despite the passage of the Alien Wife Bill, the Soldier Brides Act, the McCarran–Walter Act, and the Immigration and Nationality Act of 1965, the United States still found occasion to continue the exclusion of Asian women.

More than 30 years after the United States dispatched servicemen to Korea, it attempted to address the Amerasian question. This was the first legislative recognition of the United States's responsibility for the Amerasian children of U.S. servicemen. On January 9, 1981, the Amerasian Immigration Act was introduced. The intent of the bill was "to amend the Immigration and Nationality Act to provide preferential treatment in the admission of unmarried or married son or daughter of a citizen of the United States if [the son or daughter] was born in Korea, Vietnam, Laos, or Thailand after 1950, and was fathered by an United States citizen who, at the time of the alien's conception, was serving in the Armed Forces of the United States during active duty for the United States or for the United Nations Organization" (H.R. 808, 97th Congress, 1st Session).

The same year that Congress was considering passage of the Amerasian Immigration Act, Vincent Chin, a Chinese American, was beaten to death in Detroit, Michigan. The U.S. auto industry was beset by the import of more fuel-efficient Japanese cars. Detroit's 16% unemployment rate was blamed on Japan. In June 1982, Chin, a native born American of Chinese ancestry, went to a bar to celebrate his upcoming wedding. In the bar, two White autoworkers shouted, "It's because of you motherfuckers that we're out of work." Outside of the bar, the same two autoworkers bludgeoned Chin to death with a baseball bat.

In the interests of job protection, Simpson-Mazzoli introduced the Immigration Reform and Control Act (IRCA) that was passed in 1982. The target of IRCA was to curb, and eventually eliminate, undocumented aliens working in the United States by establishing employer-based monitoring of INS status (Kim, 1992). Along the same vein of blaming others for U.S. troubles, Congress, in committee hearings, questioned the character of Asian women who were mothers of Amerasians. Committee members were concerned that U.S. servicemen were susceptible to being seduced by Asian women who wished to immigrate if the mothers of Amerasian were allowed immigrant status with their Amerasian children.

Public Law No. 97-359, Section 1698, Preferential Treatment in the Admission of Children of U.S. Citizens, commonly referred to as the Amerasian Immigration Act of 1982, was enacted into law on October 22,

1982. The Amerasian Immigration Act established immigration preference for Amerasians. However, it continued to deny the special relationship of the mothers of Amerasians with the United States through its servicemen. Two conditions under which Amerasian children could immigrate to the United States resulted in the exclusion of women of Asian ancestry. One condition was that only the minor Amerasian child could immigrate, not the Asian mother or other family members. The second condition was that the mother of the Amerasian had to sign an irrevocable release of family rights for the child to immigrate. The release disallowed the mother any future claims on the child. This not only meant forced separation of the Amerasian child from his or her mother, but also no hope of future re-unification. Even after reaching adulthood and gaining citizenship, the Amerasian could not sponsor his or her Asian mother as a nonquota relative. Amerasians who immigrated to the United States came essentially as orphans to be fostered by American families.

The proviso of the irrevocable release made clear the United States intent of total dissociation from those Asian women who had relations with U.S. servicemen. Again, this relegated those relationships between Asian women and U.S. servicemen to the status of temporary sexual liaisons. Asian women were acceptable only as temporary romantic partners for the comfort of U.S. servicemen stationed overseas. This time, the added message was that not only were Asian women unacceptable as legitimate wives, but they also were unacceptable as mothers to rear "American" children.

Diplomatic Breakdown and Exclusion Following the Vietnam War

The popular image of women involved with U.S. servicemen in Vietnam is depicted in the play *Miss Saigon* (Behr & Steyn, 1989). This image continues the age-old U.S. concept of Asian women as temporary romantic and sexual partners. The Communist Vietnamese victory in 1975 added an additional incentive for Americans to denigrate Asians and Asian women. The loss of the Vietnam War had profound ramifications for the United States. It was a shock to American self-confidence as a military power and world leader. This resulted in the United States severing all diplomatic relations with Vietnam until 1994, thus preventing Vietnamese Amerasians from immigrating under the Amerasian Immigration Act of 1982.

On August 6, 1987, 12 years after the last U.S. servicemen left Southeast Asia, and under pressure from Vietnam, the Amerasian Homecoming Act (H.R. 3171, 100th Congress, 1st Session) was first introduced in Congress. The purpose of the bill was to permit the immigration of Vietnamese Amerasians to the United States. The bill died in the Committee on the Judiciary. It was introduced again on October 28, 1987, but met the same fate. On December 27, 1987, provisions for the immigration of Vietnamese Amerasians were passed as part the Omnibus Budget Reconciliation Act, the Amerasian Immigration Section.

Under extreme pressure from the Vietnamese government, this proviso specifically included the immigration of Vietnamese families. The Amerasian Immigration Section provided for waivers of numerical limitations on immigration for Amerasians and existing exclusionary policies. The waivers meant that adult Amerasians could immigrate and mothers of Amerasians could accompany their children to the United States. However, administrative interpretation of the legislation initially established a condition under which the Vietnamese mother could be excluded. Those family members eligible for immigration with the Amerasian included the Amerasian's spouse, child, *or* natural mother and her spouse or child. If the accompanying family member was a spouse, then the natural mother "shall not be accorded any right, privilege, or status." Amerasians initially had to choose between their mother and their spouse. Again, there existed a loophole to exclude women of Asian ancestry, once again sending the not-so-subtle message that women of Asian ancestry were not wanted in the United States.

EFFECTS OF LINGERING IMAGES

As discussed earlier, the persistent image of Asian women as erotic, temporary sexual partners for U.S. servicemen reflects the sentiments of the majority of Americans. In turn, the passage of exclusionary immigration legislation reflects and perpetuates the sexual and erotic image of women of Asian ancestry.

Stereotypic Images

The image reflected in law is not limited to Asian women living in Asia. This image also affects women of Asian ancestry born in the United States. Asian American women are exposed to the sexualized images of themselves. Two Asian American women described examples of this type of exposure.

> On a tour to Niagara Falls, other passengers kept intimating to Calvert that Yi-fong was just a girl he was taking on an extramarital fling. Although he introduced Yi-fong as his wife, they kept referring to her as his girlfriend and made snide remarks about his leaving his wife at home. People are unable to or refuse to grasp the fact that two people from different backgrounds can be married. (Sung, 1990, pp. 88–89)

> Another attitude that seems especially prevalent is the mail-order-bride mentality. Occasionally when I'm with my boyfriend—who is as Anglo

as you can get—total strangers walk up and ask him where I'm from, if I speak English. . . . The same mentality is responsible for a certain class of male that seems to think Asian women are easy to please, utterly subservient and desperately clamoring for Anglo husbands. . . . During lunch in the dorm cafeteria, [a White student] sauntered over and said (this is true), "Hello, Me see you here very long time. Me think you very pretty. I don't like American girls. I only like Asian women." (Kim, 1990, p. M4)

Erotic Images

The capitulation to this erotic image of Asian American women by the Asian American community influences the stigmatization of Asian American women in interracial relationships. "Chinese feel that women who married Americans are not decent. This is a stereotype. For me, that hurt a lot because I feel that I had to prove my character" (Sung, 1990, p. 92). "Intermarriage between Whites and Asians has been seen in recent times by some Asian Americans as evidence of racial conquest and cultural genocide rather than social acceptance and success for the Asian minority" (Kim, 1982, p. 92).

Repeated exposure to erotic imagery of oneself can have a profound effect on the development of the psychosexual identity. The incorporation of this erotic image by Asian American women has led some to feel ashamed of and reject their Asian ancestry.

> Second-class treatment like this (Asian women are easy to please, utterly subservient and desperately clamoring for Anglo husbands) has made a lot of American-born Asians ashamed of their heritage in a way that other Americans aren't. You'll probably never catch one of us with a button reading, "Kiss me, I'm Korean." In fact, there is a heavy burden on us to deny all ethnicity and to prove we're just like everyone else, i.e., real Americans. The results are sometimes pathetic. I used to present my middle name as "Susan" instead of "Suhn." (Kim, 1990, p. M4)

Identity Issues

Every Asian American woman, at some level, must contend with the image of the erotic being that is not acceptable as a legitimate partner in a long-term relationship. When Asian American women consider their identities as Americans with the elements of race, ethnicity, and gender, they do not encounter a society that encourages them to be self defined. Anti-Asian immigration legislation denigrates their worth, and erotic and sexual images objectify them. During the many years of their exclusion Asian American women were unable to participate in the legislative and political dialogue about themselves. After so many years of forced silence,

Asian American women at last can and should engage in a dialogue with the greater population of U.S. citizens through participation in the legislative process so as to shape their own images.

CONCLUSION

Federal legislation of the last 100-plus years articulates enduring images of and sentiments toward women of Asian ancestry. The most common image is that women of Asian ancestry are erotic and sexualized beings. The prevalent sentiment is that women of Asian ancestry are acceptable for temporary romantic liaisons but not as wives or mothers of U.S. citizens. This legislative presentation echoes the erotic, sexualized Asian American woman portrayed in the popular media. In looking to legislation for guidance, many Americans not of Asian ancestry may use these attitudes and images as a priori proof that Asian women are not acceptable for marriage or motherhood. Legislation can then, in turn, be used to legitimize and continue the stereotype of Asian women as erotic sex objects.

The images and sentiments presented through immigration legislation continues to be felt by Asian American women and Asian American communities throughout the United States. More positive images of Asian American women need to be articulated in a number of areas. Scientifically, qualitative research is needed on how Asian American women cope with the erotic images reflected in immigration legislation and the media. Research on the actual self-images of Asian American women is clearly needed. Social scientists need to conduct more research on the confluence of racial, ethnic, and gender identity among Asian American women. Models of identity development are necessary to guide research on gender, race, ethnic minorities, and women in the United States. Finally, more research is needed to examine the effects of these negative images of Asian American women on their relationships.

At the community level, dialogues between Asian American communities and the larger community of U.S. citizens are needed to challenge existing images and sentiments and promote new ones. Institutions of higher education need to support their Asian American female academicians and establish curricula for the teaching of Asian American women. Creative writers and makers of popular media need to develop works that truthfully reflect the lives of Asian American women in all of their complexities. Legislatively, the Asian American community needs to lobby for the elimination of legislation that denigrates Asian American women, such as the Amerasian Immigration Act of 1982. And, as citizens of a representative government, we all need to be vigilant against any legislation that either promotes a derogatory image of Asian Americans or discriminates against anyone on the basis of race, ethnicity, or gender.

REFERENCES

Amerasian Homecoming Act, H.R. 3171, 100th Cong., 1st Sess. (1987).

Amerasian Immigration Act of 1982, Pub. L. No. 97-359, 96 Stat. 1716 (1982).

Amerasian Immigration Section of the Omnibus Budget Reconciliation Act of 1987, Pub. L. No. 100-202, § 584 (1987).

Behr, E., & Steyn, M. (1989). [musical] *The Story of Miss Saigon*. London: Jonathan Cape (1991).

Bond, J. (1984). *Far Pavilions*. [television mini-series] P. Duffel (director). Washington, DC: Acorn Media.

Brier, R. (1994). Looking around. *San Francisco Chronicle*, p. 9.

Brown v. Board of Education, 347 U.S. 483 (1954).

Buck, P. S. H. (with Harris, T. F.) (1966). *For spacious skies: Journey in dialogue*. New York: John Day Co.

Cha, L., & Roscoe, J. (1989). *Eat a Bowl of Tea*. [film] W. Wang (director). Burbank, CA: Columbia Pictures.

Chinese Exclusion Act of 1882, 22 Stat. 58.

Daniels, R. (1990). *Coming to America: A history of immigration and ethnicity in American life*. New York: HarperCollins.

G.I. Fiancées Act, 60 Stat. 416 (1946).

Glenn, E. N. (1986). *Issei, Nisei, war bride: Three generations of Japanese American women in domestic service*. Philadelphia: Temple University Press.

Hammerstein, O., & Osborn, P. (1958). *South Pacific*. [film] J. Logan (director). Hollywood, CA: 20th Century Fox.

Immigration Act of August 9, 1946, 60 Stat. 975. (1946).

Immigration Act of 1917, 39 Stat. 874. (1917).

Immigration Act of 1943, 16 Stat. 682. (1943).

Immigration Act of 1982, 96 Stat. 1716. (1982).

Immigration and Nationality Act Amendments of 1965, 79 Stat. 911. (1965).

Immigration and Nationality Act [McCarran–Walter Act], 66 Stat. 163 (1952).

Immigration Reform and Control Act of 1986, 100 Stat. 3359.

Kim, A. (1990). For the last time, darn it, I am not a mail-order bride. *Los Angeles Times*, p. M4.

Kim, E. (1982). *Asian American literature*. Philadelphia: Temple University Press.

Kim, H. -C. (1992). *Asian Americans and the Supreme Court: A documentary history*. Westport, CT: Greenwood Press.

Mason, R., & Patrick, J. (1960). *The World of Suzie Wong*. [film] R. Quine (director). Hollywood, CA: Worldfilm.

Mitchner, J., & Osborn (1957). *Sayonara*. [film] J. Logan (director). Hollywood, CA: MGM Studios.

National Origins Act of 1924, 43 Stat. 153. (1924).

New York Times. (1943, November 22, p. 5). *Japanese threat to Changsha seen*.

New York Times. (1945, December 10, p. 26). *Chinese press for fleeing Chang Teh*.

New York Times. (1945, December 24, p. 4). *Glider Stowaway here with husband*.

New York Times. (1945, December 24, p. 6). *Former GI tried to swim to them*.

New York Times. (1945, December 27, p. 2). *French brides to begin Sailing for U.S. in month*.

Omnibus Budget Reconciliation Act, 100 Stat. 1329 (1987).

Shukert, E. B. (1988). *The war brides of World War II*. Navato, CA: Predidio Press.

Soldier Brides Act, 61 Stat. 190 (1947).

Sung, B. L. (1990). *Chinese American intermarriage*. New York: Center for Migration Studies.

U.S. Immigration and Naturalization Service. (1996). *Statistical yearbook of the Immigration and Naturalization Service, 1994*. Washington, DC: U.S. Government Printing Office.

War Brides Act of 1945, 59 Stat. 659.

Yung, J. (1995). *Unbound feet: A social history of Chinese women in San Francisco*. Berkeley: University of California Press.

4

WORLD WAR II INTERNMENT AND THE RELATIONSHIPS OF NISEI WOMEN

DONNA K. NAGATA

Relationships, which are such a basic and integral part of living, have received considerable attention in the psychological literature through studies on dating and marriage, family dynamics, and friendships. Such research, however, has rarely considered the impact of significant socio-historical events on these relationships. For Japanese Americans, the World War II forced removal and internment of more than 110,000 persons of Japanese ancestry from the western United States looms as perhaps the most dramatic episode of racism and injustice in their past.

Shortly after the bombing of Pearl Harbor, Hawaii, on December 7, 1941, the U.S. government ordered the internment of Japanese Americans on the presumption that they were potentially disloyal and a threat to national security. Although two thirds of the imprisoned were U.S. citizens, they were denied due process and given no opportunity for individual review. Ethnic heritage alone determined their detention within barbed-wired internment camps, where they remained for up to 4 years. Internees, who often had only 6 days' notice of their removal and could take with them only what they could carry (Nakano, 1990), suffered not only the indignity of suspected disloyalty based solely on race, but also tremendous economic and personal losses.

Despite the magnitude of this historical event, the internment remained largely absent from history textbooks and public debate for decades following the war. In 1981, some 40 years later, however, the Commission on Wartime Relocation and Internment of Civilians (CWRIC, 1997) conducted an extensive investigation of the facts and circumstances surrounding the internment and found no evidence to justify its military necessity. It concluded that a "grave personal injustice" (CWRIC, 1997, p. 459) had been committed against Japanese Americans and that the government should issue a formal apology and monetary redress to all surviving internees.

A FOCUS ON NISEI WOMEN

The upheaval of the internment has had long-lasting consequences for Japanese Americans (Loo, 1993). The experience touched all who were interned. However, gender, age, and generational differences significantly affected how individuals understood, responded to, and experienced the internment. This chapter focuses specifically on the ways in which the internment influenced the relationships of second-generation Japanese American (Nisei) women. By looking at the impact of this major historical event on the lives of Nisei women, we can better understand the intersection of history, identity, and development in women's experiences. Nisei women represent an especially interesting group on which to focus. Because they were citizens born and raised in the United States, the internment severely challenged their sense of justice, democracy, and identity. In addition, most Nisei women, who were in their teens to early 20s during the war, were at critical developmental stages. Finally, their resilience as a group, during and following the wartime experience, is impressive. An examination of their relationships in the context of the internment allows researchers and others to see how development, identity, strength, and resilience have been central to the lives of these women.

This chapter considers Nisei women as a generational cohort and, in some ways, they do represent a highly homogenous group. Restrictive U.S. immigration laws created unusually distinct generational boundaries. The majority of Nisei were born between 1915 and 1940, with the greatest number between 1918 and 1922 (Glenn, 1986). This, noted Nakano (1990), "resulted in a remarkable number of shared generational experiences and character markings in the Nisei woman" (p. 104). At the same time, both Nakano (1990) and Glenn (1986), have aptly pointed out the importance of recognizing individual differences and diversity among Nisei women, and readers of this chapter should bear this in mind as well. Also noteworthy is the fact that the internment affected Nisei women's relationships in a variety of ways. Although some effects were shared, others differed considerably. It is not possible to discuss all of the ways in which relationships were affected. Nonetheless, the examples presented in this chapter can begin to illustrate the significance of the internment for Nisei women's lives.

Nakano (1990) listed four distinct phases that marked the lives of Nisei women: (a) the pre–World War II period, (b) World War II, (c) the postwar period, and (d) the post-1960s period. This chapter uses this temporal framework, as each phase is integral to examining the impact of the internment on Nisei women's relationships. It is necessary to have a sense of their lives before the war to see how the internment changed them, during the war years to see how the internment affected their relationships, and after the war to explore enduring or long-term consequences. Each phase also considers the relationships of Nisei women within three domains: family, peers, and community. With this approach, it is possible to begin to see the effects of the internment across time and across multiple relationship roles.

The chapter draws on interview data reflecting Nisei women's experiences in their own words. These data are part of a larger Nisei Research Project (1995–1996). The majority of the interviewed women lived on the West Coast, whereas the remainder were from other parts of the United States. At the time of the interviews, interviewees ranged in age from 63 years to 78 years, with a mean age of 69 years. Their ages at the time of internment ranged from 9 years to 24 years, with a mean age of 15 years.

CULTURAL VALUES AND COMMUNITY CONTEXT: LIFE BEFORE THE WAR

Family Relations

In the years just before World War II, the average Nisei woman was in her teens to early 20s (Nakano, 1990). Her first-generation immigrant parents (Issei) often worked as farm laborers or domestic servants, or ran service-oriented businesses (Nakano, 1990). Issei mothers were responsible both for maintenance of the family and for work outside the home (Espiritu, 1997; Nakano, 1990). A strong commitment to family based traditional Japanese values embodied in phrases such as *kodomo no tame ni* (for the sake of the children) and *kazoku no tame ni* (for the sake of the family) was central. Collective effort and male dominance and privilege also typified prewar Japanese American families (Nakano, 1990). Women were raised to be *otonashi*, which translates literally into English to mean "no sound" (Smith, 1990). Although these values were evident in most prewar Japanese American families, those who lived in rural areas tended to be more traditional than those living in urban areas (Glenn, 1986).

Issei parents instilled in their children other important cultural values and behavioral norms. These included *gaman* (perseverance in the face of adversity), *giri* (sense of duty and obligation), filial piety, and *enryo* (reserve, restraint, or deference). Many also used the phrase *shikata ga-nai* to express a sense of fatalism or an acceptance of conditions that "could not be helped" (Kitano, 1969, as cited in Nakano, 1990, p. 37).

The Japanese American family also strongly valued education, and high school attendance rates for the Nisei population in 1940 were higher than those for the general population. However, young Nisei women (54%) were somewhat less likely to be attending high school than young Nisei men (60%; Nakano, 1990). This lower percentage may, in part, reflect the fact that older Nisei daughters from large farm families often had to curtail their education to help the family (Glenn, 1986).

Peer and Community Relations

Although the Nisei generation saw their primary identity as American, they were bilingual and bicultural, living what Sone (1953) called a "dual personality." The Issei supported the Nisei's allegiance to the United States, but they also expected their children to behave as "good" Japanese (Kitagawa, 1967; Nakano, 1990). As a result, tensions developed between the Issei and Nisei as the second generation tried to balance the expectations of their parents with their own desires and the barriers they faced in the larger community (Hosokawa, 1969; Kitagawa, 1967).

Most young Nisei women lived sheltered lives. "Girls learned to knit, sew, and embroider, and some took lessons in *odori* (folk dancing). [They] also . . . learned to jitterbug, played kick-the-can and baseball, and read the same popular books and magazines as their non-Japanese peers" (Matsumoto, 1984, p. 7). Despite the similarities in interests with their White peers, most Nisei lived in ethnic isolation, apart from the larger mainstream society. Many attended Japanese school as well as regular public schools, and although they might have interacted with White students in the classroom, they often maintained their primary friendships with other Japanese Americans. Urban Nisei women often joined all-Nisei church-affiliated youth groups, sports leagues, YWCA/YMCA clubs, and other groups where they could meet and socialize with their peers. Within these organizations, however, men continued to be the leaders and officers (Glenn, 1986).

Prewar peer relationships for rural women differed from those of women who lived in urban areas. Comments from Nisei Project interviewees suggest that given the great distances between houses, those who lived on family farms had significantly fewer contacts with both nonsibling Japanese American and White peers. One interviewee also noted the existence of tension between rural and urban Japanese Americans and recalled how she felt that the "city" Nisei girls looked down on her (Nisei Research Project, 1995–1996).

Both rural and urban Nisei women knew that they were expected to date and marry other Nisei. Older Nisei women frequently had prearranged marriages. Yoo (1993) researched the Japanese American ethnic press between 1925 and 1941 and found a strong emphasis on Nisei–Nisei coupling by Japanese American journalists. In addition, the message to Nisei women was "not only to marry, but to do so early to avoid the embarassment of being called an 'old maid'" (Yoo, 1993, p. 77). This emphasis on racial solidarity from within the Japanese American community interacted with the significant levels of anti-Asian hostility from the larger society and the antimiscegenation laws in most states that prohibited interracial marriages between Japanese and White Americans. Outmarriage rates before World War II were exceptionally low; only 2.3% of the women and 3.1% of the men married non-Japanese partners (Spickard, 1989). This was in contrast to the 30% outmarriage rate found for the children of European immigrants (Drachsler, 1921).

The racism and discrimination to Japanese Americans in the larger community were often mirrored in the Niseis' peer relations as well. "It was an unspoken word," commented one Nisei Project interviewee, "that you just stayed in your place." She recalled the pain of being a preteen left out whenever White friends made invitations to parties and noted a time still fresh in her memory when she entered a public swimming pool with a White friend and her mother, only to be told to leave by the lifeguard on duty (Nisei Research Project, 1995–1996).

Strength and Resilience

Although Nisei women encountered numerous economic and social restrictions in the prewar years, they also demonstrated significant strengths. Nisei women learned to balance a complex bicultural world. In addition, traditional Japanese values modeled by the Issei concerning the centrality of family, hard work, the endurance of adversity, and the importance of education gave the young Nisei an important base from which to begin their lives. Nisei women also learned the ethics of hard work from their Issei mothers, who put in long hours within and outside the home. Finally, they gathered strength from each other and their ethnic community in response to the ongoing discrimination and racism that they faced. These resources became even more important as the United States entered World War II.

PEARL HARBOR AND THE EFFECTS OF WAR

Japan's attack on Pearl Harbor on December 7, 1941, dramatically changed the lives of Japanese Americans. All of the women interviewed could remember exactly where they were when they heard the news, and many had vivid recollections of how the Pearl Harbor attack affected their relationships with family, friends, and the community.

Family Relations

The effect on family relations was devastating for those whose fathers were abruptly arrested by the Federal Bureau of Investigation (FBI) soon after the Pearl Harbor attack. One interviewee was 12 years old at the time and described the anguish of her experience:

> I really feel that was traumatic. No time for anything. Just a knock at the door, two men coming. Mother got his [clothes] and they took him . . . I still feel that was the most traumatic part of my life. How *dare* they take him when he didn't do anything wrong! To be treated so very bad. At 12, I was too young to know what was going on. I just felt the pain of my father's absence.

Tragically, when her father was reunited with the family years later, he was ill, and he died shortly after his release.

Most of the interviewees recalled very little family discussion of what was happening. Nonetheless, the FBI arrests affected the young Nisei, even if their own fathers were not taken.

> I think everybody was pretty quiet-mouthed about it all. All I can remember is before we were evacuated, some of the prominent Japanese leaders . . . were rounded up by the FBI. And, you know kids at 10, 11 [years], we used to run and find out who's going to be next? It was like run, and then run back home to give the sad news . . . Everything happened so fast, I think people (were) just more traumatized than anything else.

The Pearl Harbor attack also highlighted the citizenship differences between the Issei and the Nisei. The Issei, who were prohibited from becoming U.S. citizens, were now labeled *enemy aliens*, whereas the U.S.-born Nisei were American citizens by birth. This distinction caused many Nisei tremendous worries about their parents' futures and about the possibility that the Issei might be imprisoned or deported by the U.S. government. They did not know at the time that the eventual internment orders would include all Japanese Americans, regardless of citizenship.

Peer and Community Relations

Relations with the non-Japanese community and non-Japanese peers changed almost immediately. One interviewee recalled how customers stopped buying eggs from her father's business. Other Nisei women described a palpable shift in the social climate around them.

> You could feel the tension. People didn't know how to treat you. They kind of stood away from you and acted very strange. I suppose we did too ... I guess they all felt maybe we had something to do with it [Pearl Harbor].

Interactions at school became equally uncomfortable, as is evident from the comments of other interviewees. "The next morning [after the attack],—I was a sophomore in high school—I took the bus .... We [Japanese] all went on the bus with our heads hanging. It was a terrible day." Another woman, who was 11 years old at the time, recalled, "Friends took it out on me ... I didn't understand why they were so mad at me. I always thought I was an American! ... It was so devastating. All my friends called me a traitor." Teachers could be hurtful as well:

> They started to get very cold to us and, in fact, while in high school I remember a social studies teacher used to kind of make us upset, saying he was in a concentration camp during World War I and, "You people are gonna be in there." We couldn't, you know, we didn't believe that ... we used to hate that statement being made.

Relations with other non-Japanese groups also changed. Several interviewees remembered Chinese Americans in their schools who wore buttons reading "I am Chinese American." This created resentment for one Nisei woman, who wondered how the Chinese Americans could do this when the Chinese and Japanese had a shared history of oppression and discrimination in the United States.

Although most interviewees experienced negative changes in relation to the White Americans around them, this was not always the case. Some Nisei women noted that they had White friends and teachers who remained positive toward them after the Pearl Harbor attack and even some who maintained correspondence with them during their internment.

Strength and Resilience

The post–Pearl Harbor period generated tremendous uncertainty and concern. In response, Japanese Americans drew on their inner strengths and community ties to cope with the unfolding nightmare. The very young Nisei relied on their families to withstand the increasing hostility. Those who were older tried to maintain as much of a routine life as possible, awaiting news of their families' future, while those whose fathers were taken by the FBI stepped in to assist their Issei mothers in managing family and financial responsibilities. For the most part, however, there was little Japanese Americans could do but wait and see what would happen next.

INTERNMENT: CHANGING ROLES, AND CHALLENGING CONDITIONS

On February 19, 1942, 10 weeks after the Japanese attack on Pearl Harbor, President Franklin D. Roosevelt signed Executive Order 9066 (CWRIC, 1997), clearing the way for the removal and internment of Japanese Americans from the western portion of the United States. The internment process brought numerous changes to Nisei women's relationships. Some hurried into marriage, worried that if they did not they might be sent to a different internment camp than their loved one. Communities with large numbers of Japanese Americans were split into three or four groups for detention. Extended families were separated, and some young Nisei wives who accompanied their husbands' families spent years apart from their own parents and siblings (Nakano, 1990).

Many relationships were disrupted due to relocation. In leaving their homes and communities, Nisei women were separated from relatives, family friends, and peers (both Japanese American and non-Japanese). Most Japanese Americans were initially placed in temporary detention (assembly) centers for several months. These centers were often former racetracks and fairgrounds, hastily whitewashed before being converted into holding areas for tens of thousands of Japanese Americans. The Japanese Americans were then moved to the more permanent internment camps. Although some internees remained in a single camp until their release, others were shifted more than once to different camps during their internment. Multiple moves, along with the anxieties surrounding the internment and an uncertain future, created significant stress for the young Nisei women, many of whom were at an age when peer attachments were extremely important. One interviewee shared the following:

> I was kind of mad . . . that they could just kind of haul us around like animals. We made best friends in assembly center and then all of a sudden we were separated again. Some went to Minidoka [Idaho], and some went to Wyoming and different places.

The women adjusted as best they could, but the transitions were difficult for some, especially those who were sent to camps or detention centers where they had no friends.

> We were teenagers, trying to fit into a group that was already established. It was not comfortable trying to make friends again. And, once again, I felt the same feeling of how I felt when I was in my small

White community, trying to reach out and make friends, and of not belonging . . . And that played throughout my life.

Family Relations

Within the temporary detention centers, the Japanese Americans lived in cramped quarters, often separated only by sheets or blankets. As many as seven people lived in a single space (Nakano, 1990). These conditions, in addition to communal toilets, showers, and eating facilities, meant that there was little or no privacy. The lack of privacy was hard for the women (Nakano, 1990), and one would expect that it was particularly traumatic for young adolescent girls, who were of an age at which they were highly self-conscious about their bodies. One interviewee, who was 12 when first interned, captured well the humiliation of the detention center conditions:

> For the first time, you had public toilets and such. The building was constructed with the cheap lumber, so they had a lot of knots in there. Men would pop the knots so you'd always see some eye looking in, peeking at you. The privacy was absolutely none. Taking showers where they used to wash the horses—It was a big round area and they put this middle divider that went up about 3/4 or 1/2 way up. And the boys would always climb up that wall and be looking at you.

Conditions inside the more permanent camps continued to affect family relations (CWRIC, 1997; Kitagawa, 1967; Kitano, 1976; Matsumoto, 1989; Morishima, 1973). Entire families were confined to a single barrack room, no larger than 20 feet by 25 feet (CWRIC, 1997). Such a small space, noted one interviewee, made it difficult for older Nisei and married couples to meet their needs for intimacy. The thin walls between rooms also made Nisei mothers self-conscious about their babies disturbing neighbors, leading some to rock their infants for hours so as not to bother others (Nakano, 1990). As had been the case in the temporary detention centers, there were communal toileting, laundering, and eating facilities as well as poor food and shortages of toilet paper and milk (Matsumoto, 1984). Women with young children walked long distances to wash diapers or prepare formula at the mess hall (Nakano, 1990). In addition, because the internment camps were located in deserts and swamplands, internees faced harsh weather conditions as they went about their daily tasks.

Family unity deteriorated over time. For most Nisei, camp life meant there was more time to spend with friends and less time with their own families (Kitagawa, 1967; Morishima, 1973). Mess hall dining replaced the traditional ritual of the family meal. And, as Nakano (1990) noted, even the "literal and symbolic center of family" (p. 146), the kitchen, was lost.

Young Nisei no longer had a "home" where they could gather and invite their friends.

The Nisei faced significant changes in relation to their Issei parents as well. Issei fathers, who had been the main breadwinners and decision makers, were now inmates along with the rest of their family members. Within the camps, wives and children could earn the same meager wages for work as fathers (a maximum of $19 per month; CWRIC, 1997), and younger Nisei women found unprecedented job opportunities (Espiritu, 1997). Camp governance structure also prohibited the Issei from being elected into office, which meant that the Nisei now assumed primary responsibilities for communicating with camp officials (CWRIC, 1997). These factors served to diffuse previously well-delineated role relationships, and family members "became more inclined than ever to make independent decisions," diminishing the Issei father's status in the family as well as his ego (Nakano, 1990, p. 146). Male dominance also decreased as a result of changes in the lives of Issei mothers. Many Issei mothers, along with older Nisei women, had more free time because the duties of cooking no longer existed; they took on not only work but also a variety of recreational activities within the camps (Espiritu, 1997; Matsumoto, 1989).

One of the most painful issues to face families emerged in the early months of 1943 and centered on the so-called loyalty questions. The questions were required of all internees older than 17. One question asked men if they were willing to serve in the armed forces of the United States on combat duty wherever ordered. Women and Issei were asked whether they would be willing to volunteer for the Army Nurse Corps of the Women's Army Corps. A second question was, "Will you swear unqualified allegiance to the United States of America and faithfully defend the United States from any or all attack by foreign or domestic forces, and forswear any form of allegiance or obedience to the Japanese emperor, or to any other foreign government, power or organization?" (CWRIC, 1997, p. 192).

The questions threw families into turmoil. Although many felt little conflict in answering "yes" to both questions, others were unsure or set against answering affirmatively. The second question regarding allegiance put the Issei in an impossible position. They had been prohibited from becoming U.S. citizens yet were being asked to renounce their allegiance to their only country of citizenship. Internees worried that this was a trick question: A "yes" might be used as evidence that they had had prior allegiance to the emperor, and a "no" could be seen as a sign of disloyalty. Nakano (1990) pointed to a particular dilemma for the Nisei. If their parents answered "no" to both of the questions, and they answered "yes," they would most likely be separated from their parents. "In effect, they (the Nisei) were being asked to choose between their country and their parents" (Nakano, 1990, p. 163).

Rifts over how to respond developed among family members, between parents and children, and among siblings. Eighty-seven percent of the internees answered the loyalty questions with an unqualified "yes" (CWRIC, 1997), but those who answered "no" were segregated from the others and placed in the Tule Lake, California, camp. Nakano (1990) noted that the segregation at Tule Lake was especially taxing for women who, after working to keep their families together throughout the uprootings and hardships of camp life, now had husbands and brothers arrested for refusing to register for the draft or for political agitation within Tule Lake. The conflicts between individuals around their responses to the loyalty questions and subsequent decisions about whether to resist draft registration were so intense that they remain even today between family members and friends (CWRIC, 1997).

Peer and Community Relations

The loyalty questions generated intense conflict for many internee families. However, given their age at the time, it is not surprising that peer relations in the camps were a major focus for many Nisei women. Those who had grown up in Japanese American communities before the war found themselves interacting for the first time with Japanese Americans from other parts of the country. One interviewee was struck by the regional differences she encountered in camp. In describing these differences from her standpoint as a northwestern Nisei, she recalled thinking ". . . . Californian people, I don't know about Northern, but Southern, we were different . . . . They were more outgoing." This same interviewee went on to say that had it not been for the internment, she would never have met Nisei from California. Hence, one important outcome of internment was the exposure of Nisei to peers from other geographic areas or socioeconomic backgrounds.

At the same time, those who had lived in isolated or primarily non–Japanese American communities before the war suddenly found themselves living in confined camps with thousands of other Japanese Americans. Reduced parental supervision meant that Nisei women were freer to socialize with their peers and choose their own husbands (Matsumoto, 1989, as cited in Espiritu, 1997). "One strange thing to me," recalled one interviewee, "was seeing so many Nihonjin [Japanese]! I was 20, never had a date, never even met any boys! So, in a way, it was helpful." Dating opportunities blossomed, and it was not uncommon for Nisei women to meet their future husbands during their internment.

Over time, schools developed within the camps, including nursery schools, elementary schools, high schools, and adult education facilities (CWRIC, 1997). Peer relations changed, particularly at the high school level. All of the typical roles, such as football and basketball team captains, cheerleaders, and student body leaders, were now available to the Nisei. These were roles that had typically been filled by White students (Kitano, 1976). For the first time, "the variable of ethnicity was held constant so that competition rested primarily on qualifications and achievement" (Kitano, 1976, p. 77).

Interviewees also indicated that one of the most positive memories from the camps was the formation of deep friendships with other girls and young women. Many of these friendships have lasted into their current lives, attesting to the strong bonds that formed during that time. As internees settled in, they took jobs within the camps to keep busy and to contribute to the family savings. Nisei women met friends not only through work but also through a variety of Nisei camp activities. There were dances and a number of social groups. Many organizations paralleled those that existed before the incarceration, including the YWCA/YMCA, the Girl Scouts, student leadership organizations, and sports leagues. However, new groups also evolved in response to specific needs that developed because of the internment. One interviewee described how she and other Nisei girls, all around 15 or 16 years old, belonged to a group called The Crusaders, who assisted internees who left the camps to resettle or enter the military.

> As "Crusaders," we used to go down to the people [who] used to leave the camp, ... whether they left weekly or whether they left daily, ... a group of us girls would go down to the gate and say "goodbye" to them. We didn't exactly know them, but we gave them a little memento to take with them, such as wishbones that were painted ... wishing luck.

The Crusaders, she recalled, also reached out beyond the confines of camp by sending greetings to the Nisei serving in the military.

It is more difficult to comment on the relationships of interned Nisei women to the larger mainstream society during this period. Deliberately isolated, internees had little direct contact with the broader community, with the exception of temporary passes to go outside the camps for work or brief excursions to the nearest towns. Some Nisei women maintained correspondence with friends or others who were not interned. Letters became an important link with the outside world and a way for these women to communicate their experiences. However, as Matsumoto (1984) commented, such correspondence could be censored by the government, and it is likely that these letters did not fully convey the thoughts of those writing from camp.

Strength and Resilience

When asked how they managed these difficult times, interviewees, both those who were young and those who were in their 20s during the war years, noted that their families and the stoic strength of their Issei parents provided critical resources for coping. These, in addition to the Japanese cultural value of *gaman* helped buffer the disruptions.

Peer groups of Nisei women inside the camps such as The Crusaders also illustrate that, despite numerous difficulties, Nisei women responded to the internment with resilience and adaptation. They were determined to make the best of their situation and demonstrated this strength in a variety of ways. Some took classes in camp to advance their learning. Others sewed curtains to help create a sense of comfort for their families. Some Nisei mothers even attempted to bring food from the mess halls back to their barracks in an effort to maintain the traditional family meal. And, although the communal laundering facilities were enormously inconvenient, they eventually became a place where the women gathered to share stories and information (Nakano, 1990). The resourcefulness of women internees is also shown in more unique situations that arose. Okubo (1946), for example, published a collection of drawings from the internment experience. One picture depicts women placing huge floral wreaths on a memorial for an internee who was shot by a camp guard. What is so striking is that the flowers were all made of paper because there were no live flowers in the middle of the desert.

MOVING OUT AND MOVING ON: RESETTLEMENT AND THE POSTWAR PERIOD

By 1943 and 1944, Nisei who answered "yes" to both of the loyalty questions began to apply for clearance to leave the camps. Resettlement, however, was limited to areas outside of the military exclusion zones of the West Coast and led to a migration of Nisei from the camps to unfamiliar cities such as Chicago, New York, and Minneapolis. Those who left the camps received a one-way bus or train ticket and $25. The Nisei who resettled were primarily between 15 and 35 years old, and they took a range of menial jobs (CWRIC, 1997). Domestic jobs were among the most available to Nisei women immediately after the war (Nakano, 1990). Others, however, were able to take advantage of scholarships at colleges and universities in the Midwest and East (Matsumoto, 1989; Nakano, 1990).

Family Relations

The resettlement process affected relationships once again, fragmenting families for varying periods of time. It was not unusual for an older sibling to venture out first, become established, and then call for a sibling to join him or her. Meanwhile, Issei parents remained in the internment camps, worried about the fate of their children in the outside world. The transition was exciting for some Nisei women, frightening for others. As one interviewee recalled,

> That was a traumatic time for me because my dad put me on the train in Idaho and he didn't know whether he was ever going to see me again. He didn't know how long he'd be in camp, or what was going to happen to me.

Not all Nisei women resettled. For example, those who were very young during their internment were unable to go out on their own. As of January 1945, more than 60,000 people still remained in the camps. More than 8,000 of these were women between the ages of 20 and 40 years, and many were older Nisei women who stayed behind to care for their children, their parents, or those who were sick (Nakano, 1990). Similarly, if a Nisei daughter were an only child, she often needed to remain to look after her parents. Hence, age and family composition affected resettlement patterns.

Peers and Community Relations

Not surprisingly, resettlement brought new changes to peer and community relations. Nisei women were thrust from being internees confined within primarily all-Japanese camps into unfamiliar, predominantly White communities, negotiating jobs and establishing new lives. The support of peers and siblings who resettled in the same area helped some to cope with the challenges. However, many Nisei once again felt a loss of support by being separated from family and friends during resettlement. To make matters worse, the War Relocation Authority urged the Nisei to avoid associating with each other in order to integrate as much as possible (CWRIC, 1997). Nisei women who did resettle with friends found their lives affected in more specific ways as well. One interviewee, for example, worked as a domestic, as did her friends, and remembered how they had to plan their social events for Thursdays, because that was a designated "maid's day off." Takezawa (1995) also noted that the pressures during resettlement were so great for some Nisei that they never married.

Most of the women interviewees reported few negative experiences with overt racism or hostility in the areas in which they resettled. In retrospect, they felt that the exposure to new areas outside of the Japanese American ethnic communities had been positive. These women learned that they could survive on their own and, in the words of one project participant, "widen their horizons." One woman described the positive effect as follows:

> It showed us opportunities . . . I thought it was a learning experience . . . I learned different ways of eating, meeting different people, knowing there could be a world outside of [rural] California.

But for those who did encounter problems, the memories are still painful to recall. "When I left camp, I was 15," said one woman. "It was hot so we got off the train. There was an ice cream shop and I ran in. And the man said, 'We don't sell to Japs!'"

Most Nisei, along with their parents, eventually moved back to the West Coast after the war to reestablish their lives. There they faced housing and job discrimination and anti-Japanese violence (CWRIC, 1997). Racial taunts and outright rejection from non-Japanese peers confronted many Nisei returning to school. "People spit at us. We were shot upon, and so isolated when we went back to high school. We were seen as the enemy," recalled one interviewee. Only a few groups, particularly the Quakers and liberal church groups, extended support for returning Japanese Americans (CWRIC, 1997).

Strength and Resilience

Resettlement brought new disruptions and hardship. The dedication of those Nisei women who remained in camp to be with their parents, however, reflected both their strength and commitment to family. Nakano (1990) also saw evidence of this strength in the fact that the Nisei who resettled out of camp often called for their parents to join them as they became established. "Parent–child bonding in the Issei–Nisei family had," she noted, "already taken firm hold, and thus weathered the buffeting conditions of camp" (p. 148). This bond was to continue well into the postwar years. By the time the war ended, most Issei were too old to restart their careers. Many remained dependent on their Nisei children for the rest of their lives. This directly affected Nisei women, who were expected to care for their elderly parents. Beyond the family, Nisei women also gained strength from friendships with other Nisei as they ventured out on their own, gaining new skills and independence during the resettlement period.

REBUILDING AND REGENERATION:
POST-1960S TO THE PRESENT

Family Relations

During the 1950s and 1960s, Nisei women focused their energies on marrying and raising families. Marriage was still limited primarily to other Nisei, and most of the women stayed at home until their children were teenagers (Nakano, 1990).

The long-term effects of the camps influenced the ways in which Nisei women raised their children during this time. Most of them avoided things Japanese, encouraging their children to be model "American" citizens, and like other Japanese Americans, they did not talk about the internment years. "She [the Nisei woman] refused to discuss it, to dwell on it, wanting above all else to get on with her life" (Nakano, 1990, p. 188). Interviewee comments highlight the effect of the camp experience on the relationships of Nisei women with their children, the Sansei generation:

> The kids grew up in the East and I just didn't talk about it [the internment] because I didn't want to make them feel any different than they were. And I wanted them to be All-American. We didn't lie to them. It just really never came up because it was so far removed.

The effort to protect their children was also evident in another woman's comments:

> We raised them to be White so that they would be accepted into the mainstream . . . . We try to give our kids the best possible, protect and give them the very best they can get. To load them with scars, [like] "Gosh, you're different, herded into camp like cattle," I didn't want that. I wanted them to think *anything* is possible . . . . When you think anything is possible, it becomes possible. I think that is why I never told them about the pain, the grime . . . we went through.

Interestingly, the author's own research (Nagata, 1993) suggests that although the Nisei may have wanted to avoid talking about the internment to protect their children, that very silence had its own impact. Sansei frequently interpreted the avoidance of discussions about the camps as an indicator that there was an important and painful gap in their family histories, and some have felt the effects of their parents' internment on their own ethnic identity and self-esteem, a generation later.

Peer and Community Relations

Most contemporary Nisei now live in proximity to other Nisei. However, resettlement policies, which required that Japanese Americans leaving the camps initially remain away from the West Coast, led to a dispersal of this generation over a broad geographic range. Today's Nisei also live in communities that are predominantly non–Japanese American. Several interviewees living in areas with few other Japanese Americans reported feeling quite comfortable in their communities. Yet, the observation of one Nisei woman suggested a continued awareness of her ethnic identity and the past in her current living situation: "Here I was rejected in my White community while growing up, and here I am [living in a White community]." Such a comment indicates that the legacy of internment may continue to affect the community relationships of some Nisei women in nonobvious ways.

Peer and community relations for Nisei women have also moved into more public and political arenas (Nakano, 1990). Starting in the 1970s, Nisei women began exercising greater independence, advancing their education, or working in paid or voluntary jobs as their children entered school. They also started taking leadership roles in Japanese American community groups, such as the Japanese American Citizens League (Nakano, 1990). Nakano summarized the status of Nisei women at this time in the following way: "In short, while Nisei women were fulfilling many traditional expectations, they were also in a state of transition, easing out of some of the constraining aspects of the traditional mold" (p. 20).

Strength and Resilience

During the post-1960s period, Nisei women initially focused on the future of their children and taking care of their elderly parents. Most chose not to dwell on the past internment but rather to move ahead with their lives through self-development and, in some cases, moving into more public and political spheres.

Family discussion about the camps remained absent for decades, yet there were other ways that Nisei women continued to show their resilience to the internment. Although now in their 70s and 80s, most of the interviewed women maintained strong connections with friends that they met in the camps. These relationships have endured for decades. Many Nisei women also enjoy attending camp reunions on a regular basis, catching up on news, and reconnecting with former classmates. In these respects, the reunions seem no different from most other high school or college reunions. However, camp reunions also serve another important function for former internees. One woman, whose husband was also interned, noted that attending reunions was "a rewarding experience, kind of both [of us] going through the same thing—a camaraderie effect." Such gatherings, then, also represent a form of positive coping, reaffirming the Niseis' past internment experience in the present among peers who shared the same hardships, challenges, and memories.

The majority of interviewees did attend reunions, but there are also those who avoid them. One woman stated simply, "I'd rather forget that time." Age may also influence the likelihood of Nisei attending camp reunions. As noted by one interviewee, younger Nisei appeared less likely to go because they were too young to be socially active in camp. Another woman saw personality differences as contributing to the likelihood of attending. Outgoing and extroverted women, she hypothesized, were more likely to attend reunions. These latter points indicate the importance of remembering that there are individual differences not only in the ways in which internment affected Nisei women's lives but also in their responses to these effects today (Nagata, 1999).

RESURRECTING THE INTERNMENT AND REDRESSING INJUSTICE

Another important force influencing the relationships of Nisei women in the post-1960s period was the resurrection of the internment's importance within Japanese American communities in the late 1960s and the 1970s. During this time Japanese Americans began focusing their efforts to seek redress from the government for the injustices of the World War II internment. Numerous factors contributed to the reemergence of interest in the internment, including the Black Power movement, the emergence of an interest in Asian American ethnic identity, and the political involvement of Japanese Americans in repealing Title II of the Internal Security Act of 1950, which established the legal basis for creating camps such as those used to incarcerate the Japanese Americans during the war (Nakanishi, 1993). The writings of Nisei women about the internment also helped raise awareness about the concerns for redress. These publications include *Years of Infamy* by Michi Weglyn (1976), *Nisei Daughter* by Monica Sone (1953), and *Farewell to Manzanar* (1973) by Jeanne Wakatsuki Houston and her husband (Nakano, 1990).

By the early 1980s, Nisei women were actively participating in the redress movement. They were among the key figures who researched information to be submitted to the government commission investigating the wartime internment, and it was a woman, Aiko Yoshinaga-Herzig, who uncovered critical documents that directly challenged the doctrine of military necessity for the incarceration (Nakano, 1990). Nisei women also spearheaded grassroots and political campaigns supporting the redress movement. Hundreds testified at the CWRIC hearings held across the country (Nakano, 1990). Years of hard work by Japanese Americans, both men and women, eventually resulted in the signing of the Civil Liberties Act of 1988 (50 APP U.S.C.A. § 1989b *et seq.*), which provided for a formal governmental apology for the injustice of the internment as well as a $20,000 payment to each surviving internee.

The redress movement affected Nisei women by allowing them to see other Japanese American women in leadership roles at national and community levels. It also helped them strengthen a psychological relationship with their ethnic community and, more specifically, with their peer community of former internees. The testimonies of others who had kept their emotions hidden for 40 years affirmed the nature of the injustice that they had encountered, allowing them to examine their experience as a shared one. This sense of community stimulated by the redress effort extended across generations to include the Sansei children as well (Takezawa, 1995). Several of the interviewed women also found that the success of the movement helped reestablish their sense of relationship with the broader society and with the ideals of justice and democracy. These women felt that receiving redress increased their faith in the government and provided a sense of closure.

Others, however, had mixed reactions. "A few dollars they gave us," commented one woman, "It doesn't begin to compensate for the material (losses). No, No. What about the emotional loss, the trauma? You can't put a dollar sign on that." Virtually all of the interviewees also felt tremendous sadness that the redress bill took so long to pass. None of their parents lived to receive the apology or check, yet the Nisei women felt that it was the Issei who suffered most from the incarceration. In this sense, although the passage of the redress bill signaled a tremendous success and vindication for Japanese Americans, it also underscored the losses and suffering of the Issei that were never addressed. The Nisei still carry this emotional burden.

CONCLUSION

The comments of the women presented in this chapter suggest multiple ways in which the internment influenced the lives and relationships of Nisei women. These effects occurred across their lifetimes and helped shape their family relations, their peer interactions, and their experiences in the larger community around them. The chapter has centered on the effects of internment on the relationships of Nisei women who lived in the camps. However, it is important to recognize that the internment affected all Japanese Americans (Nagata, 1993). Those who lived outside of the military exclusion zone still faced anti-Japanese hostility and uncertainty in their lives. Others who moved inland to escape the internment endured severe economic and personal hardships in doing so. In multiple ways, the internment has been the central experience influencing the way Japanese Americans "see themselves, how they see America, and how they have raised their children" (CWRIC, 1997, p. 301). Whether interned or not, all Nisei became painfully aware of the precariousness of their rights and status in their own country. Even if a Nisei woman escaped internment, she could not ignore the fact that more than 90% of her fellow Japanese Americans had been put behind barbed wire and that she, too, would have been imprisoned had she lived on the West Coast. Similarly, many of the strengths, values, and coping responses described by the interned Nisei women can be descriptive of Nisei women more generally.

At the same time, it is important to consider the diversity of Nisei women's experiences in relation to the internment and their postwar lives.

Interned Nisei women do not represent a homogenous group. Indeed, as noted elsewhere (Nagata, 1999), there are significant differences among Nisei women in their internment experiences and their reactions to those experiences. The range of relationship effects described in this chapter do not apply to all Nisei women, nor are they exhaustive.

Finally, one should not presume that the impact of internment on a Nisei woman's relationships necessarily outweighed the impact of other noninternment factors on those relationships. Just as the internment experience varied among Nisei women, so did other life experiences that shaped their relationships with others. For example, some women were the eldest of their siblings, others the youngest, and still others the only child. Each birth status brought different family role expectations. Age at the time of internment also affected relationships with family and peers, because developmental stage provided a framework for the issues each woman faced.

Keeping these considerations in mind, this chapter provides valuable insights into the many ways in which the internment brought critical changes in the lives of Nisei women. A common theme is the importance of Japanese cultural values and behavioral norms in mediating the impact of the internment on Nisei women's relationships. From their Issei parents the Nisei women learned the importance of family and the expectation that one should persevere and make the best of adverse situations. Through it all, "Nisei women had held onto the legacy of a strong sense of family as well as other positive cultural values, which had helped sustain them" (Nakano, 1990, p. 210). Indeed, family remains a central part of their lives.

A second theme is that of resilience and coping. Feminist theorists emphasize the importance of studying women's lives in context, remaining sensitive not only to the roles, internalized expectations, and institutions that constrain their behaviors, but also to the ways in which women resist oppression and maintain personal control under those conditions (Delmar, 1986; Fine, 1983–1984; Stewart, 1994). Nisei women responded to the challenges of the internment in ways that affirmed their sense of agency. They developed strengths from their bicultural experience, learning to negotiate between traditional Japanese and American norms while coping with racism and internment. They also formed organizations that promoted social support and, through the challenges of resettlement, developed a newfound sense of independence. These strengths continued to grow as Nisei women took on active roles in the redress movement.

Finally, these Nisei women help us understand more universal themes of human response to extraordinary challenges. Their resilience during and after internment reveals a generation of women who found positive ways to cope with adversity and who have continued to focus their energies on building a better future for themselves, their families, and their communities.

REFERENCES

50 APP U.S.C.A. § 1989b *et seq.*

CWRIC, Commission on Wartime Relocation and Internment of Civilians. (1997). *Personal justice denied.* Washington, DC & San Francisco: Civil Liberties Public Education Fund, & Seattle: University of Washington.

Delmar, R. (1986). What is feminism? In J. Mitchell & A. Oakley (Eds.), *What is feminism?* (pp. 8–33). New York: Pantheon.

Drachsler, J. (1921). *Intermarriage in New York City.* New York: publisher unknown.

Espiritu, Y. L. (1997). *Asian American women and men.* Thousand Oaks, CA: Sage.

Fine, M. (1983–1984). Coping with rape: Critical perspectives on consciousness. *Imagination, Cognition and Personality, 3,* 249–267.

Glenn, E. N. (1986). *Issei, Nisei, war bride: Three generations of Japanese American women in domestic service.* Philadelphia: Temple University Press.

Hosokawa, B. (1969). *Nisei: The quiet Americans.* New York: William Morrow.

Kitagawa, D. (1967). *Issei and Nisei: The internment years.* New York: Seabury.

Kitano, H. H. L. (1976). *Japanese Americans: The evolution of a subculture* (2nd ed.). Englewood Cliffs, NJ: Prentice Hall.

Loo, C. M. (1993). An integrative-sequential treatment model for posttraumatic stress disorder: A case study of the Japanese American internment and redress. *Clinical Psychology Review, 13,* 89–117.

Matsumoto, V. (1984). Japanese American women during World War II. *Frontiers, 8,* 6–14.

Matsumoto, V. (1989). Nisei women and resettlement during World War II. In Asian Women United of California (Ed.), *Making waves: An anthology of writings by and about Asian American women* (pp. 115–126). Boston: Beacon.

Morishima, J. K. (1973). The evacuation: Impact on the family. In S. Sue & N. N. Wagner (Eds.), *Asian Americans: Psychological perspectives* (pp. 13–19). Palo Alto, CA: Science and Behavior Books.

Nagata, D. K. (1993). *Legacy of injustice: Exploring the cross-generational impact of the Japanese American internment.* New York: Plenum.

Nagata, D. K. (1999). Expanding the internment narrative: Multiple layers of Japanese American women's experiences. In M. Romero & A. J. Stewart (Eds.), *Women's untold stories: Breaking silence, talking back, voicing complexity* (pp. 71–82). New York: Routlege.

Nakanishi, D. T. (1993). Surviving democracy's "mistake": Japanese Americans and the enduring legacy of Executive Order 9066. *Amerasia Journal, 19,* 7–35.

Nakano, M. (1990). *Japanese American women: Three generations 1890–1990.* Berkeley, CA: Mina Press Publishing, & San Francisco: National Japanese Historical Society.

Okubo, M. (1946). *Citizen 13660.* Seattle: University of Washington Press.

Nisei Research Project. (1995–1996). Unpublished manuscript available from

D. K. Nagata, Dept. of Psychology, University of Michigan, 525 E. University, Ann Arbor, MI 48109.

Smith, J. (1990, February 11). Living in the U.S.A.: The troubled love story of American women of Japanese ancestry and the country that betrayed them. *The San Francisco Examiner*, pp. 9–17, 32, 34–35.

Sone, M. (1953). *Nisei daughter*. Seattle: University of Washington Press.

Spickard, P. R. (1989). Mixed blood: Mixed marriage and ethnic identity in twentieth-century America. Madison: University of Wisconsin Press.

Stewart, A. J. (1994). Toward a feminist strategy for studying women's lives. In C. E. Franz & A. J. Stewart (Eds.), *Women creating lives: Identities, resilience, and resistance* (pp. 11–35). Boulder: Westview Press.

Takezawa, Y. I. (1995). *Breaking the silence: Redress and Japanese American ethnicity*. Ithaca, NY: Cornell University Press.

Wakatsuki-Houston, J., & Houston, J. (1973). *Farewell to Manzanar*. New York: Bantam.

Weglyn, M. (1976). *Years of infamy: The untold story of America's concentration camps*. New York: Morrow Quill.

Yoo, D. (1993). "Read all about it": Race, generation and the Japanese American ethnic press, 1925–1941. *Amerasia Journal, 19*, 69–92.

5

DOMESTIC VIOLENCE IN VIETNAMESE REFUGEE AND KOREAN IMMIGRANT COMMUNITIES

CAROLEE GIAOUYEN TRAN AND KUNYA DES JARDINS

Over the past two decades, much has been written about the causes and consequences of domestic violence in the fields of psychology, social work, family therapy, law enforcement, law, and women's studies, among others. However, there is still much left to be addressed. Domestic violence remains a major social and public health problem affecting women from all racial and socioeconomic backgrounds. It is estimated that between 2 and 12 million women are beaten by their spouse each year (Kaplan & Saddock, 1991; Straus & Gelles, 1988; Straus, Gelles, & Steinmetz, 1980), and 2,000 women per year are victims of spousal homicide (Jones & Schechter, 1993). Despite increased attention to the problems caused by domestic violence, there is still a paucity of research examining how domestic violence affects ethnic and racial minority populations and specifically refugee and immigrant families in the United States. In particular,

We thank Dr. W. Ladson Hinton IV for his comments on this chapter. Carolee GiaoUyen Tran's study was funded by the Clara Mayo Research Fellowship Award from Boston University.

Asian Americans remain one of the ethnic minority groups most neglected in the psychological literature. This lack of attention to Asian American communities has been attributed, in part, to the fact that relatively few incidents of domestic violence in Asian American communities come to the attention of authorities (Ho, 1990). However, there is uncertainty about whether these low reported rates of domestic violence reflect a lower number of incidents, underreporting, low usage of public health services, or inadequate cultural and linguistic mental health resources (Bradshaw, 1994; Ho, 1990). Additionally, it is unclear how the contexts of immigration, cultural and geographic transition, and social isolation may affect domestic violence among Asian Americans.

This chapter focuses on the issue of domestic violence in two Asian American groups: Vietnamese refugee and Korean immigrant women. These groups are singled out for several reasons. First, as the nationalities of origin of the two authors, these groups were chosen for their personal as well as their professional interest. Second, because the category *Asian American* is so culturally and linguistically diverse, it is difficult to generalize about domestic violence for Asian Americans as a whole. And third, because most of the existing literature on Asian Americans focuses on Chinese American and Japanese American communities, little is known about Vietnamese and Korean women.

This chapter has three major sections. First, a multidimensional framework for understanding how sociopolitical, psychological, and cultural factors influence domestic violence in Vietnamese and Korean families is presented. The immigration histories of both groups are discussed to illustrate how the process of immigration generates conditions, such as social isolation, lack of supportive networks, unemployment, and alcohol use, that may negatively affect family interpersonal relations. How traditional cultural and social values may shape perceptions of domestic violence in Vietnamese American and Korean American communities is also examined. Second, two qualitative studies conducted with abused Vietnamese American and Korean American women are discussed to illustrate the importance of viewing the problem of domestic violence through a multidimensional framework. Third, service needs for Vietnamese American and Korean American battered women are outlined, culturally appropriate prevention and intervention strategies are proposed, and future avenues for research are suggested.

VIETNAMESE AND KOREAN IMMIGRATION AND THE STRESSORS ASSOCIATED WITH TRANSITION

The 1990 U.S. census found the Vietnamese population to be one of the fastest growing ethnic minority groups. More than 600,000 Vietnamese refugees have immigrated to the United States since 1975 (U.S. Committee for Refugees, 1976–1990). The first major exodus occurred in 1975, when nearly 125,000 Vietnamese refugees entered the United States (U.S. Committee for Refugees, 1976–1990). This initial wave of refugees included many South Vietnamese military officers, government officials, and professionals who, along with their families, were evacuated by air or boat from South Vietnam. Because this first group of refugees was well educated, had more exposure to Western culture, and had a swifter escape than those who immigrated later, they were better equipped to adjust successfully to life in the United States compared with those who arrived later.

A second major exodus began in 1978, when more than 200,000 Vietnamese refugees immigrated to the United States (U.S. Committee for Refugees, 1976–1990). Many in this group were members of business- or merchant-class families whose only route of escape was by small boats; hence, they were nicknamed "boat people." Tragically, many of these refugees suffered pirate attacks, starvation, and other traumas as they escaped to various refugee camps in Southeast Asia. Many in this group endured years in overcrowded refugee camps under horrendous conditions while awaiting sponsorship. In addition to starvation, torture, and other near-death experiences, Cheung (1984); Forbes-Martin (1992); and Mollica, Wyshak, and Lavelle (1987) reported an alarmingly high incidence of sexual violence against women in the camps as well as during their escape.

The Orderly Departure Program was created in 1979 to provide a safer, legal route of exit for a third wave of Vietnamese refugees (U.S. Committee for Refugees, 1976–1990). However, because this program was open only to those with relatives in the United States, many refugees continued to leave Vietnam illegally and in dangerous ways. A fourth and final wave of immigration included Amerasians and former South Vietnamese soldiers, many of whom had been imprisoned under extremely harsh conditions in reeducation camps (Freeman, 1989; Hinton et al., 1993). This latest influx was facilitated by immigration programs that specifically targeted Vietnamese veterans and Amerasians.

Similar to the Vietnamese, there were several waves of Korean immigration. The total number of Koreans in the United States in 1990 was estimated to be approximately 1 million (U.S. Census Bureau, 1990). The first wave occurred from 1903 to 1905, when male laborers migrated to Hawaii to work on plantations (Hurh & Kim, 1984). Many so-called Korean "picture brides" came after 1910 seeking to flee Japanese oppression or find improved economic and educational opportunities, but they came in proportionately fewer numbers than men (Takaki, 1989). Of the 8,000 Koreans who had immigrated to Hawaii and the mainland United States by 1924, only one fifth were women. Like Japanese and Chinese immigrants, these Korean immigrants were exposed to discriminatory laws such as the Chinese Exclusion Act of 1882 and the Alien Land Act of 1913 (Takaki, 1989).

The second wave of Korean immigration consisted primarily of Korean wives of American soldiers who served in the Korean War and Korean adoptees. Many Korean wives faced experiences similar to mail-order brides. They were vulnerable to domestic violence, had few financial and social resources, and suffered from U.S. prejudice against interracial marriage (Ho, 1990). Tragically, their high expectations often clashed with the harsh reality of life in the United States; their disenfranchised status often led to multiple domestic problems, including spousal abuse (Ho, 1990).

The most recent wave of Korean immigration followed the 1965 Immigration and Nationality Act, reaching a dramatic total of between 20,000 and 30,000 Koreans immigrating every year since 1968. According to Hurh and Kim (1984), this wave of Korean immigrants was different. They were one of the most highly educated immigrant groups to enter the United States, they tended to immigrate as family units (Yamamoto, Rhee, & Chang, 1994), and they usually settled in large urban areas such as Los Angeles, New York, Honolulu, and Chicago. This last group has been large enough to establish so-called "Korea-towns" with businesses, interest groups, fraternal organizations, and churches.

This brief immigration history illustrates the diverse social and family histories of many Vietnamese and Korean women currently residing in the United States. The sociopolitical and historical contexts of the different waves of immigration have had an immense impact on the adjustment experiences of individuals and may influence a family's risk for domestic violence. Those women whose immigration occurred under circumstances of war and poverty and who also were socially isolated and financially or legally dependent on their spouses are most vulnerable to domestic violence.

CULTURAL TRANSITION AND ITS IMPACT ON FAMILY RELATIONSHIPS

Research has observed that traumatic experiences and acculturation stress significantly affect mental health outcomes among refugees and immigrants (Ben-Porath, 1991; Berry, Kim, Minde, & Mok, 1987; Chambon, 1989; Hinton et al., 1993; Hinton, Tiet, Tran, & Chesney, 1997; Stein, 1979; Westermeyer, 1986, 1991; Williams & Berry, 1991). Most Vietnamese in the United States are refugees; that is, they fled a politically oppressive regime, war, or other type of political conflict in which their freedom or lives were seriously threatened. In contrast, most Koreans came as legal immigrants. Although earlier Korean immigrants came because of oppression (i.e., Japanese occupation between 1905 and 1945) or war (i.e., the Korean War between 1950 and 1953), the most recent immigrants have come primarily for education or economic opportunities. Thus, immigration status differentiates these two ethnic groups and has implications for the acculturative stress felt within them.

Stressors associated with the cultural transition of refugees and immigrants affect family life and may put families at risk for domestic violence (Rimonte, 1989). These acculturative stressors include conflicts between old and new values, identity confusion, communication problems, and experiences of prejudice and discrimination. Furthermore, the immigration process requires that new arrivals learn a new language and customs, often creating a clash of cultural values that disrupts the continuity of family life and norms. In addition, tensions within families may be exacerbated when rates of acculturation differ between spouses or between parents and children (Chambon, 1989; Westermeyer, 1986, 1991). Differential success in the workforce may also create marital tensions. For example, Chambon (1989) found that spousal conflict was associated with (a) husbands' employment instability because it led to lack of family financial security and (b) wives' employment outside the home because it led to their increased independence and less adherence to traditional gender roles. Thus, as Vietnamese and Korean women acculturate and take advantage of employment opportunities in the United States, marital tensions may increase (Rimonte, 1989). Kibria's ethnographic research (1990, 1993) provided further evidence that the process of immigration shifts the balance of power between men and women. In Kibria's study, women exercised greater influence in their families in the United States than in Vietnam because of their increased earning power and greater control over family resources. However, Kibria (1990, 1993) and T. H. Kim (1996) also emphasized that this shift in power for Vietnamese and Korean women tends to be fairly conservative because many women also strive to preserve the traditional family system and often work only out of economic necessity.

In addition, the relationship between domestic violence and unemployment has been corroborated in a variety of ethnic communities (Briar, 1983; Prescott & Letko, 1986). A longitudinal study of 1,348 Southeast Asian refugees found a causal relationship between unemployment and depression (Beiser, Johnson, & Turner, 1993). A 1980 employment survey of 605 Vietnamese heads of household (Opportunity Systems, Inc., 1981) showed high unemployment rates compared with the general U.S. population, with only about 60% of Vietnamese men and 42% of Vietnamese women participating in the workforce. Vietnamese refugees who found employment typically experienced substantial downward mobility (Stein, 1979), which Ben-Porath (1991) correlated to threats in self-esteem associated with a lower standard of living. Thus, unemployment and underemployment can negatively affect the husband's self-esteem which, in turn, can create significant tension within the spousal relationship.

Low self-esteem also has been found to be a common factor in spousal abuse in other populations (Coleman, 1980; Walker, 1979). In a comparison study of violent and nonviolent husbands, Goldstein and Rosenbaum (1985) found a significant association between wife abuse and low self-esteem among abusive husbands. Furthermore, Brenner's 1979 research, as cited in Straus (1980), showed a clear relationship between stress as indexed by unemployment rate and assault and homicide rates in the United States, Canada, and Great Britain.

Fragmentation of the nuclear or extended family as well as lack of ethnic community cohesion is common following immigration. Chambon (1989) found that Vietnamese refugee and Korean immigrant families are more vulnerable to distress and have fewer coping resources. Studies of Southeast Asian refugees (e.g., Beiser, Turner, & Ganesan, 1989) have indicated that availability of social support moderates the negative impact of resettlement adjustment among families by providing newcomers with a sense of identity and belonging. Kibria's (1993) ethnographic study showed how supportive community networks of Vietnamese women played an important role in mediating spousal disputes.

Loss experiences and family fragmentation are other hardships that immigrant families must face. Experiences of loss and family fragmentation are probably more common among Vietnamese refugees compared with Korean immigrants because Korean immigrants often came as intact family units. As a result of the dangerous and uncertain nature of escape from Vietnam, it was common for family members to leave at different times and in different groups, depending on who had the greatest chance of survival. During periods of separation, which ranged from months to years, family members often did not know whether their relatives were alive or dead (Chambon, 1989). Although the reestablishment of diplomatic relations between the United States and Vietnam in May 1995 enabled wealthier Vietnamese Americans to contact family members in Vietnam, the average Vietnamese refugee is still constrained by geographic distance and cost in reestablishing family ties. As a result, family reunions are both a time of joy as well as tremendous strain; many discover that time has changed their ability to relate to one another. Recent studies have suggested that traumatic events before or during immigration among Vietnamese refugees can manifest in the form of symptoms of posttraumatic stress disorder (PTSD), predisposing Vietnamese refugee men to act out their distress in aggressive ways. For example, Hauff and Vaglum (1994) found a relationship between PTSD and interpersonal sensitivity and aggression in a study of 104 Vietnamese men, suggesting increased risk for aggressive behavior toward their wives and children.

SUBSTANCE ABUSE AND DOMESTIC VIOLENCE

Yamamoto et al. (1994) found a higher rate of alcohol use among elderly Korean men in the Los Angeles area compared with the general population. Of 51 men studied, 21.6% met the criteria for alcohol abuse, and 13.7% met the criteria for dependence. This finding was corroborated in a St. Louis, Missouri, study of Korean and White American elderly men as well as in a study of men in Korea. Higher alcohol use in the Korean community may be associated with increased risk for domestic violence, just as it is in the general population (Walker, 1984). In a 1997 study by Tran, 24 of 51 battered Vietnamese women attributed the abuse to their partner's addiction to alcohol, drugs, or gambling.

INFLUENCE OF CULTURAL VALUES ON DOMESTIC VIOLENCE

Traditional Vietnamese and Korean cultural values may shape beliefs and attitudes toward domestic violence. These traditional cultural values may (a) influence an attitude of acceptance toward wife abuse, (b) support the minimization of wife abuse, and (c) influence women to endure spousal abuse.

Group-Focused Social and Familial Norms

Vietnamese and Korean attitudes toward domestic violence are very much rooted in and intertwined with traditional and patriarchal values about family, marriage, and sex roles. One basic difference between Confucian-based Asian cultures and Western culture is that in the former, the individual is group focused and less self-focused; that is, the needs and desires of an individual are secondary to those of the family (Jamieson, 1993; Timberlake & Cook, 1984). This fundamental difference stems from the influence of Confucian philosophy and teaching throughout much of East and Southeast Asia. Confucianism emphasizes the importance of harmony between various familial and social relationships, social order within and outside of the family, and close family bonds. Because independence and individual autonomy are discouraged, individuals feel greater pressure to behave and conform to social and familial expectations and roles (Jamieson, 1993; Shon & Ja, 1982).

The emphasis on close family bonds creates an interdependence between an individual and his or her family. A person's behavior reflects not only on himself or herself but, more important, on his or her nuclear and extended family; consequently, concepts of guilt and shame have different meanings than they do in Western culture (Jamieson, 1993; Kibria, 1993;

Shon & Ja, 1982). The Asian concept of "loss of face" implies that the entire nuclear, as well as extended, family loses respect and status in the community when an individual family member behaves inappropriately (Jamieson, 1993). Although there are significant benefits to interdependence, it also constrains individuals to adhere to social norms, to keep harmony, and to minimize conflicts in interpersonal relationships. Consequently, family pathologies such as domestic violence are likely to be kept secret because revealing such problems outside the home would bring shame to the entire family (Rimonte, 1989).

Oppression of Women in Traditional Gender Roles

Confucian ideology, which has molded Vietnamese and Korean cultural values and defined traditional gender roles and human relationships, is based on men's dominance over women. One major Confucian principle, the "Three Submissions," states that women should be subservient to their fathers when young, to their husbands when married, and to their oldest son when widowed (Jamieson, 1993; Shon & Ja, 1982). The notion of male superiority and female inferiority is reflected in popular Vietnamese sayings such as: "One boy, that's something; ten girls, that's nothing" and "A hundred girls aren't worth a single testicle" (Jamieson, 1993, p. 18). Strict adherence to this aspect of Confucian ideology oppresses women and may tacitly promote domestic violence.

Women's inferior status to men is reflected in many cultural practices and attitudes common in traditional Confucian societies. The birth of a male child, for example, is of greater importance than the birth of a female child. Furthermore, women bearing sons were rewarded with higher status in society and in their husband's family. Historically, it was also legal for husbands to divorce wives who could not produce sons. In such situations, the wife was publicly shamed by having to find her husband a new wife who could bear sons. Thus, the higher status of men in Confucian societies often came at the expense of the pain, humiliation, and subjugation of women.

Because women are considered inferior to men in Confucian societies, they have not been allowed the same level of education as men (Kibria, 1993; Song, 1996). Women usually were discouraged from gaining abilities and talents that might be useful for a career outside the home because it was assumed that men would be the primary breadwinners. Despite the fact that many women worked, they had little or no control over the family's economic resources. The subordination of women was also reflected in their absence from political and leadership positions; traditionally only men were heads of towns and family groups (Kibria, 1993).

Various cultural ideals about what makes a "good woman" also convey the message that women should be submissive to men and that striving to attain this ideal is a positive virtue. Accordingly, an ideal Vietnamese woman is supposed to possess four basic virtues: (a) be a good housewife, (b) be physically attractive, (c) speak well but in a careful and soft manner, and (d) be a person of good character (Kibria, 1993). In addition, good women are expected to retain their purity before marriage by preserving their virginity, lest they be stigmatized as "damaged goods." In sum, a good Vietnamese or Korean woman should be subservient, obedient, quiet, and pure. These virtues promote the subordination of women by glorifying passivity and submission to male authority.

Suffering and perseverance are also virtues viewed as fundamental to building strong character for Vietnamese and Korean women. These virtues are derived from Buddhism (Jamieson, 1993). Although the value placed on enduring suffering has, in some respects, been adaptive for women in oppressive societies, these virtues also encourage women to passively accept sexual inequalities, thereby promoting the status quo. Women are also given support and recognition for enduring hardships and discouraged from speaking up or taking action to change oppressive situations. Traditional Vietnamese and Korean folklore has dramatized and glorified in songs, poems, stories, and movies the ideal wife as someone who is completely devoted to her husband, her children, and her two sets of parents. This complete devotion is measured by her numerous self-sacrifices and ability to endure, suffer, and persevere under the worst mistreatment and circumstances of war, poverty, and family abuse.

Furthermore, according to Buddhist beliefs, the acceptance of one's fate is viewed as positive rather than negative; it is believed that one should not challenge one's life situations because they are determined by fate (B. Kim, Okamura, Ozawa, & Forrest, 1981; Kitano & Kikumura, 1976). Thus, the combination of patriarchal values, cultural practices, and gender role expectations of women may support and maintain the existing family order, even when women are suffering spousal abuse.

The Institution of Marriage

Historically, most marriages in Vietnam and Korea were prearranged, making it difficult for women to choose their own husbands (Jamieson, 1993). A marriage usually involved the exchange of money and gifts from the man's family to the woman's family in the form of a dowry. After marriage, the wife usually had limited contact with her family, as she was considered to be property paid for by her husband and belonging to his family. A good wife was expected to be chaste, submissive, self-sacrificing, frugal, uncomplaining, and completely devoted to her husband and his family. A woman generally entered her husband's home as a stranger and was expected to please and serve her husband as well as his entire family.

The double standard used to judge the sexual conduct of men and women conveys to women the message that they have no right to expect marital fidelity. Although women are expected to be pure and faithful, their husbands are allowed to be promiscuous, have multiple wives, and visit prostitutes. In fact, traditional legal codes sanctioned polygamy, which was a mark of affluence and prestige for men (Kibria, 1993); consequently, many men had affairs to demonstrate their prowess and superior status. Furthermore, many women felt that they could not divorce because marriage was considered permanent and they feared loss of their children. Under traditional Vietnamese and Korean customs, only the husband could initiate divorce (Kibria, 1993). Women who were divorced or widowed typically did not remarry; those who did remarry often were stigmatized and ostracized by their communities.

Although these gender roles characterize Confucian societies in general, Ho (1990) found differences in the degree to which different Asian ethnic groups adhered to them. Ho conducted focus groups and surveyed attitudes about domestic violence among Laotian, Cambodian, Chinese, and Vietnamese refugees and found that men's domination of women was more openly accepted among Vietnamese groups. Vietnamese men described a sense of ownership over their wives and considered them property. Vietnamese women felt that they had to tolerate their husbands' extramarital affairs and were more tolerant of physical violence than Chinese women (Ho, 1990). Interestingly, T. H. Kim (1996) found similar themes in her qualitative study of Korean men and women.

These studies illustrate how certain traditional Vietnamese and Korean cultural values may (a) influence an attitude of acceptance toward wife abuse, (b) support the minimization and concealment of wife abuse, and (c) influence women to assume that they have to endure domestic violence. Furthermore, the above model of domestic violence emphasizes the importance of including other factors such as immigration, acculturation, and substance abuse when considering domestic abuse in Vietnamese and Korean families.

DOMESTIC VIOLENCE AMONG VIETNAMESE REFUGEE AND KOREAN IMMIGRANT WOMEN

Two studies explored attributions of abuse from Vietnamese (Tran, 1997) and Korean (Song, 1996) women in terms of (a) why the abuse began, (b) why it continued, and (c) what contributed to the women staying in the relationships. Interestingly, the studies revealed striking similarities in the qualitative findings for the two groups.

The Vietnamese Refugee Sample

Tran (1997) studied 65 Vietnamese women from an urban New England area. Participants were drawn from an Asian domestic violence agency and a Vietnamese American civic association. On average, the women were about 38 years old, were married, had been in the United States for less than 5 years, had low English proficiency, had less than 9 years of education, and were not employed.

Of the 65 women, 51 reported physical and/or verbal abuse within the past year. Of those, 92% reported being physically abused, 80% reported being verbally abused, and 73% reported both types of abuse. The abused women differed from the nonabused women in several respects: They were less educated, were more likely to be separated from their husbands, and reported that their partners drank more frequently and if employed were less satisfied with their occupation. These women reported suffering the following types of physically abusive acts: 55% reported being hit with a closed fist, 45% reported being slapped, 24% reported being choked, 33% reported being threatened with a gun or knife, and 47% reported feeling that their life was in danger.

"About 90% of battered women reported that they have problems speaking English." (Song, 1996, p. 107).

The Korean Immigrant Sample

Song (1996) conducted her study with a nonclinical community sample of 150 Korean immigrant women from the Chicago area. These women were recruited from various Korean community agencies, churches, Buddhist temples, newspapers, shops, bookstores, travel agencies, and grocery stores using nonrandom sampling. On average, the women were about 36 years old, were married, had been in the United States for about 5 years, had at least a high school education, and were employed.

Although verbal abuse was not included in this study, 90 of the 150 participants reported physical abuse within the past 2 years. Types of abusive acts endured mirrored those in the study of Vietnamese women (Tran, 1997): 57% reported being hit with a closed fist, 42% reported being slapped, 24% reported being choked, 20% reported being threatened with a gun or knife, and 2% reported that their spouses made actual attempts to kill them. Similar to the Vietnamese cohort, these abused women reported that 58% of their partners had experienced occupational downward mobility. Battered women were twice as likely as nonbattered women to attend church. It is interesting to note that, within this group, three times as many women experienced battering during the 3rd to 5th years of residence in the United States. This is consistent with other studies suggesting that abuse occurs after the initial cultural shock of immigration has passed, that is, after the first couple of years, when the harsh realities of the new environment become more evident.

QUALITATIVE RESULTS OF ATTRIBUTIONS TOWARD ABUSE

Qualitative analysis of the two studies (Song, 1996; Tran, 1997) shows strikingly similar results. Four main attribution categories emerged as to why the abuse began, why it continued, as well as why the women remained in the relationships with their abusers: (a) patriarchal perspective that supports and sustains abuse; (b) cultural transition, including disempowerment and unemployment; (c) partners' promises to change; and (d) partners' addictions.

Patriarchal Perspective That Supports and Sustains Abuse

Although Vietnamese and Korean cultural and social values do not explicitly encourage men to mistreat or abuse their partners, the fact that they are rooted in a patriarchal perspective influences and supports the subjugation and abuse of women. Often these cultural and social values are used to justify the abuse by both men and women alike.

The highest virtues of a good Vietnamese or Korean woman include her ability to persevere; to be obedient; and to devote her entire life to her parents, husband, and children. Juxtaposed to this are traditional cultural beliefs that men are superior and the ultimate authority in their homes and thus are more highly valued in society. These cultural ideals, held by both men and women, are echoed in the narratives of the battered women in Tran's (1997) and Song's (1996) studies.

Song (1996) categorized attitudes toward Korean traditionalism and found that, compared with nonbattered women, battered women were significantly more likely to endorse traditional attitudes that a Korean woman:

should not leave her husband once she is married
should always obey her husband
['s] place is to be married, stay home and have children (p. 97)

Several Vietnamese women's narratives conveyed the similar belief that women need to be controlled (Tran, 1997). Trang,[1] age 30 and still with her abuser, said, "He beats me because he thinks that once he married me he can hit me whenever he wants and I have to endure it" (p. 18). Quynh, age 33 and separated from her abuser for 4 months, said

He told me he hits me because I talk too much; I didn't stay quiet when he ordered me to. He thought that he could just continue to beat me and control me like he did in Vietnam, like how most Vietnamese men control their wives. (p. 18)

---

[1]Names have been changed to protect study participants.

Six women from the Vietnamese sample spoke of how their abusers' family members or friends supported and encouraged the abuse as a way to discipline the woman and ensure her obedience. Khanh, age 44 and at the shelter, said,

> His sister and mother told him that he should beat me up if I disobey him; they told him that a man should not put up with any disobedience from his wife. (p. 18)

Most of the women in these studies faulted themselves and attributed the abuse to their inability to be a good wife. The Vietnamese women felt that their husbands were justified in hitting them because they had failed to obey or submit to their demands, even when the demands were abusive or unreasonable (Tran, 1997). The Korean women felt that they had provoked their husbands' aggression and were critical of themselves for not controlling their own emotional outbursts or not putting up with their husbands' inappropriate actions (Song, 1996).

The issue of male infidelity appeared as a major theme in the narratives of the Vietnamese women. Many women internalized the expectation that they should tolerate their partners' affairs. Consistent with traditional cultural attitudes toward marriage, this cultural expectation was used to justify the abuse by some women. Fifteen women in Tran's (1997) study related stories of physical abuse by their partners because they had asked about, found out about, or protested against their partner's extramarital affairs. Nga, age 27 and Vietnamese, became so despondent by her husband's extramarital affairs and his abuse of her that she attempted suicide. At the time of the interview, she was living with her parents and had been separated from her spouse for 2 weeks. She said

> You see, he has had a few women, not just one.... He wanted me to accept his affair and allow him to go back and forth with her. He even brought her home to sleep with him while I was working. I was the only one supporting all of us! I just couldn't stand it anymore! When I told him he can't have both of us, he beat me up really bad; he told me I was a worthless wife because I did not give him what he wanted. I became very sad and tried to kill myself. (p. 20)

Although some women reacted to their husbands' affairs with protest, others implied that perhaps they deserved to be beaten because they should have kept quiet about them.

Many of the Korean men in Song's (1996) study accused their wives of being unfaithful, a phenomenon common among abusive spouses in general. Many of the Korean women reported being tired both physically and emotionally because they were employed outside of the home and solely responsible for all child rearing and household tasks. This exhaustion contributed to their avoidance of sexual contact, which further provoked their husbands, who then accused their wives of adultery.

Cultural Transition: Disempowerment and Unemployment

These studies (Song, 1996; Tran, 1997) also corroborated the hypothesis that differing rates of acculturation between spouses may lead to marital tension and put women at risk for abuse. Clashes between traditional Vietnamese and Korean patriarchal ideals and American ideals of equality between the sexes were particularly evident in the narratives of five women as they spoke of their abuse experiences. Moreover, although abuse may have started in Korea for some of the Korean women, it tended to become worse once they were in the United States (Song, 1996). The Vietnamese women conveyed the assumption that their partners beat them because they were angry over their lack of power in the United States compared to Vietnam (Tran, 1997). This theme was illustrated by Mai, age 44, who was still living with her abuser. Her husband began abusing her after being in the United States for several months. Her awareness of women's rights in the United States led her to realize that she did not want to be abused anymore.

> He beats me because he wants to control me, keep me at home. He tells me that he can beat me like how Vietnamese men can beat their wives in Vietnam, that coming to America should not change this. But I don't want to put up with this beating anymore. I know that women don't have to put up with this in America. I want to go out and work in the community. . . . He tells me he hates the U.S. society because men here don't have enough power like they do in Vietnam. Here, men get restraining orders when they hit their wives or kids. He thinks this is ridiculous. (p. 21)

Many of the Korean men complained about the unfairness of U.S. domestic laws and felt that government agencies had no right to interfere in the private affairs of married couples. For Vietnamese refugee men, the reeducation camp experience and often traumatic immigrations further added to their frustration at unemployment and the severe financial strains many experienced in the United States. Hanh, a 49-year-old Vietnamese woman whose husband was unemployed in Vietnam after 1975, said

> The Communists lied to us; they told us to go into the new economic zone to do farming so we can earn good money. This was not true. Our work in the forest was very dangerous because there were many mines left over from the war. Many of us got hurt because the mines exploded while we were working on the land. I still have scars on my head from two of the explosions. During this time my husband blamed me for our hard economic conditions and his unemployment. He began hitting me and told me it was my fault that he could not find a job because I had convinced him to go to the new economic zone. (p. 22)

Several women also spoke of how the reeducation camp experience had changed their partners' personalities, making them more irritable and abusive.

Downward mobility and unemployment appeared to be significant factors characterizing the batterers and contributing to abuse. Many of the Vietnamese men had experienced job discrimination after their release from the reeducation camp and were treated as pariahs because of their past affiliations with the non-Communist government. Several women whose husbands became unemployed in the United States shared how their partners' prolonged unemployment contributed to the abuse (Tran, 1997). Although most of the Korean men in Song's (1996) study were employed, there were significant decreases in job status, with a shift from white-collar, professional positions in Korea to manual-labor jobs in the United States.

Addictive Behaviors Among Abusive Partners

Within the Vietnamese sample (Tran, 1997), almost half of the battered women attributed their abuse to their partners' addiction to alcohol, drugs, or gambling. Luu, age 19 and separated from her abuser for 1 month, conveyed that her boyfriend's drinking and gambling addiction made him abusive. Another woman attributed her abuse to her ex-partner's cocaine use. Lien, age 29 and in hiding for 7 months at the time of the interview, said

> His personality and behavior became strange, abnormal, and unpredictable after he began smoking cocaine. He began hitting me after he started using cocaine. He never had enough money, always demanded money from my mother or I. I was always scared because I never knew what kind of mood he would be in. He sometimes used his gun to threaten my mom and I so we would give him more money. (p. 24)

The above examples illustrate how various addictions may be seen as not only precipitating abusive behavior in some men, but also exacerbating the severity of abuse among already-abusive men. Although Song (1996) did not address alcohol or substance abuse in her study, arguments over partners' use of alcohol were reported as the precipitant to abuse in 26.7% of the cases in her study.

STAYING IN ABUSIVE RELATIONSHIPS

Factors that contributed to women staying in abusive relationships fell into three major categories: (a) obligation to family and children, (b) limited financial and social resources, and (c) partners' promises to change. Many of the Vietnamese and Korean women did not leave their abusive relationships for reasons similar to battered women in general: They were too afraid to leave, and many feared retribution. In addition, these women conveyed how various traditional cultural values further contributed to their staying.

Obligation to Family and Children

The importance of family cohesion and harmony, the priority of family needs over individual needs, and the cultural expectation that women will endure any hardship to preserve family cohesion all contributed to the women staying in their abusive relationships. Moreover, leaving the relationship would highlight their shortcomings and bring shame to their entire nuclear and extended family. The most common reason given for remaining in an abusive relationship was for the sake of the children. More than 30 of the Vietnamese women (Tran, 1997) spoke of how they sacrificed their own happiness and endured the abuse to preserve their family's cohesion. Hoang, age 58 with five children who had endured more than 18 years of physical and emotional abuse, illustrates this common sentiment:

> I stay with my husband because I think about my children. I don't want them to be without a father. If I endure the situation, my children will love me. If I leave their father they may blame me later for taking them away from him. (p. 25)

Other women feared that a divorce would cause them to lose custody of their children because this is a very real phenomenon in their countries of origin, where divorced women do not have the right to keep their children. Most were unaware of U.S. law, which has historically favored the mother. Korean family law gives custody to fathers when couples divorce, and women's rights to visitation are restricted until the children become adults.

Many women also reported that they decided to remain with their abusers because of pressures from family members, friends, and religious advisors. Many of the Korean women spoke of saving face and not wanting to hurt their family's reputation by exposing the abuse or divorcing (Song, 1996). A 26-year-old Vietnamese woman in the shelter with her two young children said

> My parents and their friends told me that children need their fathers; they told me that I should swallow my pride and forgive him so my kids can be with their father. (Tran, 1997, p. 26)

Whereas some women reported that they stayed because they did not want to bring shame to their families, others reported that they stayed mainly because they feared ostracism and judgment from others in the community. One Vietnamese woman, Khuyen, age 41 and Catholic, said, "I had stayed because I thought about my religion and my parents. I did not want to fail my parents or shame them" (Tran, 1997, p. 27). Korean church ministers often encouraged women to return to their husbands and forgive them as good Christians (Song, 1996). Thus, religious and cultural value also became tightly interwoven with women's reasons for staying with abusive partners. These cultural values often influenced a woman's decision to stay in an abusive relationship and for others in her support system to deny, hide, and minimize the enormity of the problem. The tolerance of wife abuse and lack of strong community and familial sanctions against domestic violence has discouraged and prevented some women from getting help.

Limited Financial and Social Resources

Limited financial and social resources, including difficulty speaking English, employment inexperience, social isolation, and lack of financial or community support, are factors limiting the ability of women in abusive relationships to obtain their independence. Many of the women studied had young children and little or no money for child care services even if they found employment. Xuyen, age 26 and Vietnamese with four young children, said

> I want to leave so much but I don't have a way to escape. I have no one and no money to help me leave. I cannot speak English and I don't have any money. Sometimes, I think the only way I can escape his beatings and become free of him is to kill him. But I know I cannot do that because of my children. (Tran, 1997, p. 28)

Even when women worked, their pay was often not enough to cover basic living expenses. In Song's (1996) study, none of the women remained in the relationships because they wanted to, but because of unavoidable circumstances. Korean women were employed more out of economic necessity than choice. At the same time, all the women were solely responsible for all household tasks and raising their children, which did not allow much time for engaging in social activities outside of the home. Although more than half of the battered Korean women in Song's study participated in Korean church activities, this involvement did not afford a buffer against domestic abuse.

Some women said that they stayed with their abusers because they were unaware that battered women shelters existed. Moreover, they tended to see shelters as short-term solutions (Song, 1996). One Vietnamese woman who fled her abuser once she found out about the shelter said

> I had to stay with him because I had absolutely no place to go and he threatened that he would kill me if I ever tried to leave. You see, I have no family here and I never made any friends because he always followed me everywhere, wanted to know exactly where I was every

minute. I never even knew there were shelters for women until very recently. (Tran, 1997, p. 29)

Partners' Promises to Change

Another major reason that women gave for staying with their partners was because their partners had promised to change (i.e., they hoped that their partners would stop being abusive). Chi, age 25 and Vietnamese who had recently reunited with her husband, said, "I want to give him another chance because I love him. He has promised to be good and change. I hope it can happen" (Tran, 1997, p. 29). Ngoc, a 40-year-old Vietnamese woman who had endured more than 17 years of physical abuse, said

> I have stayed because I think about my kids. Also, each time we fight and I leave him, he begs me to come back. He promises that he would not hit me again. He asks our friends and relatives to talk to me and convince me to return home. (p. 30)

Reasons for remaining in abusive relationships among Vietnamese and Korean are common to battered women of other racial and socioeconomic backgrounds: fear of retribution, concern for children, obligation to family, partners' promises to change, concern over what family and friends might say, shame, and lack of financial independence. Cultural traditions based on Confucian values regarding the role of women and Buddhist philosophies about fate and destiny often are used to justify abuse and hinder Vietnamese and Korean women from leaving abusive relationships. These pressures are compounded by immigration histories that elicit sense of loss, racism and prejudice from the larger society, language barriers, limited social networks, and little political or economic power. Consequently, for these women, challenging their abusers threatens not only their physical safety, but also their only source of financial and emotional support. As Song (1996) pointed out, challenging abuse can be a threat to a woman's very sense of ethnic and cultural identity.

TYPES OF SERVICES NEEDED

What is clear from both studies is the need for mental health services that are sensitive to the particular difficulties of refugee and immigrant women and to the power relationships and cultural values inherent in abusive relationships. Multiple barriers exist for women of color in accessing services. One significant obstacle is the knowledge that mental health services and battered women's shelters exist. Seventy percent of the women in Song's (1996) Korean sample were not aware of formal services to help them. Thirty-seven percent of Tran's (1997) Vietnamese sample said that regular home visits or periodic telephone calls to check in with them would be a great help. Many Vietnamese women expressed how they often felt isolated and depressed and would greatly appreciate ongoing contact with service providers who could empathize with their situation. Many did not have friends or family members close by or could not confide in others about the abuse.

Given their limited ability to speak English, most of the women had little ability to interact with the outside world. Thus, it was not surprising that 28% of the Vietnamese women suggested that translation services be increased (Tran, 1997), and 65% of the Korean women reported that language difficulty was a major reason for not seeking services (Song, 1996). Many Vietnamese women reported that they often relied on their abusers or children to translate for them because it often was difficult or impossible to get a translator.

The need for more English as a Second Language (ESL) programs was also cited. Many women reported that they were unable to attend ESL classes because the programs were too far away, had long waiting lists, or were held during hours when they could not obtain child care. Need for child care was reported by 22% of the Vietnamese women (Tran, 1997). Many emphasized the need for government-subsidized child care programs to enable them to pursue self-advancement activities (i.e., ESL classes, job training, prevocational programs, job placement), that in turn would improve their chances of becoming employed. Many of the women expressed their hope for the future; more than 55% reported wanting to go to work or be enrolled in ESL or vocational programs.

The types of services described speak of the need for support for women on a number of different levels, all of which would make them somewhat less financially and socially dependent on their abusive partners. They raise issues of empowerment which, to be relevant, must be viewed within the context of cultural beliefs and philosophies and emphasize the prevention of domestic violence.

IMPLICATIONS FOR PREVENTION AND CLINICAL SERVICES

Prevention and Outreach

The social characteristics of abused women in the Vietnamese and Korean studies (Song, 1996; Tran, 1997) suggest that these women are extremely isolated from social support systems and have few financial and personal resources. More resources must be made available to refugee and immigrant battered women to provide them with opportunities to leave abusive relationships. Additionally, more support to families will offer a greater range of options to prevent abuse. Clearly, these women could benefit from comprehensive job training programs that include child care services, ESL classes, vocational skills training, and job placement.

Given the identification of partners' unemployment and job dissatisfaction as significant risk factors for abusive behavior, it seems equally important that policies be established to ensure that unemployed men as well as all new refugee and immigrant arrivals are provided with comprehensive job training programs. Given the tendency for downward mobility, training should include not only ESL classes, skills training, and job placement, but also retraining and ways to negotiate the transfer of existing skills to the U.S. job market. Under current immigration rules, all refugees are expected to find jobs within 8 months after their arrival without proper training or adequate English language proficiency.

Prevention programs could go a long way toward reducing domestic violence if they offered active outreach to women and their families, to community leaders, and to community organizations. Education of both men and women about the problems of and risk factors associated with domestic violence, information about U.S. laws regarding domestic violence, and information regarding resources available to help families is important, especially for newly arrived refugees and immigrants. Prevention and education programs must also address and confront the cultural beliefs and social values that support the subjugation of women and reframe those beliefs in ways that are empowering to both men and women.

Education and prevention programs must also emphasize the teaching of communication and anger management skills to facilitate nonviolent forms of communication. Community education and prevention programs should discuss how cultural values may discourage and hinder abused women and their families from seeking help. It is hoped that the process of community education and prevention would empower families to seek help early and decrease the fear and shame that families may feel about getting help.

Because Korean churches and ministers have a tremendous influence on Korean community life, outreach and education to ministers, church elders, and parishioners could significantly affect views of domestic violence and promote open discussion and modify behaviors regarding domestic violence.

Intervention and Treatment

Culturally sensitive shelters staffed with advocates fluent in Vietnamese, Korean, and other languages are greatly needed. Culturally sensitive treatment programs must also be developed for men who are abusive. Few shelters or treatment programs are currently available for refugee and immigrant populations. Culture- and language-specific treatment programs must be made available to challenge cultural norms and social values that support the subjugation and abuse of women. Batterer programs must focus on ways to help men take responsibility for their violence; in particular, refugee and immigrant men should not be allowed to use their cultural traditions as excuses for abusive behavior. Therefore, treatment programs must teach and train batterers to behave in nonviolent ways. Relaxation, emotional awareness, anger management, communication skills, and cooperative decision-making skills training would help these men to be more attuned to their aggressive impulses and equip them with nonviolent ways of expressing their feelings of anger and helplessness. It is acknowledged, however, that getting men involved in these types of programs is extremely difficult. Men of all cultural backgrounds have been unlikely to self-refer for treatment or intervention related to domestic violence except on court order.

Thus, education and prevention programs need to find creative and less pathologizing ways to reach abusive men. It is possible that job training, language programs, or civic activities could include discussions about life stresses related to immigration, cultural transition, and prejudice and the risks for domestic violence, thereby giving men a context for discussing the interrelationship of these problems.

Because Vietnamese and Korean cultural values discourage public disclosures of family problems, individual psychotherapy may initially be preferred over group therapy for women who are actively dealing with abuse. Many women in Tran's (1997) sample reported that they often felt sad and wanted ongoing contact with counselors who could understand their situations. A therapist's ability to be respectful of and empathic to a woman's struggles allows the woman to recognize that she does not have to continue to endure and be silent. The therapist can provide multiple contexts for the woman to make sense of her experience of violence. These may include various cultural, economic, religious, acculturation, and immigration factors. However, T. H. Kim (1996) made an important point when she cautioned that the therapist must be sensitive to the complex dynamics involved in the relationship between the abused Korean woman and her partner:

> Given that her identity may be integrally defined in terms of the traditional value system—however repressive that might be—the act of rejecting her abusive situation may be accompanied by tremendous psychological loss (that is, in terms of cultural rejection, loss of self esteem). (p. 133)

Thus, traditional Western methods of empowerment need to be tailored specifically for Vietnamese, Korean, and other women raised with more rigid or overtly patriarchal values. *Empowerment*, T. H. Kim (1996) suggested, may in this context be defined as the development of skills that allow victims of domestic violence to develop significant interpersonal influence and more effective support systems.

Furthermore, clinicians must seriously consider the appropriateness of many traditional Western therapeutic approaches given that many Asian refugee and immigrant women are not familiar with Western psychological theories or the process of therapy. In general, a holistic and flexible approach to therapy may be more helpful. For example, therapists may want to intersperse sessions of talk therapy with other forms of intervention such as meditation, art, and psychoeducation. This is not to imply that Vietnamese, Korean, or other Asian refugee and immigrant clients lack the ability or insight necessary for successful responses to traditional Western approaches to psychotherapy. But, as in all cases, assessment of the needs of the client should take place with the awareness that a holistic view of the individual in a community context may be more productive than a traditional, limited view. Additionally, clinical interventions may be more useful when they incorporate cultural values that can be used to empower change in women. For example, the value given to close family ties can be used to mobilize family members to provide emotional, financial, or physical support to an abused woman. Thus, although individual therapy may be a powerful first phase of intervention with abused women, later phases may include family members and friends who can assist the abused woman. Finally, therapists should continually assess the appropriateness of their interventions and consult with other therapists who are knowledgeable about issues pertaining to the specific issues for Vietnamese refugees, Korean immigrants, and other ethnic and racial minority communities.

It also should always be emphasized that there are inter- and intraethnic differences among Vietnamese refugees, Korean immigrants, and members of any other specific group. As Asian Americans are not one monolithic group, length of time in the United States, wave of immigration, acculturation level, community characteristics, economic status, and specific individual factors related to trauma or other life stresses will influence how women perceive and relate to providers. Clinicians and other providers can strive to use their cultural knowledge to inform their clinical practice rather than define it.

CONCLUSION

The problem of domestic violence among Vietnamese refugees and Korean immigrants is multidimensional. Traditional Vietnamese and Korean cultural and social values may shape and influence the way domestic violence is perceived. Preliminary findings indicate that more Vietnamese and Korean women experience domestic violence and more severe acts of violence compared with others in the general U.S. population (Lockhart, 1987; O'Leary, Vivian, & Malone, 1992). Qualitative results clearly demonstrate that the issue of domestic violence among Vietnamese refugees and Korean immigrants is complex. Multiple factors including cultural, economic, political, and psychological perspectives encourage women to remain with their abusers and influence others in their support systems to deny and minimize the problem of domestic violence.

It is hoped that these preliminary findings will generate further research and encourage education, outreach, and discussion to facilitate the development of culturally sensitive interventions for Vietnamese, Korean, and other abused women and their families. Avenues for further research include (a) examining specific links between alcohol and substance abuse and domestic violence within Vietnamese, Korean, and other Asian American communities; (b) addressing the impact of witnessing violence or experiencing physical abuse in childhood on domestic violence in adulthood within other Asian American communities; and (c) determining the impact of prejudice and racism as contributing factors to domestic violence.

Additionally, given the prevalence and severity of domestic violence within Vietnamese and Korean communities, it would be extremely important to investigate resiliency factors among Vietnamese and Korean families in which domestic violence does not occur. Studies to promote the reduction of domestic violence and the social and economic structures needed to reduce domestic violence should be given further attention. Despite gains that have been made, there is much left to do to end the profoundly damaging effects of domestic violence.

REFERENCES

Beiser, M., Johnson, P., & Turner, J. (1993). Unemployment, underemployment and depression affect among Southeast Asian refugees. *Psychological Medicine, 23,* 731–743.

Beiser, M., Turner, J., & Ganesan, S. (1989). Catastrophic stress and factors affecting its consequences among Southeast Asian refugees. *Social Science Medicine, 28,* 183–195.

Ben-Porath, Y. (1991). The psycho-social adjustment. In U.S. Department of Health and Human Services (Ed.), *Mental health services for refugees, Refugee Mental Health Program, U.S. Department of Health and Human Services* (pp. 1–23). Washington, DC: U.S. Department of Health and Human Services.

Berry, J. W., Kim, U., Minde, T., & Mok, D. (1987). Comparative studies of acculturative stress. *International Migration Review, 21,* 491–511.

Bradshaw, C. K. (1994). Asian and Asian American women: Historical and political considerations in psychotherapy. In L. Comas-Dias & B. Greene (Eds.), *Women of color.* New York: Guilford Press.

Briar, K. H. (1983). Unemployment: Toward a social work agenda. *Social Work, 28*(3), 211–216.

Chambon, A. (1989). Refugee families' experiences: Three family themes—

Family disruption, violent trauma, and acculturation. *Journal of Strategic and Systemic Therapies, 8*(2), 3–13.

Cheung, F. K. (1984). *Assessment and recommendations for Indochinese refugees in Southeast Asia (Special focus on boat people suffering violence in Thailand, Philippines, Indonesia, Singapore)*. Washington, DC: Bureau for Refugee Programs, U.S. Department of State.

Chinese Exclusion Act of 1882, act of May 6, 1882, 22 Stat. 58, c. 126, as amended July 5, 1884, 23 Stat. 115, c. 220. Repeal of the Chinese Exclusion Act by act of December 17, 1943, ch. 344 § 1, Stat. 600.

Coleman, K. (1980). Conjugal violence: What 33 men report. *Journal of Marital and Family Therapy, 6,* 207–213.

Forbes-Martin, S. (1992). *Women refugees*. London: Zed Books.

Freeman, J. (1989). *Hearts of sorrow: Vietnamese American lives*. Stanford, CA: Stanford University Press.

Goldstein, D., & Rosenbaum, A. (1985). An evaluation of the self-esteem of maritally violent men. *Family Relations, 34,* 425–428.

Hauff, E., & Vaglum, P. (1994). Chronic posttraumatic stress disorder in Vietnamese refugees: A prospective community study of prevalence, course, psychopathology, and stressors. *Journal of Nervous and Mental Disease, 182,* 85–90.

Hinton, W. L., Chen, J., Du, N., Tran, C. G., Lu, F., Miranda, J., & Faust, S. (1993). DSM-III-R disorders in Vietnamese refugees: Prevalence and correlates. *Journal of Nervous and Mental Disease, 181,* 113–122.

Hinton, W. L., Tiet, Q., Tran, C. G., & Chesney, M. (1997). Predictors of depression among Vietnamese refugees: A longitudinal study of new arrivals. *Journal of Nervous and Mental Disease, 185,* 39–45.

Ho, C. (1990). An analysis of domestic violence in Asian American communities: A multicultural approach to counseling. *Women and Therapy, 9*(12), 129–150.

Hurh, W. M., & Kim, K. C. (1984). *Korean immigrants in America: A structural analysis of ethnic confinement and adhesive adaptation*. Rutherford, NJ: Fairleigh Dickinson Press.

Jamieson, N. (1993). *Understanding Vietnam*. Berkeley CA: University of California Press.

Jones, A., & Schechter, S. (1993). *When love goes wrong*. New York: Harper Perennial Publishers.

Immigration and Nationality Act of 1965. P. L. 89–236 §§ 8, 24, 79 Stat. 916, 922. Appears generally at 8 USCS §§ 1101 *et seq*.

Kaplan, H., & Saddock, B. (1991). *Synopsis of psychiatry*. Baltimore, MD: Williams and Williams.

Kibria, N. (1990). Power, patriarchy, and gender conflict in the Vietnamese immigrant community. *Gender and Society, 4*(1), 9–24.

Kibria, N. (1993). *Family tightrope: The changing lives of Vietnamese Americans*. Princeton, NJ: Princeton University Press.

Kim, B., Okamura, A., Ozawa, N., & Forrest, V. (1981). *Women in shadows*. La Jolla, CA: National Committee Concerned With Asian Wives of U.S. Servicemen.

Kim, T. H. (1996, Summer). Cultural aspects of marital violence. *Progress: Family Systems Research and Therapy, Phillips Graduate Institute, 5*. 127–137.

Kitano, H., & Kikumura, A. (1976). The Japanese American family. In C. H. Mindel & R. W. Havenstein (Eds.), *Ethnic families in America*. New York: Elsevier.

Lockhart, L. L. (1987). A reexamination of the effects of race and social class on the incidence of marital violence: A search for reliable differences. *Journal of Marriage and the Family, 49*, 603–610.

Mollica, R. F., Wyshak, G., & Lavelle, J. (1987). The psychosocial impact of war trauma and torture on Southeast Asian refugees. *American Journal of Psychiatry, 144*, 1567–1572.

O'Leary, K. D., Vivian, K., & Malone, J. (1992). Assessment of physical aggression against women in marriage: The need for multimodal assessment. *Behavioral Assessment, 14*, 4–14.

Opportunity Systems, Inc. (1981). *Ninth wave report: Indochinese resettlement operational feedback*. Washington, DC: Author.

Prescott, S., & Letko, C. (1986). Battered women: A social psychological perspective. In M. Roy (Ed.), *Battered women: A study of domestic violence* (pp. 72–96). New York: Van Nostrand Reinhold.

Rimonte, N. (1989). Domestic violence among Pacific Asians. In Asian Women United of California (Ed.), *Making waves: An anthology of writings by and about Asian American women* (pp. 327–336). Boston: Beacon Press Books.

Shon, S., & Ja, D. (1982). Asian families. In M. McGoldrick, J. Pearce, & J. Giordano (Eds.), *Ethnicity and family therapy* (pp. 208–229). New York: Guilford Press.

Song, Y. I. (1996). *Battered women in Korean immigrant families: The silent scream*. New York: Garland.

Stein, B. N. (1979). Occupational adjustment of refugees: The Vietnamese in the United States. *International Migration Review, 13*, 25–45.

Straus, M. (1980). Social stress and marital violence in a national sample of American families. In F. Wright, C. Bahn, & R. W. Rieer (Eds), *Forensic psychology and psychiatry*. New York: New York Academy of Sciences.

Straus, M., & Gelles, R. (1988). How violent are American families? Estimates from the National Family Violence Re-Survey and other studies. In G. Hotaling, J. T. Kirkpatrick, & M. A. Straus (Eds.), *Family abuse and its consequences: New directions in research* (pp. 14–36). Newbury Park, CA: Sage.

Straus, M., Gelles, R., & Steinmetz, S. (1980). *Behind closed doors: Violence in the American family*. New York: Doubleday/Anchor.

Takaki, R. T. (1989). *Strangers from a different shore: A history of Asian Americans*. Boston: Little, Brown.

Timberlake, E. M., & Cook, K. O. (1984). Social work and the Vietnamese refugee. *Social Work, 29*(2), 108–112.

Tran, C. G. (1997). Qualitative analyses of domestic violence in Vietnamese refugee women. Manuscript submitted for publication.

U.S. Bureau of Census. (1990). *Statistical yearbooks of the immigration and naturalization service.* (1981–1988). Washington, DC: U.S. Government Printing Office.

U.S. Committee for Refugees. (1976–1990). *World refugee survey.* New York: American Council for Nationalities Service.

Walker, L. (1979). *The battered woman.* New York: Harper & Row.

Walker, L. (1984). *The battered woman syndrome.* New York: Springer.

Westermeyer, J. (1986). Migration and psychopathology. In C. L. Williams & J. Westermeyer (Eds.), *Refugee mental health in resettlement countries* (pp. 39–59). Washington, DC: Hemisphere.

Westermeyer, J. (1991). Psychiatric services for refugee children. In F. L. Ahearn & J. L. Athey (Eds.), *Refugee children: Theory, research, and services* (pp. 127–162). Baltimore, MD: Johns Hopkins University Press.

Williams, C. L., & Berry, J. W. (1991). Primary prevention of acculturative stress among refugees: Application of psychological theory and practice. *American Psychologist, 46,* 632–641.

Yamamoto, J., Rhee, S., & Chang, D.-S. (1994). Psychiatric disorder among elderly Koreans in the United States. *Community Mental Health Journal, 30*(1), 17–27.

III

BICULTURALISM:
INTERACTIVE DUALISM
IN RELATIONSHIPS

Role expectations and stereotypes influence the lives of Asian Americans and inevitably affect their relationships. Asian cultural values define the order of relationships primarily from a male-oriented perspective. In Confucian philosophy, the five hierarchies of relationships dictate social decorum and order for men and women in relation to men. Although the degree of conformity to these rules of social order varies among Asian American women according to generation and ethnic group, the existence of a group unconscious and group memory influences perception, behavior, and values in the formation of relationships. Moreover, Western values, both influencing and influenced by stereotypes of Asian American women and men, again affect the formation of relationships. Cultures and societies are not static; for example, the values and practices of Confucian philosophy differ today from those of preceding generations. As Asian women immigrate to the United States, they both influence and are influenced by its culture.

In essence, the bicultural experiences of Asian American women have a significant impact on their relationships. The concept of biculturalism is preferred over acculturation because it suggests the interactive nature of and dual direction in which culture influences behavior, roles, and experiences. This process includes beliefs, practices, and values that influence the formation of self- and cultural identity as well as the development of interpersonal relationships.

The chapters in this section cut across generational, cultural, and historical boundaries. Chao's ancestor altars (chapter 6) and Chin's examination of mother–daughter relationships in literature speak to the images, stories, and memories carried by Asian American women and their impact in sustaining and influencing the relationships of Asian American women (i.e., nurturing, connections, and love). Moreover, it is the strength of identity that is both sustaining of self-esteem and self-image. For Asian American women, this self-identity generally is intricately interwoven with cultural identity. However, it should not be confused with identity problems, confusion, or conflict. In other words, these self- and ethnic identities and ancestor altars are to be viewed as developmental rather than pathological phenomena. This is not to say that pathological problems and maladjustment may not develop, nor is it to suggest that these phenomena do not create conflict and tension, as suggested by Kakaiya (chapter 8). However, they do provide support and connectedness, such as in friendships and social networks, as discussed by Serafica, Weng, and Kim (chapter 9).

There are several trends and questions to consider. Are today's families and societies shifting from patriarchies to matriarchies? What is the legacy being left as cultures and societies evolve; for example, as Asians become Asian Americans, as women achieve greater equity in the workplace, and as a feminist perspective becomes more dominant? The biculturalism of Asian American women is more prominent in the formation of relationships given the significant differences between Asian and Western cultures and the physical and racial differences between Asian and White women.

The term *interactive dualism* describes the evolutionary and historical perspectives; the oppression of socioeconomic and sociopolitical contexts; and the diversity of experiences of cultural groups that come together, interact, and influence one another with the concept of biculturalism. Moreover, it reflects the tendency of these forces to interact yet retain an inherent tension in their inability to eliminate and amalgamate differences and the dynamic nature of this process. Consequently, the earlier concept of a melting pot is inadequate and inappropriate, whereas the idea of a "garden salad" is more applicable in describing the evolution of the bicultural identity of Asian Americans and other ethnic groups.

6

ANCESTORS AND ANCESTOR ALTARS: CONNECTING RELATIONSHIPS

CHRISTINE M. CHAO

Ancestor altars are not simply interesting collections of antique photos of dead relatives. Rather, they are powerfully symbolic containers of psychologically and culturally necessary energies. Likewise, one's ancestors are not there simply to give one a pedigree about which to brag. They stand ready to offer connection and relationship. Ancestors and ancestor altars are a crucial and central psychological reality of the Asian psyche.

Although the psychological and spiritual functions served by ancestor altars are similar across ethnic groups, there are many differences in the specific ways that altars are conceived and constructed. For example, a Vietnamese altar will differ from a Chinese altar. A Japanese altar in Japan might look very different from one constructed by a third-generation Japanese American in the United States which, in turn, may look very different from a Korean altar in either the United States or Korea. In fact, the noncreedal aspect that characterizes much of Asian spirituality allows for significant individual expression in the construction of ancestor altars such that each person's altar will be unique. This chapter, therefore, is in no way an in-depth or exhaustive study of the role of altars in any one

Asian community. Furthermore, this chapter should not be taken as a theological or anthropological treatise on altars or on practices that have come to be labeled as *ancestor worship*. My interest in altars has come from a heart place, a dream place found within myself and the clients with whom I have worked. From here, with all the attendant limitations of application and generalizability, I offer this work.

This chapter encompasses three areas. The first is a brief exploration of the psychological role played by ancestors in the Asian community and how this dynamic is operative in people's psychological makeup (i.e., looking for the ancestors). The second addresses what the actual keeping of an ancestral altar has meant and how the creation of altars reflects both a history of conflict as well as a harmonious fusion of beliefs and practices in the Asian community (i.e., syncretism and transformation). Throughout the chapter there is discussion of the applicability of these issues for clinical practice. The third section provides descriptions of some of the ancestor altars kept by Asians in the United States (i.e., serving the soul).

LOOKING FOR THE ANCESTORS: REMONSTRATIONS AND REVERENCE

My father kept an ancestor altar, but it was in his heart. He listed all of his relatives who had died, and each day he would pray to them or pray for them, a theological distinction that reflected his status as a convert to Catholicism in China. His ancestors were intercessors between the deity and him. They were his go-betweens. But he also gave them honor and he remembered them.

My father was Eurasian and a Chinese-kibbei. My grandfather, Ci Fong, could not become a U.S. citizen because of the Chinese Exclusion Act of 1882 (Hong Kingston, 1980), so he made sure that his sons were born in the United States, thus giving them U.S. citizenship. My father was then raised between New York and Hong Kong, with trips to mainland China, where he survived a smallpox epidemic in Shanghai in the 1920s.

One day late in his life, when he was battling lung cancer, my father showed me the paper on which he had written, in very precise groupings, the names of all his ancestors. He used this piece of paper to pray each day. First came his mother and father, followed by his grandparents on both his mother's and father's sides; then came aunts and uncles, followed by cousins who had died. Then, included in their own group, were my mother's parents, her brother, and her aunts. A separate grouping held his favorite saints designated as his spiritual ancestors. My father never erected a formal altar to these ancestors. If I had suggested, however, that what he was doing was just that, he would have told me to stop engaging in romantic notions, go to church, and study harder.

How many first-, second-, third-, or fourth-generation Asian Americans have heard similar admonitions to do better, work harder, study more? These are not just our parents' voices; they also are the voices of the ancestors that underlie a Confucian hierarchy that demands obedience. They are the echoes of what our parents heard, what their parents heard, and what our great, great grandparents heard, and so on, down through the ages. This is particularly true of those Asian communities with Confucian and Buddhist roots: Korean, Vietnamese, Chinese, Japanese, Cambodian, Laotian, and South Asian (Indian), to name a few.

Psychological Dynamics

The psychological dynamics at work are made clear in the following passage by the Chinese American author Gus Lee, writing of the festival of Ching Ming in his 1991 book *China Boy*. The particular content is Chinese, but the overarching function can be seen throughout Asian society and is very much operative in the Asian psyche:

> Anyone can relate to other people, but traditional Chinese honor the dead. *Ching Ming*, which means "shiny bright," is a ritual of paying homage to ancestors. . . . Graves are swept, flowers placed, food offered, meals arranged at the headstones. The living explain new developments, emphasizing accomplishments to the dead. Apologies are offered for imperfections in a Confucian world that expects flawless behavior. An unforgiving managerial continuum reaching from the father to the oldest remembered paternal relative sits in stony judgment.

> Ching Ming is probably the reason that so many Asians have succeeded in school, since honoring professors is simple compared to pleasing people who have been dead for centuries and who have nothing to do but judge your behavior according to the pickiest standards known. (pp. 39–40)

Clinical Implications

The clinical implications of this make it important that whatever genogram a therapist creates with a client, time and space need to be made for exploring and understanding the client's immediate and not-so-immediate ancestors and the role that they play in her or his life. Many times Cambodian refugees, who have survived the so-called "killing fields," have been queried as to how they managed to survive physically or hold on emotionally. Their reply often is simply, "My ancestors."

When working with Asian and Asian American clients, ancestors need to be approached as living members of a person's immediate family.

They can be warm and supportive, providing psychological stability and nurturance, or they can be recalcitrant and critical. Psychology talks about the dynamic of the negative voice of the internalized mother or the internalized father and how this can interfere with a person's self-esteem or undermine areas in which a person consciously vows they want to achieve. Again, with Asian clients, this concept needs to be expanded so that the voices of the ancestors can be explored as well. For example, an Asian American client, who may be either third- or fourth-generation, may be in deep conflict about whether to pursue a career in the fine arts as opposed to one in the more respectable arenas of law, medicine, or education. It is not just that Mom and Dad, grandparents, and aunties and uncles disapprove. Often the client as well as the family has unconsciously polled the ancestors, and they do not approve. This disapproval can wreak internal emotional havoc, and we do our clients a disservice if we ignore it.

ESCAPE CLAUSE

It is also important to point out that there is a sort of escape clause found within the strictures of filial piety, which can be defined as the "honor, reverence, obedience, loyalty, and love owed to those who are hierarchically above you" (Chao, 1992, p. 159). This escape clause is found in the *Great Learning*, also known as the *Analects*, which are the collected sayings attributed to Confucius, who can be said to be one of the great ancestors standing behind Asian philosophical thought. Paradoxically, Confucius reminds the reader that one can be both a filial daughter or son and at the same time follow the dictates of his or her own heart:

> The Master said, "In serving his parents a son may remonstrate with them, but gently; when he sees that they do not incline to follow his advice, he shows an increased degree of reverence, *but he does not abandon his purpose*; and should they punish him, he does not allow himself to murmur." (Confucius, 1979, p. 74)

To not abandon one's purpose, while at the same time loving and honoring those who do not understand or who actively disapprove of one's course of action, speaks directly to a dynamic resolution that many Asians have come to use consciously. Jeanne Wakatsuki Houston (1980) wrote of arriving at this bicultural solution that allows her to be true to both her Japanese self and her Western self, which emerged from growing up in the United States. Questions such as where should she sit in relation to her husband and whom should she serve first made social engagements such as dinner parties a confusing clash of cultures. She has, more or less, resolved her struggles over whether she should serve the men or women first and whether she should sit next to her husband or at the head of the table:

Now I . . . entertain according to how I feel that day. If my Japanese sensibility is stronger I act accordingly and feel comfortable. If I feel like going all-American I can do that too, and feel comfortable. I have come to accept the cultural hybridizes of my personality, to recognize it as a strength and not weakness. (p. 24)

Would her ancestors approve? Very likely. And they probably would deem her extraordinarily smart for her adeptness at flowing between two worlds. This is, in part, because the ancestors live in two worlds. They are here, but they are also there. They are the bridge linking and connecting the present with the past, and the past with the future. The ancestors offer both a sense of identity and the assurance of belonging. The extended family goes outward, encompassing grandparents; aunts; uncles; cousins, including cousins many times removed; and so forth; and then backward to realms unseen.

ON BECOMING AN ANCESTOR

There is a hexagram in the *I Ching* (Baynes, 1950) labeled *ting* or *the cauldron*. The ting was more than just a pot or soup tureen. Cast of bronze, with a handle and carrying rings, it was a ceremonial vessel used to hold cooked foods at banquets and in the halls of the ancestors. The commentary on the ting hexagram reads in part "All that is visible must grow beyond itself, extend into the realm of the invisible. Thereby it receives its true consecration and clarity and takes firm root in the cosmic order" (p. 194). This can be seen as a psychological comment on the process of a person becoming an ancestor. The ancestors are those once-visible family members who now are literally in "the realm of the invisible." They are taking "root in the cosmic order" and thus can potentially play a profound psychological role in the life of a family or an individual. Thus, Grandfather, who has died and is an ancestor, will still be present with his likes, dislikes, prejudices, and shortcomings, but he also will be rooted in a cosmic order with a Buddha nature that has come to the forefront.

For Japanese Buddhists, at death one becomes a buddha and the family obtains a Buddhist posthumous name. When the origin of this custom is examined, one can see the striving for what psychologists might label *self-actualization* or *individuation*.

The term for the custom used in the Jodo-shin sect is *homyo* (*ho* is the Law). . . . This term originally referred to a lay title given in recognition of strict observance of the Buddha's Law. A man or woman who went to a temple or monastery to undertake a religious regimen received a certificate bearing a title reflecting the degree of the austerities practiced. Originally, then, these were not posthumous names at all. The pieces of paper on which they were written may well be the prototypes of the wooden memorial tablets. . . . (Today) . . . the posthumous name has lost its early meaning and can be purchased for everyone who dies. (Smith, 1974, pp. 84–85)

Some people may cynically decry that the monetary amount a family can afford to spend, as opposed to a person's true nature, determines how exalted or elaborate a name is obtained. I posit, however, that there is a psychological dynamic at work whereby the person's ascent to the position of ancestor holds the potential for healing and nurturance of the family and its members who are left behind. To paraphrase the *I Ching*, as an ancestor, the actual family member has perforce "grown beyond" himself or herself, entering into the realm of the sacred. To take one's place in the realm of the sacred is to be "consecrated" into an ancestral "cosmic order." The ancestor now has entered into another sort of hierarchical arrangement, with all its attendant responsibilities. To illllustrate this, a friend whose mother had died when she was in her early teens recalled that not too long before her father died, her mother came to her. Whether this was a dream or a visit by her mother's spirit was immaterial. Although her mother did not say anything directly, my friend said she knew it meant that she must return to Korea to be with her father.

HUNGRY GHOSTS, OR QUAN YIN SMILES ON ME WITH MA-MA'S FACE

It is perhaps only fair that attention be paid to the possible negative dynamics that might be operating. A Freudian argument might emphasize that deep in a person's ancestral memory, along with conscious feelings of love, he or she also harbors secret feelings of hate because the other person stands in the way of an inheritance. Thus, negative projections create angry ancestral spirits (i.e., hungry ghosts) that must be appeased by offers of food. Additionally, guilt, engendered because of these negative emotions, also leads to placating the ancestors by creating special places for them, again with offerings of food and drink, the lighting of candles, and the burning of incense.

Finally, someone might ask, what of the ancestor who physically or sexually abused a child? Is their memorial tablet to be placed on an altar? What if a child simply couldn't stand a parent? A friend related the story of a Southeast Asian man, an oldest son, who had a terrible relationship with his father. Now living in the United States, the son kept no altar for his father, but instead had a picture of him tacked on the wall in his basement.

These are some of the issues that arise frequently in clinical practice. How does a person resolve simultaneously loving and hating a parent? Should he or she forget? Should he or she forgive? How does a person get past the trauma and get on with his or her life? Whether it is in a therapist's office or on an altar, the ancestors are always present. One can see operating on an ancestor altar many of the same psychological and existential dilemmas that occur in a therapist's office. Who has a place on the altar and who does not, as well as who made those decisions, can reveal much about the psychological operations of an individual or a family.

An 11-year-old girl wrote a prize-winning essay in honor of her great-grandmother in which she remembered watching her "Ma-Ma" in front of her altar. In the essay, Jessica tells the story of her great-grandmother's life and relates how both her great-grandmother's presence and memory sustain her. The words, put down on paper, constitute an ancestor altar:

> Ahhh. . . . The sweet aroma of incense. . . . It beckons my memory to when I was little, watching my Great-Grandmother burning incense to Quan Yin (the Chinese Goddess of Mercy), Sahm Bo Fut (the Three Gods), and for the loss of her husband, Chung. She would put a little tiny spoon of cooked rice in three tiny bowls, and she would put tea in three other tiny cups.

Jessica also recounts stories her great-grandmother told her:

> What makes Ma-Ma so special to me is that she would always explain about how she came from China, about my ancestors, and my Chinese heritage. Ma-Ma told me lots of stories. She also told me about her life in China.

Jessica also shares the psychological benefit that she derived from this wonderful great-grandmother, now her ancestor:

> I remember she would encourage me to bear through my problems, especially when my parents were divorced and my dad wouldn't come to see me. When my cousins made fun of me because I wasn't full-blooded Chinese, and I didn't look Chinese, Ma-Ma would sing to me and tell me that it was okay to be a multicultural person. She would cry with me and tell me to keep my head high and be proud of who I am.

> Now the sweet aroma of incense is fading away, and Ma-Ma has gone with it. But I'll always remember her and treasure her in my heart. . . . Quan Yin smiles on me with Ma-Ma's face. (Oliver, 1996, p. 6)

ALTARS: SYNCRETISM AND TRANSFORMATION

A number of years ago, an elderly Southeast Asian woman was brought by her family to see me at an Asian mental health center. The woman had suffered terribly during the war years in Vietnam. Her family said that she was babbling; she made no sense. She was "acting like a crazy lady," they said. When she came in, eyes downcast, supported by her son and daughter-in-law, the first thing she did was grab at something that lay in the dusty corner, something that had missed the wastepaper basket. It was a long, thin piece of black plastic from which objects had been snapped off, leaving flat pieces that jutted out at regular intervals. She snatched at the plastic and animatedly began speaking in Vietnamese. Her son tried to take it out of her hands, and I did not need a translation to know he was saying something to the effect of "Ma, drop that junk . . . that's just trash!" She retorted with a long stream of angry words. This, I realized, was something to which I should pay attention. I told the son to tell his mother that I would be honored if she kept the black plastic object, and I asked the family to let me know what the mother wanted. The mother wanted the object to place on the ancestor altar.

No altar, however, had been erected in their home in the United States. The son and his wife worked long, hard hours at jobs with pay and status far beneath their previous educational attainments. That they had escaped from Vietnam was a miracle in itself. Their children were consumed with fitting into their American schools and learning English. The pressing needs of survival precluded any ideas of putting up an altar. Besides, Americans didn't have altars in their homes, and the son and his wife would find questions about an altar embarrassing. For them, Vietnam was the old way of life; the United States was the new. However, for the mother, the absence of an altar was significant. Ever since meeting that woman, I have made a point of inquiring about ancestor altars with Asian clients.

Since I started asking about altars, I have learned many things. Some refugees and immigrants have told me that since coming to the United States they have made a conscious decision to, in the words of one client, "give up my old gods and take your country's gods." Some people have told stories of deep rifts occurring within their families because of this. An example would be a Southeast Asian refugee family who had been sponsored by a U.S. Christian church. Out of a sense of gratitude and respect, as well as a desire to show honor to their sponsors' gods, the family or some of its members will begin to attend church services. (Historically and philosophically, Asians have been able to syncretize and incorporate numerous spiritual legacies and feel no conflict between the various spiritual systems.) Frequently, some family members formally convert to the denomination of the sponsoring family. They then announce to the remaining, non-Christian members of their family that they can no longer be involved with offering food to their ancestors or even erecting altars or caring for them because their pastor had told them that the practice was idolatrous and the food offered was "devil food." Because they were now Christians, they could no longer participate in the practices in which nonbelievers engaged.

This often was the beginning of painful rifts in many families, with family members voicing dismay at those who seemed to have turned their backs on the very people (their ancestors) who helped bring them safely to this new country. To not honor one's dead mother, father, grandmother, or grandfather is unthinkable, the highest form of arrogance and conceit. This frequently results in one part of the family cutting off ties with another part at the very time the family needs absolute cohesiveness to handle the stresses and strains that face them as they adjust to a new country and, in some cases, attempt to recover from traumatic experiences.

These examples are not to imply that every first-generation Asian family experiences this kind of conflict. A Roman Catholic friend from Vietnam, whose Christian roots go back a number of generations, explained that he simply places his "God altar" first and on top of his ancestor altar. A friend born in Japan who also had Roman Catholic family members recounted that before a test she would go and bow at the family's Shinto altar, their ancestral altar, and the Catholic altar. If she did well on the exam she would return to each altar, bow, and share the information of her success. None of this, she reported, felt contradictory.

This seemingly easy, ecumenical coexistence has had a long evolution in Asia. Buddhism, which originally came to China and Japan as a foreign religion introduced from India, became intermingled with Confucianism, Taoism, and older native religious systems. Ancestral veneration appears to be universally present throughout Asia. As Ching (1993) noted:

> The coexistence of all three religious traditions, and the possibility for the same people to be involved in all of them, testifies to a certain pluralism within the Chinese—and the East Asian—civilization, a pluralism that was hardly known by Europe and the Middle East. (p. 233)

In addition to the fact that this syncretistic pluralism could not be fathomed by Western missionaries, imperialistic motives combined with racist underpinnings so that historically the veneration of ancestors was suspiciously regarded, labeled *ancestor worship*, and then roundly condemned as idolatry. The roots of this condemnation are to be found in what is known as the "rites controversy," which raged for several centuries beginning in China in the 1500s when a debate started about whether or not Christian converts would be permitted to carry out the rites and rituals involving veneration of their ancestors. The Jesuit Matteo Ricci (1552–1610), who had learned Chinese and was respected as a Confucian scholar, approved of the veneration of ancestors. Subsequent Jesuits were assured by the emperor K'aang-hsi (who reigned from 1661 to 1722) that the rites involving family members who had died were memorial rites that fulfilled the obligations of filial piety and not worship of gods. However, other Roman Catholic missionary groups deemed these rites pagan, idolatrous, and superstitious. These latter groups won out, and in 1742 Pope Benedict

XIV issued a papal decree condemning the Chinese rites. Catholic missionaries in China were required to take an oath to oppose the rites. The decree was not reversed until 1939, when Pope Pius XII issued another decree allowing Catholic Christians to practice the ancestral rites (Ching, 1993, 1997).

This clash of cultures and theological misunderstandings became intertwined with the dynamics of power and control. What happened in China and throughout Asia 3 centuries ago is still alive, and the tensions are still operative with Asians arriving in America. A Hmong shaman who relocated to Chicago spoke to an ethnographer (Conguergood, 1989) about this issue:

> I still believe Hmong religion
> In my country Laos none of my cousins changed to Christian
> But now all my cousins come to America
> And all of them change to Christian . . .
>
> I shall never forget my own culture
> I am Hmong
> My father and mother gave me birth
> I shall call to feed their spirits . . .
>
> When you feed the spirits of your father and mother
> Grandfather and grandmother
> You say, Come to eat
> Come to defend
> Come to protect
> Close the mouths
> Stop the tongues of the evil spirits
> Do not allow them to take hold of anyone
> Come to us
> Shelter us from sickness (p. 18)

Not very long ago, power and control fueled the racist deportation of Americans of Japanese ancestry into internment camps (Exec. Order No. 9066, 1942). On February 19, 1942, President Franklin D. Roosevelt authorized the incarceration of 120,000 West Coast Americans of Japanese descent, 80% were U.S. citizens by birth. The commemoration of the 50th anniversary of the closing of the Tule Lake, California, internment camp was recently observed. Among those returning was the actor George Takei, who achieved fame as Mr. Sulu in the television series *Star Trek*. The picture accompanying the news story showed him bending to light incense at an altar (Lin, 1996). Eleven people died while interned at the Tule Lake camp. Takei said, "America betrayed American ideals at this camp. We must not have national amnesia; we must remember this" (p. 7).

A story that needs to be researched and told is what happened to many of the altars that existed when Japanese Americans were forced to relocate to internment camps during World War II. Many family pictures of relatives in traditional Japanese dress were burned because their presence was considered too incriminating when Japanese Americans felt that proving loyalty to the United States was essential. (It should be noted that not one Japanese American was ever found to be a spy or in any way disloyal to the United States.)

Although taken from a novel about a Japanese family in Hawaii, the following scene rings true:

> The Buddhist altar ... also worried her during the war years and so she hid it on her closet floor behind muu muu dresses, bringing her rice offerings to the closet and praying they wouldn't come to take her husband away. (Ida, 1996, p. 85)

How might the above vignette be interpreted? Is it about a woman who sneaks food into a darkened closet and then starts to talk to beings who are not there? If she's not delusional, is she merely naive or childish? Perhaps it is best to escape the problem by saying that this is in the realm of the spiritual and therefore not an area for psychologists, social workers, psychiatrists, or counselors. I offer, however, that to do any of these things would be to miss what has the potential to be psychologically transformative.

To enter the realm of the ancestors, to be present at the altar of the ancestors, is to place yourself at the juncture where the spiritual and the psychological meet. Or, to put it another way, the spiritual and the psychological are laid out on continua that overlap and intertwine. Ancestor altars are located where the two meet. In the West, we have striven to make psychology a "hard science," an "exact science," but in entering that arena of psychology in which therapy occurs we are probably closer to shamans, to monks, and to priests. When a person goes to the altar of his or her ancestors, he or she becomes, in many ways, his or her own shaman, monk, or priest. They are at the place at which this world and the other world touch and meet. They are also at a potentially therapeutic place, a place in which their hearts can be attended to. The literal Chinese for the character of *psychologists* translates into "the doctor of the inner heart" (Chao, 1992, p. 160). At the altar of his or her ancestors, then, a person can become his or her own psychologist, his or her own doctor of the inner heart.

To understand what is transformative about the altar, it is necessary to realize that the altar is where the ancestors reside and that the person who constructed the altar has participated in the delineation of sacred space. To function within sacred space is to open oneself up to the possibility of transformation. In psychological terms, the altar provides a meeting place for the conscious and the unconscious; it allows a conduit to be constructed between the conscious and the unconscious. The altar allows for an encounter with the psyche. You go to the altar to talk with the ancestors, to dialogue with the sacred, to experience what is numinous. This is not to say that every visit to an ancestral altar will result in a "peak experience." Nor should you be disappointed, as my daughter was when she was 4 years old, wanting to know why the mooncake we had placed on our altar very near my father's picture, did not have any bites taken out of it. The creation of an altar means we leave the realm of the literal and step into the world of the symbolic. We give up what the Jewish mystic Martin Buber (1970) termed "I–it" relationships for the connectedness experienced in an "I–Thou" relationship.

The existence of an altar also means that a person is partaking in and creating ritual. Ritual consists of two parts: movement and form. The movement aspect of ritual is the process. It involves what one does: erecting, creating, building the altar. The physical space must be lined out, set aside. This "doing" part also involves actions such as bowing, sitting in meditation, lighting incense, chanting, and praying.

Ritual also involves objects. You select ancestral tablets; you place pictures; you cook food and put it on the altar. In effect, almost anything has the potential to be an object that can be placed on an altar. That object becomes a symbol and, as such, the conduit for the psychological or spiritual power residing in it. Swiss psychiatrist Carl Jung (1955) wrote of ritual:

> In the ritual action man places himself at the disposal of an autonomous and "eternal" agency operating outside the categories of human consciousness. . . . How something eternal can "act" at all is a question we had better not touch, for it is simply unanswerable. (p. 249)

THE ALTARS OF ASIANS IN THE UNITED STATES: SERVING THE SOUL

The altars that Asian Americans keep, if they choose to keep them at all, vary tremendously. In many instances, the person who keeps the altar is not the oldest son, who in China, Korea, Japan, Vietnam, and so forth, would be obligated to erect and maintain the altar. For Asians in the United States, a daughter often chooses to do this. Some altars are very traditional. Some altars reflect the bicultural resolution of many Asian Americans. Other times altars are utterly new things that are created as the person flows among many streams; that is, defining themselves within their particular ethnic group and defining themselves within the umbrella appellation of *Asian American*.

A number of years ago, at a meeting of the Asian American Psychological Association, I constructed an altar as part of a professional presentation. I also distributed a questionnaire and asked people to share with me their experiences with altars. Before the meeting, I also distributed this written request to colleagues, associates, and friends. In response to my request, many people shared their experiences.

A third-generation (Sansei) Japanese American woman living in Colorado recalled the altar kept at her grandparents' house and spoke of hotokesima—the Buddhist sense that "we're all interconnected, there's a sense of continuity" (D. J. Ida, 1995, personal communication). She spoke of her grandparents, who had memorized the sutras and each morning would go in front of their butsudan. (*Butsu* is the Japanese word for a buddha. *Butsudan* means the Buddhist altar and serves as the home altar in which memorial tablets for the dead are enshrined.)

> When a pot of fresh rice was made the first scoop off the top was put in a little brass bowl and set before the altar. It was the same with the first fruits or if someone brought a big bag of candy, the first candy went on the altar.... When my grandfather died I was 10 years old. My grandmother said, "Grandpa is now part of *hotokesima*." It felt very comforting. (D. J. Ida, 1995, personal communication)

A 73-year-old engineer, a naturalized U.S. citizen who was born in China to parents of Mongolian, Chinese, and Basque ancestry, recalls his parents, who were killed by bombing raids during the Sino-Japanese wars:

> I don't keep the altar up all year. I put it up for the New Year. I have my father's and mother's picture and my grandparents on both sides. I put a white rug before the altar. [This was one of the few items he was able to take out of China after his parents' woolen factory was bombed.]

> We kou tou. I put oranges and stacks of Chinese grapefruit, which are symbols of wealth.... I put the things which I knew my father and mother liked. They both liked vegetables very much: green peppers, onions and green beans. (E. D. A. Corl, 1995, personal communication)

Although this altar is not kept up all year, it is taken out as needed by family members:

> When anything happens, my son, who is 56 years old, comes to me and says, "Pop, can we put up the altar?" I put the white prayer rug out for him. I put out the pictures, one candle for each and incense and food. I put out mantou (buns) and then rice. Rice was very expensive when my parents were alive ... and oranges, pomeros, but no vegetables. My son puts things he wants.... Putting up my altar is serving the soul. It's part of you. It's like eating. (E. D. A. Corl, 1995, personal communication)

A third-generation (Sansei) Japanese American man spoke of developmental changes within himself over time: "In my 20s I was individualistic. Now, family continuity and making sure that values get passed down [are] important" (J.S. Mio, 1996, personal communication). He recalled that when his grandmother died at the age of 95, he asked his mother for the altar (*butsudan*) that she kept. He has many vivid memories of his grandmother loving to play cards and going to Las Vegas, so he decided, in her honor, to put playing cards on the altar. He has inherited and is creating anew. Actually, he is carrying on his grandmother's tradition of melding the old with the new. He reported that his grandmother used to fill a sake cup with coffee every morning and place it on her altar. He has taken a wasabi bowl that his mother made and, like his grandmother, is doing an old–new thing by filling this with coffee and putting it on the altar. Describing his altar, he writes:

> At the top is a picture of the statue of the Buddha in my family's church. Inside of the shrine is a picture of the infant Buddha. At the bottom is the bowl of ashes where incense is burned. To the right is the gong. The box at the far right has extra incense sticks. On top of that is an older picture of my Grandmother. The vase at the left contains sticks of incense. I have a blue lighter next to it. The little brown bowl on the tissue paper is a wasabi bowl my mother made, but I put coffee in it every morning for my ancestors. The playing cards are next to this bowl. . . . Right behind the cards is a picture of my uncle who died last year. Next to him is my Grandfather, who died 20 years ago. Behind my uncle is my Grandmother. . . . She died last year. To the right of her is my cousin who died 10 years ago. Behind them . . . is an uncle who died 2 years ago. Finally, in the back is an uncle who died 26 years ago. He and the first uncle were uncles by marriage. All others are blood relatives. All of these people are those who died in my lifetime, whom I remembered. I have an Aunt and two cousins who died in Japan whom I never met. (J. S. Mio, 1995, personal communication)

In China, the ancestral tablets and scrolls were kept in a special "hall of the ancestors." In the United States, that hall may look seemingly profane yet actually contain what is special and sacred. A Chinese American writes:

> My dad passed away in 1988, my mom in 1991. My altar to them is a special photo of the two of them I happened to find as I was sorting through their stuff. They were standing inside a church, all dressed up for a relative's wedding; smiling directly at the camera. What I like about the photo was the happiness on my parents' faces, and how everything seemed to be in its place. I had the photo enlarged to 8″ x 10″, consulted with a Chinese expert about matting and framing (perhaps because I am Chinese and wanted to observe tradition on such matters), and then had the photo framed. It now sits on top of my piano in the living room, amidst (and in a way "looking over") other photos of my wife, kids, and other relatives. Each morning when I

meditate, I sit facing these photos, including of course, the one of my mom and dad. (D. J. Lam, 1996, personal communication)

The next description is that of a memory of an altar. It is a memory, however, that remains deeply vivid for the writer, who now lives in the United States as a naturalized citizen but who grew up in Indonesia and is of Chinese ancestry:

> Inside the innermost chamber of my parents' house in Kudus, Indonesia, there was an ancestor altar. It was 8' tall, 6' wide and 2 ½' deep. It was made of teak wood, marble top and mirrors with colorful dragon paintings on them. The altar was originally built by one of my mother's wealthy uncles, in memory of their parents. Eventually, the pictures of my grandparents from both sides were added, because my father was the oldest son and my mother was the oldest daughter. On top of the altar there were three silver urns containing ashes in which burning joss sticks were placed.
>
> Once a month on a certain evening, tea in small porcelain cups was served and joss sticks lit. Every year there were a number of festivities when the altar was covered with a variety of dishes, fruits, cookies, cups of rice-wine, and tea. The altar had an extra leaf that would be pulled out to make it twice as large. With each offering, there was always an extra bowl of rice and a cup of tea on each side of the altar. Extra joss sticks were also placed on both sides. The left side was to remember all our overseas ancestors and the right side for those remaining in China.
>
> As children, my brothers, sisters and myself played around and under the altar, but always quietly and in a hush-hush. It was a place to behave and be respectful not only toward the dead but also toward the older generations in my family.
>
> The ancestor altar that I knew when growing up always gives me nostalgic memories. I have not, consciously, created an altar, real or spiritual. But I know deep in my heart there is an ancestor altar that continually gives me my sense of identity and belonging to my family, past, present, and no doubt also future generations. (R. Lie, 1996, personal communication)

Now that others have allowed me to share their stories, let me share mine. One day a physician friend called and asked if I would be home for the next hour. Hearing that I would, she said she was stopping over with something for me. When she arrived, she handed me a beautiful rattan tray on which was arranged a variety of fruits and announced, "This is for your altar," and then headed out, saying she was late for rounds at the hospital. It was the eve of the lunar new year, and I was actually cooking food for a big party and putting "lucky money" in red envelopes for the children. I stood with the tray thinking, "But I don't have an altar." And then I realized I did. There on our mantelpiece I had pictures of the family, although the dead were mixed in with the living. I separated them. I grouped them: the dead of my family, the dead of my husband's family. The ancestors. I placed my friend's tray of fruit. There was a pineapple on it. My friend later explained that the Vietnamese word for *pineapple* is a homonym for the word *smoke*, which in turn relates to incense. Incense carries our prayers to the ancestors. Incense purifies. Incense commemorates. I lit joss sticks. When and how had I gotten them? I don't remember, but it didn't matter. I needed them and they were there. I arranged a bouquet of flowers. I lit a candle. I placed dishes of the foods I had cooked. I bowed in front of the assemblage. I prayed for them. I prayed to them. I remembered those I had known and loved with all my heart. I grieved anew. I looked at those I had never known personally. I felt comforted. I thanked them. My friend was right. I had an altar.

ALTARS OF OTHER CULTURES

Awareness of altars in Asian culture has led me to the altars of other cultures: the altars of Dias do los Muertos (Days of the Dead), the altars of Kwanzaa, and the Passover seder table, to name a few. I think many people, especially women, create altars almost unconsciously: collections on tabletops, on window sills above sinks, on the corners of desks. Here among the ancestors is a place to bring one's innermost heart. Here is a place to receive assurance, confirmation, and sustenance. Here is a place of connection.

The African American acappella group, Sweet Honey in the Rock, sings to us:

> Listen more often to things than to beings.
> Listen more often to things than to beings.
> 'Tis the ancestors' word when the fire's voice is heard.
> 'Tis the ancestors' word in the voice of the waters.
>
> Those who have died have never, never left.
> The dead are not under the earth.
> They are in the rustling trees.
> They are in the groaning woods.
> They are in the crying grass.
> They are in the moaning rocks.
>
> Those who have died have never, never left.
> The dead have all pact with the living.
> They are in the woman's breast.
> They are in the wailing child.
> They are with us in the home. (Sweet Honey in the Rock, 1988)

REFERENCES

Baynes, C. F. (1950). *The I Ching or book of changes* (R. Wilhelm, Trans.). Princeton, NJ: Princeton University Press.

Buber, M. (1970). *I and thou* (W. Kaufman, Trans.). New York: Scribner.

Chao, C. M. (1992). The inner heart: Therapy with Southeast Asian families. In L. Vargas & J. Koss-Chiono (Eds.), *Working with culture: Psychotherapeutic interventions with ethnic minority children and adolescents*. San Francisco: Jossey-Bass.

Ching, J. (1993). *Chinese religions*. New York: Orbis Books.

Confucius. (1979). *The analects* (D. C. Lau, Trans.). New York: Dorset Press.

Conguergood, D. (1989). *I am a shaman: A Hmong life story with ethnographic commentary* (X. Thao, Trans.). (Southeast Asian Refugee Studies Project, Center for Urban and Regional Affairs Occasional Paper No. 8). Minneapolis: University of Minnesota Press.

Exec. Order No. 9066 (1942).

Hong, K. M. (1980). *China men*. New York: Alfred Knopf.

Houston, J. W. (1980). Beyond Manzanar: A personal view of Asian American womanhood. In R. Endo, S. Sue, & N. Wagner (Eds.), *Asian Americans: Social and psychological perspectives* (Vol. 2). New York: Science and Behavior Books.

Ida, D. (1996). *Middle son*. New York: Doubleday.

Jung, C. (1955). *Collected works. Vol. II, Psychology and religion: West and East* (R. F. C. Hull, Trans.). Princeton, NJ: Princeton University Press.

Lee, G. (1991). *China Boy*. New York: Dutton.

Lin, S. C. (1996, July 12). Painful memories: Internees commemorate 50th anniversary of Tule Lake camp closing. *Asian Week: The Voice of Asian America*, p. 13.

Oliver, J. (1996, May 3). Remembering Ma-Ma. *Asian Week: The Voice of Asian America*, p. 6.

Smith, R. J. (1974). *Ancestor worship in contemporary Japan*. Stanford, CA: Stanford University Press.

Sweet Honey in the Rock. (1988). Breaths CD. Flying Fish Label. Lyrics adapted from the poem "Breaths" by Birago Diop, music by Ysaye Barnwell, © 1988. Y. M. Barnwell. Recorded by Sweet Honey in the Rock. Reprinted by permission: Barnwell's Notes Publishing.

7

MOTHER–DAUGHTER RELATIONSHIPS: ASIAN AMERICAN PERSPECTIVES

JEAN LAU CHIN

Culture defines many role expectations and behaviors related to gender. As women's roles evolve within a changing society, who women choose for their role models, how they develop their identities, and how they form interpersonal relationships often stem from that first relationship between mother and daughter. As Asian American women in the United States grapple with the bicultural aspects of their lives, the dynamics of the mother–daughter relationship can become intense.

For example, what happens when an Asian American daughter achieves middle-class educational and economic status and, in doing so, attains a social standing never dreamed of by her immigrant mother? How does an Asian American daughter establish a mother–daughter bond when she cannot fathom the trauma of separation, abandonment and death experienced by her immigrant mother because of war, poverty, and immigration? These are the experiences of many Asian American immigrant mothers and their daughters.

How does an Asian American mother adapt to the world in which her daughter lives and advise her of that which she has not experienced?

Culture and gender roles are not static. They have evolved with sociopolitical changes from Confucian times to the present. Yet Asian American women often wrestle with these changing roles while believing in their stability. Immigrant mothers often struggle to maintain their Asian culture in the United States as aspects of their identity while their Asian American daughters may view their immigrant mothers as resistant to change. How do Asian American women establish a mother–daughter bond within this context? There are few empirical studies addressing this issue. Even if there were, how could they reflect the intensity of affect, the complexity of issues, and the depth of meaning as captured through folklore and story. Themes illustrative of mother–daughter relationships can be viewed and analyzed through folklore and story.

THE CONTEXT OF POWER AND CONNECTIONS

Feminist theory has struggled with questions about women's roles and their development, often returning to the basic question of whether women are inherently different from men. In the formation of relationships, nurturance and connectedness often characterize feminine relationships, whereas power and dominance often characterize masculine relationships. However, these elements coexist in most relationships.

What differences exist among Asian American women? Sociocultural, political, and immigration history provide common contexts for Asian American women and often contribute to the unique nature of their mother–daughter relationships. Although the immigration experience is not unique to Asian Americans in the United States, race and cultural differences between Asian and Western cultures can result in particularly dissonant adjustment experiences. Although the structure of Asian cultures, as prescribed by Confucian philosophy during pre-Communist times, rendered women dependent on men, immigration often resulted in mutual dependency between husband and wife and a reversal of dependency between immigrant parents and their American-born children because of language and other accultural factors.

Values of modesty, reciprocity, and filial piety common to Asian cultures historically prescribed roles for Asian women that were subservient to men within interpersonal and familial relationships. Patriarchal dominance within Asian cultures defined a woman's social status by her marital status and the position of her husband within the family hierarchy. Bound by cultural expectations, Asian women historically played a self-sacrificing, subservient role to achieve the Confucian ideal of the virtuous female. However, interpersonal connectedness was the basis on which Asian women created a respected social status and maintained the integrity of the family unit.

Chinese immigrant women often experienced the hardships of famine, poverty, and war before coming to the United States. Because of high infant mortality rates and poor socioeconomic conditions, abandonment of children was common in pre-Communist times. Although social conditions improved in post-Communist times, the value placed on sons has persisted from Confucian times; abandonment of daughters was common given the one-child-per-family national policy established since the cultural revolution to address the geometric birthrate in China. For those impervious to the experiences of starvation and poverty, these practices may appear brutal, cruel, inhumane, or otherwise uncaring. For those who witnessed loved ones die of starvation and disease, such practices were the sacrifices made for survival and protection of remaining family members. Although immigration to the United States was often an escape to freedom and improved economic conditions for most Chinese, they never forgot their obligations to those left behind. Chinese immigrants came with strong cultural values, beliefs, and practices derived from Confucian philosophy. Many Chinese women came to join husbands who had immigrated earlier. In attempts to recreate a family, home, and community within an unwelcoming host culture, they developed a culture and way of life that was uniquely Chinese American while believing that it was still wholly Chinese.

WHAT IS DIFFERENT FOR ASIAN AMERICAN WOMEN?

Mother–Son Relationships

The emphasis on mother–daughter relationships in Western cultures is in contrast to the prominence of mother–son relationships within Asian cultures. A close mother–son relationship is not devalued in Asian cultures as it is in Western cultures as in the image of the "mama's boy." Rather, it is valued as representing the filial piety of the son to the mother. In marriage, it grants the mother-in-law the highest power and status achievable within traditional Asian cultures.

Prominent during Confucian times, Asian American daughters often resent the constant deference to male siblings and displays of favoritism. Daughters are frequently reminded of the son's importance in carrying on the family name and his role in protecting the family. Sons often have been catered to and receive extra privileges. Although daughters may not always accept these premises, they later understand that the family is viewed as the source of survival, identity, and pride for everyone. Daughters are expected to defer to sons because this preserves the integrity of the family unit. A strong family with a strong male gives status and power to the entire family. Daughters ultimately accept this special mother–son relationship when they realize that it does not preclude a strong and unique bond between themselves and their mothers. Mothers share with their daughters the stories of experiences that made them strong, the skills they need, and the values that are central to their identities.

Sacrifice of Mothers

The ideal of maternal sacrifice is classic in Asian folklore. By Western standards, it may appear extreme and self-negating. However, reinforced by Confucian philosophy in Asian cultures, it emphasizes placing others first with the expectation that others will provide support when needed; it is supported by a social order that emphasizes reciprocity between individuals and devalues exploitation. For Asians, unlike Westerners, it is not viewed as self-denigrating but as reflective of the ultimate willingness to nurture and protect one's family.

This sacrifice is illustrated by Asian mothers giving the best food to her children while reserving the least desirable food for herself. It is conveyed by her frugality in saving and recycling everything, a trait considered both a virtue and a necessity during hard economic times. This sacrifice is demonstrated by her giving freely of food and gifts to family and friends while living within limited means. When viewed through a Western lens, however, Asian daughters often resent this sacrifice because the mother seems exploited and self-denigrating. Western culture embraces a different mentality; one does not give unless given to.

The traumas commonly experienced by Asian mothers in the past included the witnessing of children dying or abandoned because of famine and disease, and explains their irrevocable fear and drive to protect and nurture their children. According to the tenets of reciprocity within Asian cultures, Asian mothers have strong expectations of repayment with honor and respect from their children. Given this unspoken reciprocity inherent in Asian cultures, a mother's sacrifice represents the highest level of character development.

Prominence of Familial Relationships

The emphasis on male–female relationships in Western interpersonal contexts is in sharp contrast to the prominence of familial relationships within Asian cultures. Unlike Western social gatherings and dinners, which often are male–female oriented (i.e., characterized by the number of couples present), Asian social gatherings are often family oriented (i.e., characterized by the number of families present). For Chinese immigrant women, for example, this difference often meant large family gatherings in which Asian women shared the cooking. These gatherings provided strong images of Asian mothers as nurturers and of extended families with mothers as anchors. They also emphasized the connectedness among families.

The sharing and giving of food, especially during holidays and festivals, was a ritual of many Chinese American immigrant women. These women made extra pastries and cakes during holiday and festival times to give to friends and relatives; during earlier immigration periods, when there were fewer women in the United States, this meant nurturing the men whose wives and families had not yet immigrated. Daughters shared in these rituals with their mothers as they helped make the pastries and do the cooking. Although changing immigration patterns have modified these behaviors, influences of Confucian philosophy persist even among Asian Americans today.

MOTHER–DAUGHTER RELATIONSHIPS IN POPULAR LITERATURE: *THE JOY LUCK CLUB*

Psychological Analysis

The Joy Luck Club (Tan, 1989) is a novel about mother–daughter relationships and the influence of culture and character on the psychological development and adjustment of Chinese immigrant and Chinese American women through generations. It is the story of four Chinese immigrant women and their American-born daughters bonded by their weekly mah-jong and investment club. This bond is psychological while serving social and financial interests as well. Analysis of its themes captures many aspects of mother–daughter relationships among Chinese American women. There are several prominent themes in the novel: the overpowering influence of family secrets, the trauma of separation, the transmission and continuity of dynamic issues from one generation to the next, and the oppression of women coupled with their resilience. Symbols and metaphors reflecting the elements underlying Taoism—wood, water, metal, fire, and earth—are characteristic of a woman's personality and fate. The influence of war, poverty, and starvation on the lives and relationships of Asian women permeate the novel. Ultimately, the resolutions between the mothers and daughters illustrate the resilience of and bonds among Asian American women.

Jing-Mei and Suyuan Woo

Jing-Mei Woo's mother was forced to abandon her two babies when she fled Kweilin China because of the Japanese invasion. In the United States, she starts a mah-jong and investment club to keep the pain and fear of reality at bay, but she is left with a lifelong yearning for reunion with the children that she abandoned, not an uncommon phenomena among Asian immigrant women. She often recounts her story to her daughter, Jing-Mei, frequently with a different ending. Jing-Mei is angry and willful as a child, refusing to be changed by her mother, whom she perceives as demanding. Jing-Mei's mother's hopes and dreams lie in her wish for Jing-Mei to play the piano; Jing-Mei is determined not to try and, finally, she shames her mother in a recital in which she deliberately plays terribly. This mother–daughter relationship plays out the mother's expectations of obedience and the daughter's rebelliousness. When Jing-Mei finally makes peace as a woman, she realizes that in disappointing her mother and trying to "follow her own mind" she has lost her culture. It is symbolic of their bond that her mother gives Jing-Mei her "life's importance" (p. 208), a jade pendant on a gold chain. It is only after mother's death that Jing-Mei realizes her mother's wisdom in describing her character through an analogy in which during dinner she carelessly chooses the crooked crab (i.e., her character) that no one picks because everyone else wants the best quality. Jing-Mei comes to terms with her mother by fulfilling her mother's long-cherished wish to find her abandoned babies. Jing-Mei is able to accept the Chinese part of herself (i.e., obedience) in the reunion with her long-lost half-sisters.

An-Mei Hsu and Rose Hsu Jordan

An-Mei Hsu is raised by her grandmother and aunt with ghost stories and threatening tales. These stories are part of an oral history tradition transmitted by Asian mothers. Her grandmother constantly recounts the story of a greedy girl whose belly grew fatter and fatter; this girl poisons herself after refusing to say whose child she carried (i.e., taboo against premarital sex). When the monks cut open her body, they find inside a large white winter melon. An-Mei's grandmother continues with statements such as "When you lose your face, it is like dropping your necklace down a well. The only way you can get it back is to fall in after it." This is an allusion to suicide. An-Mei later finds out that her mother ran off to marry a rich man after An-Mei's father died, bringing shame to the family. Although cast out of the family, An-Mei's mother returns home to see the dying grandmother for the last time. In the ancient tradition, she cuts off a piece of her flesh to cook as a medicinal potion to heal her mother though knowing that it is hopeless. This is symbolic of the highest sacrifice. As An-Mei runs to reach her mother, against her grandmother's wishes, she spills a pot of hot soup on herself, causing deep, lifelong scars. An-Mei joins her mother and when they return home finds that she is the fourth wife and concubine of a man who raped her as a ruse to bear him sons. An-Mei's mother's shame, depression, and lack of choice lead her to commit suicide. Because she could not speak up or run away, she poisons herself 2 days before the lunar new year; she plans her suicide to take advantage of Chinese beliefs to force her husband to revere her and her children or run the risk of her returning to haunt him as a vengeful spirit.

An-Mei's element is water, an aspect that dominates her life development and that of generations to follow. Rose Hsu Jordan's mother–daughter story is dominated by the irony of her mother's faith in God's will. Rose's mother, An-Mei, believes her faith is responsible for keeping good things coming although she is unable to pronounce "th," causing Rose to confuse *faith* with *fate*. During a family outing to the beach, a tragedy occurs, affecting the entire family. Rose was to care for and watch over her brothers; however, her 4-year-old brother (the only child not named after a Bible character) drowns, causing the entire family to feel guilty for being selfish. In her grief, Rose's mother tells the following story: "An ancestor of ours once stole water from a sacred well. Now the water is trying to steal him back" (p. 129). Rose's mother brings out her Bible and tries to entice the sea to release her son by offering it another treasure in a hopeless attempt to bring back her son. When this fails, she responds with despair and horror for being "so foolish to think she could use faith to change fate" (p. 130).

In adulthood, Rose divorces after 17 years of marriage. She was attracted to her husband because "he was different from the Chinese boys. He was brash, assured and opinionated. He was angular and lanky, and his parents came from Tarrytown, not China." Not surprisingly, the marriage was met with disapproval from both families. The relationship becomes one in which Rose is always being rescued emotionally and protected by her husband; she is dependent on him and indecisive. In rethinking her marriage, she compares it to her drowned brother, that is, how she knew he was in danger and let him drown. She sees "fate shaped half by expectation, half by inattention. But somehow, when you lose something you love, faith takes over. You have to pay attention to what you lost. You have to undo the expectation. Water is symbolic in this relationship, with separation as a theme throughout the generations" (p. 131).

In her marriage, Rose plays out her mother's need to be rescued. She becomes depressed and suicidal over the divorce and takes an overdose of sleeping pills—replaying the helplessness of her grandmother, who resorted to suicide as a way to free herself from a shameful marriage and rescue her daughter. With her mother's support, Rose is able to take a stand by refusing to move out of her house. The use of metaphor characterizes Rose's development. She is told, "A girl is like a young tree, you must stand tall and listen to your mother standing next to you" (p. 191). Her mother said she was born without wood so that she listened but let the words blow through her. The reunion between mother and daughter is symbolized by the planting of new seedlings among the weeds running wild throughout the garden (p. 196). The garden is nurtured by water, thereby resolving An-Mei's inability to rescue her own mother from her fate.

Lindo and Waverly Jong

Betrothed at age 2, Lindo is turned over to her mother-in-law's household at age 12 following a flood of the family property. She is married at 16 to a husband who is intellectually limited, spoiled, and ineffectual. Her mother-in-law is dominant and superstitious and expects a daughter-in-law who will be obedient, raise proper sons, care for old people, and sweep the family burial grounds. When leaving, Lindo's mother gives her a red jade necklace and the message to be true to herself, which Lindo decides is strong like the wind and pure like genuine jade.

When the marriage is not consummated after several years and there are no offspring, Lindo is blamed by her mother-in-law as being too balanced with metal (i.e., gold). The mother-in-law removes all sharp things from the room because they are cutting off the next generation. Lindo finally devises a way to get her husband's family to dissolve the marriage by using their own superstitious beliefs against them. Lindo fabricates a dream in which a vision predicts her fate that brings together details she has observed about her in-laws. The wind had blown out the candle during their wedding night, so the marriage is doomed and her husband will die if he stays in the marriage. To prove this prediction, she claims that the ancestors planted signs to show the marriage is rotting. In her dream a man with a long beard and a mole on his cheek identified (one of the ancestors) three signs: (a) a black spot on her husband's back would eat away his flesh as it did the ancestor's face, (b) Lindo's teeth would fall out, (she already has cavities), (c) a seed planted in the womb of a servant girl who was really of imperial blood and Lindo's husband's true spiritual wife. Believing this so-called dream, the mother-in-law readily agrees to allow Lindo to leave the family if she swears not to tell the story.

Being born without metal, Lindo is balanced by his mother in her marriage with gold and learns to use the wind as a powerful but unseen force to set direction. Waverly Jong is taught by her mother the art of invisible strength (i.e. wind). She goes through life attentive to innuendoes. She becomes fascinated by the strategy of chess and goes on to become a champion chess player. Waverly's mother's comment on chess is that it is played by American rules, analogous to immigration (i.e., they [Americans] know the answers and won't tell you). Waverly learns why not to reveal "why" to others (i.e., a little knowledge withheld is a great advantage). Her mother proudly watches, but with proper Chinese humility calls Waverly's success luck. As her mother begins treating her special, Waverly resents her mother's standing over her, taking credit for her winning, and showing her off on Saturday market days. She retaliates, only to find that her mother ignores her and that as her mother stops standing over her like a protective ally as a result, she begins to lose games and loses interest in chess altogether (i.e., her mother had won again; the "strongest wind cannot be seen," p. 100).

The game of chess is symbolic of the characters of mother and daughter. Waverly picks up her mother's traits of strategy and shrewdness, although the mother–daughter relationship is characterized by battle and struggle. The powerful support of the mother reflects silent but powerful maternal pride. However, it is a strong battle of wills between mother and daughter. Waverly resents her mother's ability to see black where there is white and vice versa and her mother's strength and strategy in trapping her into getting angry. Ultimately, she comes to realize that the battle with her mother has been fought within herself. As a scared child, she saw a formidable foe in her mother; as an adult, she finally sees what was really there: "an old woman, a wok for her armor, a knitting needle for her sword, getting a little crabby as she waited patiently for her daughter to invite her in" (p. 184).

Ying-Ying and Lena St. Clair

Ying-Ying was a spoiled rich child cared for by an amah who had given up her own baby son when her husband died and she was forced to become a nursemaid. Ying-Ying was taught never to ask to have her needs met as this was selfish and viewed as unfeminine. On a fishing trip, Ying-Ying gets her dress dirty as she watches a lady chop fish. Fearful that she will be punished, she smears fish blood over her dress, frightening her amah, who thinks she is hurt. Threatened by her amah that she will be banished to Kunming, Ying-Ying runs away, gets lost, and is picked up by some fishermen. Her fears worsen; she is afraid that she will turn into a beggar girl without her family. Frightened and wet, with nowhere to go while waiting to be found, she watches a performance of The Moon Lady, a classic play of eternal life, wantonness, and feminine weakness, not unlike the story of Adam and Eve. An eternity had passed since the Moon Lady saw her husband, for this was her fate—to stay lost on the moon, because she dared to seek her own selfish wishes. This story has deep significance both physically and emotionally for Ying-Ying, who was told never to ask. Ying-Ying wishes to be found. She later marries an Irish-English man who believes that he saved her from poverty when, in fact, she had more riches than he could ever have dreamed of.

Lena St. Clair was told by her mother that her great-grandfather had sentenced a beggar to die in the worst possible way. Later, the dead man came back and killed him, or he died of influenza. Her mother was fearful of her environment and became overly protective of Lena. She told Lena horrendous stories of what would befall her if she did not obey (e.g., threats of being sold, being eaten). Lena remembers that after falling in the basement at age 5, her mother told her a threatening story that escalated her fearful imagination of seeing things. Although her mother never talked about her past in China, her father believed that he saved her from a terrible life and changed her name and birthdate on the immigration papers. "So, with the sweep of a pen, my mother lost her name, and became a dragon instead of a tiger" (Tan, 1989, p. 104). Lena's father apparently was oblivious to mother's true feelings and needs because he could not communicate with her in Chinese. He would put words into her mouth. Lena also ended up making up lies to her mother when she translated for her.

After the family moved to an apartment on a hill, Lena's mother was fearful, particularly after having been accosted by a drunk. She holds tightly to Lena, always thinking that there is danger lurking nearby. Lena's mother is anxious that this new house has poor feng shui; is imbalanced; violates all the basic principles of harmony. She constantly rearranges the furniture, saying, "When something goes against your nature, you are not in balance" (Tan, 1989, p. 108). Lena eventually learns that her mother deteriorated after the death of a child and feels guilty for having killed her baby. This guilt apparently derived from the earlier abortion of a child from her first husband when the restrictiveness in China made for few options. Lena is awed by her mother's astute intuition and her ability to read signs and predict things before they happen. However, she also realizes that the threatening stories and her mother's strange behavior are the results of her psychosis or the loss of spirit. Lena describes her mother's behavior as ghostlike and her father's obliviousness to her mother's true nature as that of the Ugly American.

When Lena was young, her mother told her to finish her rice or marry a pock-faced husband. Lena took this to mean that she was destined to marry Arnold, a mean neighborhood boy with tiny pits in his cheeks. She deliberately leaves more rice in her bowl and starts sacrificing food to try to do him harm; she becomes anorexic. She later learns that Arnold died from measles at age 17; this scares her and she begins to gorge herself, becoming bulimic.

Lena marries Harold, a colleague and architect, and moves into a renovated barn with a mildew-lined pool on 4 acres of land covered with redwood trees and poison oak. She becomes a doormat for Harold; they split the rent and all other expenses. She is grateful to him for helping her out. She does not tell him that she is actually paying more than her share, rationalizing what a good deal she has. She continually fears that Harold will realize that she is not good enough and how underserving she is; she fears that she will be exposed. She ends up supporting his career and working for him while continuing to rationalize that this is equal and that it does not matter. Meanwhile, Harold is oblivious to all this and thinks that he is being fair; he is unable to recognize his selfishness.

Lena's mother sees through everything and points out the absurdity of their financial balance sheet and how Lena is getting the raw end of the deal. Lena begins to despair and gets confused because she had so rationalized the arrangement as part of her equality and independence.

During the tour of their house, Lena laments, "My mother knows, underneath all the fancy details that cost so much, this house is still a barn" (p. 151). The balance in life emphasized by the mother as so important gets played out pathologically in Lena's balance-sheet marriage. Additionally, the mother's uncanny intuition and prophetic ability to point out things before they happen is paralleled by the marital relationship in which father is oblivious to the mother's true nature. Her mother's prophetic admonition of "Why don't you stop it?" to Lena about her marriage contradicts her own inability or refusal to "stop it" by allowing things to take their course in her own life; she acts by her silence.

Lena gives her mother the guest bedroom when she visits; her mother smiles. This is contradictory to the Chinese way of thinking, in which the guest bedroom is the best bedroom or the master bedroom. Lena's mother tells Lena her story: that she came from one of the richest families in Wushi and her marriage at 16 was arranged. When she was 18, her husband left her for an opera singer; she felt shamed and suicidal and aborted the baby conceived with her husband. She then goes to live in the countryside among the peasants. After 10 years, she goes to work in the city and becomes pretty again. Lena's father thinks that he saved Ying-Ying from the poor country village, not realizing that he had waited patiently for 4 years "like a dog in front of a butcher shop" (p. 250) until she was ready. She has felt like a ghost (i.e., without spirit) in her marriage, and she has married a ghost (i.e., what Chinese call White people). In contrast to Lindo's favorable use of winds as strategy and strength, Ying-Ying's winds are destructive and sweep things away. Devoid of anger and affect after having been abandoned by her first husband and having aborted a child, Ying-Ying allowed things to happen passively but in doing so made choices.

Crosscutting Themes

Mother–Daughter Relationships

The special bond between mothers and daughters is manifested in each of the four relationships depicted in *The Joy Luck Club* (Tan, 1989). As the daughters struggle for autonomy and identity, rebelliousness against maternal guidance, intergenerational misunderstandings, and cultural dissonance between mother and daughter are played out. Closure is found as the daughters come to terms with their Chinese identity, the learning transmitted from mother to daughter, and the inculcation of culture with character.

Many influences reflective of Chinese culture are illustrated in the nature of these mother–daughter relationships. Child rearing is characterized by the use of stories and threats to illustrate moral principles and guide behavior. Maternal pride is characterized by overt modesty against a backdrop of silent pride; mothers are openly critical of their daughters in a typically Chinese way of getting others to object and compliment their daughters. Maternal guidance is typified by the mandate to be obedient. The tension between mother and daughter is prominent throughout the novel. The mothers feel that they know what is best and cannot understand how their daughters can know something if they did not teach it. The daughters, on the other hand, rebel against their mothers' control and expectations. However, each of the daughters comes to realize the perceptiveness of her mother. Each comes to terms with what she has gained from her mother and comes to identify with her.

Multigenerational Influence on Character and Psychological Adjustment

The influence of each mother's history, character, and development on her daughter is striking. The stories show that the daughters are unable to escape the origins and fates of their mothers. History repeats itself despite the contextual change of the cultural setting and the daughters' active and conscious wishes to devoid themselves of their Chinese culture at certain points in their lives. There are parallels in character despite each daughter's attempt to be her own person. The influence of the five elements of Taoism on the life adjustment of mother and daughter, on the forms of pathological adjustments, and on the coincidences of fate are clearly illustrated. The elements are metaphors for defining characteristics of adjustment and pathology.

Culture and Immigration as It Shapes Psychological Development

The environment serves as a context for how the women of *The Joy Luck Club* (Tan, 1989) make adjustments in their lives. These include reactions and experiences related to the war in China and immigration and adjustment to the United States. The many contrasts between U.S. and Chinese traditions influence the conflict experienced by the mothers and daughters. This gets played out in the marriages of the daughters and is described by Jing-Mei as "moving West to reach East" (p. 184).

Superstition in traditional Chinese culture as described in the novel is probably more intriguing because of its novelty and exotic quality. Important, however, is its analogy to superstitious beliefs in Western culture during times when science and technology were in their early stages, infant mortality was high, and control over natural disasters was minimal. Consequently, fate, faith, and superstitious beliefs played a more prominent role in hopes, dreams, and fears.

Symbolism is both central to the Chinese culture and prominent in the dynamics of the novel. The five elements of fire, water, wood, earth, and metal are the core of Taoism; they are used to predict and decide major events. The balance of these elements is important to character and fate.

Tracing the symbolism of these elements for each of the women shows interesting coincidences and relationships to character development and psychological adjustment. Feng shui is alluded to frequently in its importance to guiding the women's behavior.

DEVELOPMENTAL PROCESSES FOR ASIAN AMERICAN WOMEN

Chinese American daughters often are puzzled by the modesty of their mothers and their tendency to put themselves down in front of others as an Asian virtue. Only when daughters realize the strength of their mothers' Asian pride do they understand that this modesty is merely a way of "fishing for compliments," as one might say.

The dependency of Asian women is often highlighted in the feminist movement as an example of how women are kept powerless. From a Western viewpoint, Asian women appear to be dependent, subservient, and deferent to their husbands to preserve a patriarchal hierarchy. From the Asian perspective, however, these behaviors are often viewed as interdependence with a mutuality between husband and wife as they negotiate a new society and culture. Immigration, with its new economic and social conditions within a bicultural context brought about change and uncertainty in gender roles and expectations. For example, Asian women in the United States often got jobs and acquired English-language skills more readily than their husbands did.

As second-generation Asian American women struggle with choosing between being housewives, or working women, they have options not available to their immigrant mothers. Sociocultural changes and cross-cultural perceptions influenced a developmental process for Asian American women that is often depicted by Westerners as the choice between a liberated, Western role and a restricted, subservient Asian role. From an Asian perspective, these choices should reflect the developmental process of change and the evolution of women's roles without implying that a woman must give up her cultural identity.

Chinese women worked side by side with their husbands in the rice fields in China and toiled without their husbands who were in the United States as laundry or garment workers. Although the closed society typical of the villages from which many of the early Chinese immigrants came was partially replicated in the United States, immigration itself created many new options. Mobility and economic independence decreased the significance of ostracism from the family and village for violating social taboos. Chinese American immigrants defined their extended families more broadly in response to their separation from more immediate family members in China. Chinese American women could survive outside the family because society was no longer defined by the family clan. Immigrant parents accepted and encouraged the educational goals of their American-born daughters as a means of economic mobility despite the dissonance engendered by cultural prescriptions.

What did Asian immigrant mothers communicate to their daughters in their conduct and behavior? Although there may have been pathological consequences for some, false pathological aspects are played up when Asian American women are viewed strictly in terms of Western beliefs because they fail to take into consideration the underlying values and positive supports within Asian American cultures. Some Asian American women will accept these "pathological" concepts and reject Asian gender roles in a false attempt to be liberated and modern. Some Asian American women will be confused and unable to negotiate a syntonic gender and cultural identity because of competing and conflicting cultural values and obligations.

CONCLUSION

This chapter considers the strengths of the mother–daughter bond for Chinese American immigrant women and their daughters. As understood from analysis of a literary piece it has implications for many Asian American women who can and have incorporated the positive aspects of both Western and Asian cultures, learned to value their derivation and differences, and formulated individualized bicultural identities. As immigrant mothers struggled with the ravages of poverty, losses, and separation from loved ones, the stresses of immigration, and adjustment to a bicultural environment, they communicated strength despite limited means and education, nurturance amid the demands of a patriarchal society, and connectedness in establishing communities and families where they did not exist.

After immigration, many early Chinese American immigrants continued to live in poverty, often amid abundance. Chinese immigrant mothers taught their daughters the frugality and industry that they felt was needed to survive. They taught modesty of character and the sacrifice of motherhood. Chinese American daughters learned of the special bonds of women cooking together, nurturing others, and sacrificing for children and family while remaining modest about achievements and resolute in creating and maintaining supportive families and communities. As mothers and daughters learned to struggle with the contradictions, laugh at the ironies, and lament over the gaps, forging ahead with the love and nurturance, they established mother–daughter bonds that were uniquely Asian American.

REFERENCE

Tan, A. (1989). *The Joy Luck Club*. New York: Putnam.

8

IDENTITY DEVELOPMENT AND CONFLICTS AMONG INDIAN IMMIGRANT WOMEN

DIVYA KAKAIYA

The United States is seen as the land of opportunity, but for many Indian women this opportunity comes with both many joys and a heavy price. The lives of Indian women in the United States are complex. The first large wave of Indian immigrants came after 1965 when the immigration laws were relaxed (Immigration and Nationality Act of 1965). This particular generation of women has now been in the United States for more than 3 decades. There is now a well-defined second generation that is looking to be heard and understood. Family tensions are at an all-time high, with both mothers and daughters attempting to negotiate new rules and new boundaries as Indian women form their identities as Indian Americans.

The history of Indian immigration provides the context for understanding generational issues among Indian women. Also affecting the roles and identities of Indian women in the United States has been the Indian women's movement.

Conflicts faced by Indian women in the United States as they form their identities range from assimilation concerns; financial and social adjustment issues; the development of a bicultural identity; the challenge of balancing professional, personal, and ethnic lives; domestic violence; emotional and verbal abuse in relationships; and divorce. Conflicts affecting the second generation have to do with the disparity of values between parents and children, pressure in sexual relationships, dating, peer pressure, alcohol, and drugs. Communication between the generations is lacking, resulting in alienation and thereby increasing the risk for maladaptive behavior.

IMMIGRATION HISTORY

Early 1900s: Farm Laborers From Punjab

The earliest Indian immigrants came to the United States during the early 1900s, mostly from the state of Punjab in the northern part of India. They came as farm laborers, and their experiences were very different from those who immigrated later. They experienced discrimination and segregation. Most married Mexican women, as it was against the law for them to marry White women. Because they were nonprofessionals and they intermarried so quickly, they were soon fully assimilated. Consequently, little is known about this group. The greatest amount of research regarding Indian immigrants is emerging from the group that immigrated during the late 1960s. Most second-generation Indian Americans are the children of these immigrants.

1965–1980s: Highly Educated Professionals

The 1965 Immigration and Nationality Act resulted in thousands of Indian families coming to the United States. It was through the men that the families immigrated; most of them were highly educated professionals or technically skilled individuals. They were highly valued in the United States and were eager to assimilate. Agarwal's (1991) study of these families showed that their primary reasons for immigration were the economic, educational, and professional opportunities available in the United States. In Agarwal's sample, the original intention for many was to complete their education, work for a few years, make a lot of money, and then move back to India. However, after having children and settling, most of these immigrants decided to remain in the United States. Frequent trips back to India became a common phenomenon among this generation. Fear of losing their cultural identity appears to keep them connected to Indian cultural events and activities. Children often take Indian classical dance lessons and language classes. Psychological adjustment was hard for this group, particularly because of the loss of extended family and kinship ties.

The adjustment for women was particularly difficult because most of the husbands were at work all day while the women were alone at home. For many of these women, assimilating into the White culture was intimidating; many did not speak English when they came to the United States. Although many of these women had professional degrees, they came to the United States because their husbands wanted to, not because they chose to.

This group often described themselves as "extremely hardworking, determined to succeed, aggressive, risk-taking, money minded, and family oriented" (Agarwal, 1991). The rise up socioeconomic levels was quick because most had been among the most highly educated professionals in India. This was reflected in the May 1997 issue of *India Currents* magazine, which featured a cover story on the Indus Entrepreneurs, who helped to trigger the Silicon Valley boom. The formation of an organization called TiE (The Indus Entrepreneur), whose goal is to be a forum for business-people from the South Asian subcontinent and a means for them to get acquainted, was chronicled. For example, the group organizes an annual weekend-long conference for its members to learn business skills. Although the majority of conference attendees have been men, more women are starting to attend.

Post–Mid-1980s: Business-Oriented Immigrants

An additional influx of a different group of Indian immigrants occurred in the 1980s and 1990s. Many were extended family members of the original group who came in the 60s; others were those who applied for immigration directly. This new wave of immigrants is the more business-oriented people. Most lack professional backgrounds, but own businesses such as motels, liquor stores, franchises, gas stations, and so forth. The women in these families are poorly educated and generally do not assimilate into the mainstream American culture. The children of these immigrants tend to be more traditional in their value systems and maintain stronger ties with India.

THE WOMEN'S MOVEMENT IN INDIA

Women Under Hinduism: The Caste System

Indian culture has been characterized as having a hierarchical worldview that is grounded in the Hindu caste system. The caste system operates at the level of social relationships and at the level of ideas and values (Everett, 1981). There are a large number of social segments of castes (jati) in which membership is ascribed. A person is born into a jati; jati are endogamous; and to preserve the ritual status of the jati, there are norms governing the behaviors of each member. In the fourfold caste system there is a distinction between religious authority and political power; the Brahmins are the priests, and the Kshatriyas are the rulers.

This hierarchical worldview has significant implications for the women's movement. There is a high level of tolerance for different groups living side by side but the expectation of norms to rank and separate them. Therefore, if any women were to be involved in any political or religious activities, they would naturally tend to be from the high-status groups. Therefore, many women consider it their fate that they are born into a certain caste and must abide by its rules. These women would not consider taking the risk to engage in any rituals or activities performed by women from the higher castes.

In the book *Daughters of Independence* (as cited in Liddle & Joshi, 1986), Paul Thomas characterized the impact of Hinduism on the development of the Indian women's movement as both "complex and contradictory." Men were seen as superior, with male heirs being necessary to ensure the salvation of deceased ancestors. In the four stages of life (i.e., student, householder, hermit, and wandering ascetic), women were excluded from the last two stages and were expected to focus on their roles as mothers and housekeepers.

Many components of the Hindu value system contributed to the lesser status of women and the extreme subordination of women to their husbands. There was early marriage and *sati* (i.e., the burning of the wife at her husband's cremation pyre). There was the Hindu Shastric tradition that prescribed that intercourse should occur at the time of the girl's first menstrual period. Widows were treated as outcasts and prohibited from remarrying. *Sati* was practiced by several castes before it was declared illegal by the British in 1829. In both India and the United States, widows are required to wear white saris, symbolizing that any adorning was only for the benefit of the husband. Without a husband, a woman's life is considered colorless.

Shakti, or Power and Male–Female Dualism Under Hinduism

On the other hand, there is a principle of male–female dualism in Hinduism (i.e., *Shakti–Shiva*) and a religious tradition of male–female equality that provide for improved status for women. In the Vedic period (1500 B.C.–500 B.C.), women had religious equality with men, women were educated and participated in public affairs, and child marriage was not practiced.

As social scientists attempt to generalize about gender differences and the position of women in India, the paradoxical aspects of this duality are puzzling. In Hindu cosmology all animating power is female. The word for power is *Shakti*, and it can be used to refer to energy or strength. It is also the name of a Hindu goddess. Nandy, a social psychologist recounts in the essay "Woman Versus Womanliness in India" (as cited in Liddle & Joshi, 1986) how womanliness is associated with energy, animation, and creative artistry—not weakness.

These two aspects of Hinduism, the religious dualism and the equality of men and women in the Vedic period, were emphasized by the Hindu revival movements of the late 19th century. The Arya Samaj called for a return to Vedic principles; the Ramakrishna mission emphasized the female aspects of Hinduism. These two revivalist movements placed women in a position of honor, expressed concern over the position of women, and enlarged the number of religious and social activities in which women participated.

Interestingly, the paradox of this duality is further highlighted by the classical Hindu book of moral law, *The Laws of Manu*, which states that male kin must subject a woman to lifelong control. If women have an excess of power according to the definition of *Shakti* and, therefore, a corresponding excess of sexuality and the potential to swell into angry goddesses, then men would have a strong interest in restraining them (Gold, 1994). This explains the urgency to marry daughters before they attain puberty, the stigma against widows, and the pervasive male fear of women draining them of their vital fluids. Consequently, a pattern of male biological, political, and economic dominance much like the patriarchal orientation of the Western world emerged.

Patrilineal Joint-Family System

The patrilineal joint-family system is featured strongly in the Brahmanical Hindu law, which states that a Hindu son should bring his bride to live in his family home. Consequently, Indian women are socialized from a very young age not to regard the family into which they are born as their family. They are taught to think of their husband's family as their permanent family; thus, attachments with their families of origin are discouraged. This concept of joint families has been far more common in the higher castes, which follow the Brahmanical law, than among the lower castes.

The emergence of the joint family contributed significantly to the differential status of men and women. Several generations of men may bring their brides into the family to live together under the same roof. There is a strict hierarchy based on age and sex, with the mother-in-law's position the most highly valued family position for a woman. Once a woman attains this status, she often tends to be just as oppressive as the men. Older women in the joint family discourage younger ones from participating in social activities outside the family, a phenomenon that was even stronger when *purdah* was practiced.

Purdah, or Female Seclusion, Under Muslim Rule

The status of women deteriorated significantly with the arrival of Muslim rule. When *purdah,* the Muslim custom of female seclusion, was adopted by middle-class Hindus, child marriage (or intercourse at a girl's first menstrual period) and *sati* became more common. What is interesting is that although *sati* is very much associated with Hinduism, there actually are no references to it in Hindu mythology.

According to leading Hindu theologians, *sati* had its roots in ancient Greece. Pyre sacrifices similar to *sati* also were prevalent among the Germans and Slavs. Most probably, the practice of *sati* came to India during the year 1 A.D. through the Kushans, a central Asian race that ruled the northwestern part of India. *Sati* was never practiced anywhere in southern India. Even in northern India it was practiced only among the warrior tribes called Rajputs. The Rajputs were fanatical Hindu warrior tribes who were constantly in battle with the Muslims as well as among themselves. It is likely that this practice developed because the Rajputs had many young widows who posed serious ethical and moral problems to a monogamous society. Instead of allowing men to have more than one wife as the Muslims did, the Rajputs used the "easy" solution of eliminating unwanted widows by *sati* (Viswanathan, 1992). Although these customs (i.e., *purdah* and *sati*) were purportedly created to protect women from intruders during war times, they continued to be practiced during times of peace.

Purdah also implied a division of labor by sex (Papanek & Minault, 1982). A woman's sphere of activity was domestic (i.e., she managed the home, prepared the food, and took care of the children). The man's sphere of activity was external (i.e., he provided for the family economically and participated in any other interactions outside the family). With the exception of ceremonial events, such as births, marriages, deaths, or religious festivals, women did not leave the home.

Ahimsa, or Infinite Love, Under the Hindu Revival Movements

The Hindu revival movements of the late 19th century led to the reemergence of women in a more honored position. The segregation of women through *purdah* under Muslim rule actually created the rudimentary formation of women's associations; it provided opportunities for women to socialize among themselves. Groups formed to improve the position of women; leaders from educated and politically active backgrounds emerged. In addition, a strong nationalist movement had formed to promote Indian liberty from British rule. A new nationalist identity emerged, with many of the educated men actually encouraging women to be educated. The early feminists in India from this period were the daughters and wives of the educated elite.

An important figure in the women's movement during this time was Gandhi, who was very respectful toward women. He conceived the concept of *satyagraha*, or pressure for social and political change through friendly passive resistance, as especially fitting for women because of their moral character and capacity for self-suffering. For Gandhi, woman was the incarnation of *ahimsa*, meaning infinite love and infinite capacity for suffering. He elevated the self-deprecating characteristic of female suffering of earlier periods to a higher standard to which all men should aspire.

From this brief historical analysis, it can be seen that the relationship between the evolution of Hindu tradition and the emancipation of Indian women has been convoluted. For a culture that, until recently, burned widows with their deceased husbands, change has come slowly. Factors influencing these changes include the dramatic rise in the literacy rate among women in India and the degree of exposure to other cultures and practices. The backgrounds of the women immigrating to the United States from India have been diverse. Educational differences, urban versus rural differences, and differences in degree of exposure outside the family and culture make generalizations difficult.

CONFLICTS FOR INDIAN IMMIGRANT WOMEN

Women's Karma: Adjustment to Immigration

For most Indian women immigrating to the United States after 1965, it was not by choice. They followed their karma (i.e., their husbands decided to immigrate and they had no choice but to follow their fate). The acculturation process for these women was slower than for the men because they stayed in the home and had very little contact with the world outside. A number of these women were highly educated professionals; however, they chose to remain at home to raise their children. Their primary goals were to support their husbands and look after the domestic needs of the family. It was not until the 1980s, when many of the educated women began Indian women's organizations to address the issue of domestic violence in Indian families, that this began to change.

Acculturation is the process of maintaining an identity with one's culture of origin while adapting to the host culture. For Indian families in the United States, acculturation depended on education, class, caste, family size, economic support, connections to their traditional culture, degree of religiosity, immigration history, and degree of acceptance of the loss of their country of origin (Almeida, 1996).

Historically, many Indian men came to live in the United States for only 2 to 5 years before going back to India; they then located a suitable bride through an arranged marriage and brought her back to the United

States. This phenomenon was met with mixed feelings by most Indian women. As much as a woman may be excited about moving to a foreign country, she is also leaving behind her kinship ties and much of her identity. Given that segregation of the sexes is still so widely practiced in India, she also leaves behind her entire support network. Because women who leave India to follow their husbands to the United States are admired and revered in India, most are not able to express their true feelings of fear and insecurity about moving so many thousands of miles away. Typically, a woman also may not have any idea of what awaits her in the United States. The isolation an Indian woman experiences in the United States is often overwhelming, particularly if she came from a village or did not speak English before immigrating.

Because the husbands often are more assimilated by virtue of their education and employment, they typically end up teaching their wives all sorts of things: how to dress, how to carry themselves, and how to handle their finances. If a wife does not speak English, her husband often will be her translator. This places the husband in the powerful position of being able to mold his wife into whatever he wants her to be.

Because Indian women are raised with the concept and expectation of sacrifice, they often will bend completely to what their husbands expect of them. Thus, there is a significant imbalance of power in these early marital relationships. Because the wife often is so dependent on her husband for financial support, mobility, and so forth, the risk for domestic violence is high when the husband's expectations are not met. Often the husband controls all the finances such that the wife may not have access to any money of her own or to any of the legal documents that could allow her some autonomy.

Assimilation and Loss of Cultural Identity

For many of these women, a friendship with an American woman may be their first and only attempt at assimilation. Often these friendships offer a firsthand experience of the U.S. culture with the opportunity to see how this other world lives. First-born children in these families often end up as translators for their parents and as mediators for their siblings. Not unlike other immigrant groups, children's school friendships become a means of expanding their exposure to American ways, often resulting in intergenerational conflict. Indian children often want their mothers to learn American ways so that their friends can be understood and welcomed into their homes, whereas Indian mothers struggle with how to maintain their Indianness.

Some Indian families have been so eager to adapt and assimilate that they later regret having assimilated so quickly at the expense of their culture. In their eagerness to adapt and assimilate, they did not speak the

Indian language with their children or maintain their culture at home, with the result that intermarriage with non-Indian men or women is high. Again, not unlike other immigrant groups, this is lamented by the elders of the society, who often are very vocal about their regrets in not having incorporated Indian values into their children's upbringing or not having encouraged biculturalism.

Many Indian families have reacted to this loss of Indian identity with a renewed interest by parents in maintaining the Indian language, culture, and arts. Unlike in the past, religious traditions and rituals are now making a strong presence in many Indian families, with frequent religious events common phenomena for most Indian families. Many metropolitan areas with large Indian populations, such as Los Angeles, San Jose, San Diego, New Jersey, Chicago, and Houston, now have language classes in which Hindi, Gujarati, Urdu, or Sanskrit are taught. Additionally, many Indian girls are now being trained in Indian classical dance forms and musical instruments. It is not uncommon for Indian parents to be taking their children to Bharat Natyam classes and sitar lessons as well as with ice-skating and swimming classes.

At the same time, many of these mothers often will not have had any formal training in these classical dance forms or musical instruments themselves. However, they take tremendous pride in their children being raised with such a strong Indian heritage. The children, on the other hand, often feel pressured by the demands of the two cultures. Although many do develop a healthy biculturalism, some may pay the price of a life that feels compartmentalized.

MOTHER–DAUGHTER RELATIONSHIPS, ADOLESCENT IDENTITY FORMATION, AND FAMILY CONFLICT

Another developmental crisis for immigrant Indian women occurs when their daughters reach their teenage years. A common phenomenon is that parents who may have involved their daughter in all sorts of extra-curricular activities will suddenly become very fearful of the daughter's emerging sexuality. Many mothers, who may have parented in a very re-laxed way, now become hypervigilant in monitoring for possible signs of their daughter "going on the wrong track."

This usually means that the daughter has started to indicate interest in boys, wants to imitate her American friends with regard to dating, and wants to go to school dances and proms. At this point, fathers often begin to examine the clothes worn by their daughters for appropriateness, and both parents begin to nag their daughters about maintaining modesty in their dress, particularly when attending primarily Indian functions. Many second-generation Indian adolescents describe how tiresome it is when their parents "lecture" them. For parents, this pervasive fear of "losing" their children to the dominant (i.e., American) culture often results in obsessional rumination over these issues with their children in a strong, disciplinary manner. None of these factors make for a comfortable parent–child relationship.

As girls reach puberty, parents develop strong fears that their daughters will get pregnant. These fears are sometimes overexaggerated, based on parents' fears of the unknown. As immigrant parents not having experienced life as a teenager in the United States, they often base their expectations on what they hear and read in the media; consequently, they expect the worst. Becoming pregnant while unmarried is one of the biggest taboos in the Indian culture in both India and the United States. This is apparent in the Indian movie industry, which has focused on the theme of the young woman exploring her sexuality as a family crisis. Deceit and secretiveness are usually portrayed in these popular movies, reflecting the significant fears and concerns of the parent audiences.

An interesting phenomenon has been noted among the Indian community in England. The rate of suicide among Indian teenage girls is very high. If Indian parents discover that their unmarried daughter is pregnant, they often will tell their daughter that they would rather she kill herself than have her bring the shame of an unwed pregnancy to the family.

The rate of eating disorders among Indian Americans is also on the rise. Kakaiya and Kassam (1997) conducted a preliminary study to explore the incidence of eating disorders among the Indian community in southern California; they found that 18% of the women in the sample had an eating disorder.

Indian families take pride in achievement, are success driven, have high moral standards of behavior, are appearance conscious, are enmeshed, discourage autonomy, and avoid conflict. Additionally, special meaning is attached to food. Open expression of conflict is not allowed, particularly for young women. Therefore, in a classical paradoxical situation, these young women are expected to be successful, yet not assertive.

The relationship between parents and Indian adolescent girls in the United States is often very conflicted. Many parents show an outward expression of flexibility and openness (e.g., stating that they communicate very well with their children), yet they often are shocked to discover that their daughters have gone to great extremes to lie to them to get their individual needs met. Most Indian families do not encourage independence and autonomy; it is not permitted for girls to express their personal needs or interests. Interdependence and cohesiveness are highly valued in Indian families. American therapists often mislabel these phenomena as *extreme enmeshment*, thereby running the risk of incorrect therapeutic interventions if there is not an understanding of how deeply rooted in Indian culture this value of needing to belong is.

Indian mothers place a high value on education and attending prestigious schools. They often will encourage their daughters to pursue graduate school studies at any cost. Nevertheless, sons are given much more support and flexibility as to the opportunities they can pursue. Therefore, adolescent girls often experience the conflict of sons being more highly valued.

Indian mothers are discouraged from expressing feminist ideas lest they risk being viewed as loose, immoral women or family breakers. The female friends of an Indian woman with feminist ideas will tell her to "tone it down" because expression of such ideas may adversely affect her adolescent daughter's development. A classic example of this is a quote from the feminist mother–daughter team of Shamita Das Dasgupta and Sayantani Dasgupta in their chapter from the book *Dragon Ladies: Asian American Feminists Breathe Fire* (1997). Both mother and daughter speak candidly about their experiences as feminists in a South Asian culture that does not encourage the voices of women:

> Because my daughter and I started writing on feminist issues, our picture appeared on the cover of the national women's magazine Ms. Although our community friends maintained a stony silence, one of my husband's colleagues sympathetically warned him about the danger of such explicit declaration of our politics. Since no one in our community takes kindly to a non-traditional woman, the colleague explained, my feminist daughter was really hurting her chances of marriage. Besides, who would want to establish a marital alliance with someone whose mother was a feminist?

In the same book, Sayantani Dasgupta expresses her feelings about being raised as an Indian American. She describes during her childhood of always being ultra-aware of her brownness, her strangeness, and her difference. As a grown woman, she describes the experience of coming up with a list of eligible men for herself only to have her friends joke about how much easier it would be if she were a lesbian, thus implying that women are more likely to think like her than men and that most men, even second-generation ones, would be threatened by her feminist ideas.

Indian mothers are often caught between their husbands and their daughters during this process of adolescent development. Reminiscent of their own struggles with immigration and oppression they may have experienced in India, many are empathic with and encouraging of their daughters' strivings while caught in the dilemma of being bound by the traditions of the Indian culture. Many end up acting as mediators between father and daughter as conflicts emerge. In many instances, Indian fathers may not even be aware of the degree of flexibility given by mothers to their daughters. It is not uncommon for a crisis to develop in a family when a father accidentally discovers that his daughter has gone to prom night or a party with male friends with permission from her mother. These "discoveries" often represent significant developmental steps in the lives of Indian American families.

BICULTURALISM AMONG COLLEGE-AGE WOMEN

A trend is emerging among young Indian women to seek colleges away from home, with the clearly articulated reason that they are looking to get away from the repressive home environment. Many feel that they will have the best of both worlds by attending colleges 2 or 3 hours away. This way, they will have the freedom to date, to socialize, and to stay out as late as they want to away from the watchful eyes of their parents while at the same time minimizing the frightening experience of leaving home.

College is a time of significant developmental growth for all women. Among young Indian women, it often is the first time they get to test their own values and ideals without parents looking over their shoulders telling and them what they should and should not do and how they should or should not dress. College often is the first time for a serious relationship and for a young Indian woman to have her first sexual contact. Indian women are expected to remain pure before marriage. The pressures inherent in statements such as "Virginity is a necessity for any Indian woman to be successfully married," which are heard by most Indian women pose challenges and conflicts among these young women with regard to intimacy and sexuality.

Indian women often will date American men because they do not want to be viewed as loose among the Indian groups on campus. Additionally, dating an American man often represents a young Indian woman's rebellion because it is the epitome of separation and autonomy from parental values and Indian culture. Because defiance and rebellion are absolutely not tolerated within most Indian families, this dating behavior is often done in secret and hidden from parents. Young Indian women often have a code of silence among themselves whereby they will not reveal any personal information about their friends even to their own parents for fear that it will be disclosed.

To date, there are no known studies on the incidence of date rape among Indian women on college campuses. It is likely to be high and underreported given the psychological phenomenon discussed in this chapter. As a result of the sheltered adolescences of many Indian women, they often are not equipped with the skills necessary for assertiveness in dating situations.

After college, young Indian women must face returning home, as is expected of unmarried women within the Indian tradition. Returning home to the tight rules and overprotective environment is now made difficult by the less restrictive experiences of college. Therefore, many Indian women choose to continue on to graduate school to delay their return to the family home. Because education is so valued, they know that this choice will receive positive responses from their families.

MATE SELECTION

The next developmental milestone is seeking a mate to marry. Given the Indian tradition of arranged marriages, many Indian women face the dilemma of including their parents in locating a mate, especially if they did form a significant relationship in college. A modified version of the traditional arranged marriage exists in the United States. There is a booming industry in the personal ad section of local Indian newspapers and larger, widely circulated newspapers. A typical ad reads as follows: "Parents seeking a suitable mate for their 24-year-old-daughter, MBA, tall, fair. Prefer a doctor or a lawyer. Should be well settled." This type of ad reflects many of the strongly held values carried from Indian society to the United States. Fair-complexioned women are preferred over those with darker complexions. Other values about the ideal Indian woman are often communicated; the word *thin* indicates the value of thinness in the Indian culture. A woman is considered more marketable for marriage if she is educated; consequently, educational accomplishments are often highlighted. Parents seek for their daughters husbands who will provide material comforts.

Despite their prevalence, little research has been conducted on these matrimonial ads. For example, what percentage of these ads result in the finding of suitable mates? Also, what is the incidence of divorce among those finding their mates in this manner? It is noteworthy that more of these ads are for women than for men. It is likely that men have greater latitude in mate selection and therefore are more likely to advertise.

The stigma of divorce is subtly emphasized in these ads when a divorced person describes himself or herself as "innocently" divorced. The implication is that it is the fault of the other party. Given the frequency of arranged marriages, many divorces occur precisely because second-generation Indian American men have been encouraged by their parents to marry women from India; after a couple lives together, however, the marriage fails because the differences between husband and wife are so radical given that they were raised on two continents.

Internet marriage bureaus have recently become flourishing businesses. The early marriage bureaus easily led the way for the establishment of others. Many Indian Americans now register through the Internet and have their profiles listed in the specific sites for Indian matrimonial ads. Interested parties have the option of contacting each other by phone or

E-mail. This confidential user-friendly approach appeals to many who feel that it provides them with participation in the selection process. One local marriage bureau in Southern California has approximately 4,000 individuals registered.

A more modernized version of the arranged marriage system now exists whereby young people are allowed to go out with each other 3 or 4 times before deciding whether they want to marry. Many young Indian men prefer to marry women from India because they want a wife who will be less modern, less assertive, and more likely to fit in with the values of the extended family network. Most of these young men will have already dated American women extensively, but they expect their Indian brides to be pure and chaste.

INTERGENERATIONAL CONFLICT

Clinicians will see increasing numbers of Indian families coming into treatment with parent–child issues as the tensions between the generations increase. The voices of the second generation are becoming clearer and louder, as evidenced by growing numbers of articles in Indian newspapers addressing intergenerational conflict. For example, the *India Journal* has a section titled "Jivan," which means *life and youth* in Hindi. This section is edited by second-generation Indians and contains extremely candid and vocal articles on the subject. A very strong sense of wanting to be seen and heard is reflected in titles such as "Pros and Cons of Arranged Marriages" and "Dating Indian Style." Biculturalism is prominent as a theme in this magazine through the integration of Indian value systems into the discussions. However, most of the articles are by college students presenting selected worldviews.

CLINICAL THEMES WITH INDIAN WOMEN
AND ADOLESCENTS

Desperation

If an Indian woman enters therapy, it is because she is feeling very desperate about her situation. In India she would have had an extended network of other women in the household with whom to vent her frustrations. In the United States, Indian women are isolated from such networks and are completely dependent on their husbands. An Indian woman also would be reluctant to share her feelings with her friends because of the need to preserve a positive image.

Many women enter therapy without their husbands' knowledge;

therefore, the therapeutic relationship begins under a shroud of fear and secrecy. Most Indian men are threatened by the thought of their wives going into treatment because of fears that she may grow into herself and decide that she is dissatisfied with the marriage. An Indian woman entering therapy should be given a tremendous amount of acknowledgment and support for overcoming both cultural and sexual boundaries in seeking treatment.

Subdued Anger

Therapists must also be keenly attuned to the fact that, for most Indian women, direct expression of anger has been subdued in their personality formation. Therefore, an Indian woman may have repressed her frustrations and anger for many years. She may present with years of suppressed hostility as well. With such a heightened level of anger toward her spouse or in-laws, the Western-trained therapist may experience an immediate countertransference and may quickly jump to the conclusion that the situation has progressed too far for any therapeutic interventions to be effective. The therapist may immediately suggest separation or divorce as a solution. A Western-trained therapist should keep in mind that the laws of karma and dharma play a very active role in an Indian client's experience of distress. An Indian woman may initially come to treatment only to vent. Later, after she feels the therapist understands her value system, she may be willing to take small steps in the direction of acknowledging her needs.

Reluctance to Engage Husbands

Additionally, if a client presents with a marital issue and the therapist quickly suggests that she bring in her husband she is likely not to return to therapy. Indian men are extremely resistant to the idea of exposing private issues in public, and they also tend to be rigid in their perspective. Men from the second generation are much more open to the counseling process and may even be the ones to initiate therapy. This clearly illustrates the assimilation process that has occurred within the second generation.

Depression

Symptoms of depression will be manifested as an alternative way of dealing with stress and the repression of anger and hostility. When the Indian woman comes to the United States and makes friendships with American women, she is exposed to a different worldview. The deference to her husband and her elders she had never questioned now may be seen in a different light. The dilemma that this conflict poses is strong, and many women will experience somatic distress. However, this conflict can take a long time to emerge, and many women will seek treatment but not make the changes needed to facilitate personal growth. The therapist must understand that the Indian culture is collective in nature, not individualistic. The concept of self-fulfillment is very alien to an Indian woman. She will probably want to learn ways to better tolerate and accommodate her situation. The therapist must be comfortable with the fact that the client may not make the changes he or she recommends.

CLIENT–THERAPIST RELATIONSHIP

The relationship with the therapist can be central to the healing process for the Indian client entering therapy. The therapist can be a role model of biculturalism as well as a sounding board for frustrations and disappointments within the marital relationship. As part of the process of feeling comfortable with the therapist, the clients may ask an Indian therapist many questions about his or her personal background. Sharing personal information, such as about immigration and marriage may be helpful. For non-Indian therapists, consultation with an Indian therapist is recommended to enable the therapist to understand what specific factors may affect the presenting problems.

Once an Indian family "adopts" the therapist, he or she will be given a place of honor in the family. Indians traditionally will hold prayers at the local temple or at their house to mark special occasions, and invitations to such events may be extended to the therapist. The therapist's presence can be taken as a sign of bestowing blessings on the family, and it can greatly enhance the therapeutic alliance. It is imperative, however, that the issue of confidentiality be reviewed so that the family feels safe in that their confidentiality is maintained. They may introduce the therapist as a friend of the family. The limitations of the Western ethics codes when working with an Indian family are readily apparent.

In conclusion, a non-Indian therapist's seeking consultation from an Indian psychotherapist could greatly enhance the Indian client's ability to feel understood by the therapist. It is important that the therapist keep in mind that for someone from a culture that is nervous about losing its ethnic identity, the actual step of seeking counseling means that the level of distress is severe. Therefore, it is likely that a more directive, hands-on, open approach will work extremely well with Indian clients.

REFERENCES

Agarwal, P. (1991). *Passage from India—Post 1965 Indian immigrants and their children.* Palos Verdes, NM: Yuvati Press.

Almeida, R. (1996). East indian families. In M. McGoldrick, J. Giordano & J. K. Pearce (Eds.), *Ethnicity and family therapy* (2nd ed.). New York: Guilford.

Dasgupta, S. D., & Dasgupta, S. (1997). Bringing up baby. In S. Shan (Ed.), *Dragon ladies—Asian American feminists breathe fire*. Boston: South End Press.

Everett, J. (1981). Approaches to the "woman question" in India: From maternalism to mobilization. *Women's Studies International Quarterly, 4*, 169–178.

Gold, A. (1994). Gender, violence and power: Rajastani stories of Shakti. In N. Kumar (Ed.), *Women as subjects—South Asian histories*. Charlottesville, University of Virginia Press.

India Currents. (1997, May).

Kakaiya, D., & Kassam, S. (1997). *The incidence of eating disorders among the Indians in southern California*. Unpublished manuscript.

Liddle, J., & Joshi, R. (1986). *Daughters of independence: Gender, caste and class in India*. London: Zed.

Papanek, H., & Minault, G. (Eds). (1982). *Separate worlds: Studies of* purdah *in South Asia*. Columbia: South Asia Books.

Viswanathan, E. (1992). *Am I a Hindu?* San Fransisco: Halo Books.

9

FRIENDSHIPS AND SOCIAL NETWORKS AMONG ASIAN AMERICAN WOMEN

FELICISIMA C. SERAFICA, ALICE WENG, AND HYOUN K. KIM

In the behavioral and social sciences literature, the relationships of Asian American women usually have been conceptualized in kinship terms. Studies of Asian American women in relationships typically have been about their filial relations, conjugal relations, sibling relations, and relations with other relatives (e.g., Yanagisako, 1977, 1985). Empirical studies of their friendships and social networks are rare despite the significance of these relationships as proposed by theorists and revealed by studies of women from other ethnic groups.

Several theories (e.g., Erikson, 1963, 1980) have pointed to the importance of interpersonal relationships, particularly friendships, for adult psychosocial development and adjustment. In studies of White Americans, it has been found that women's friendships provide rewards that are very different from the rewards of parenting or marriage (Duck & Wright, 1993; Larson, Mannell, & Zuzanek, 1986). Besides offering companionship, women's friendships are major sources of intimacy, nurturance, and identity; they provide emotional support, acceptance, and social validation and are a strong component of physical and psychological health (Adams &

151

Blieszner, 1989; Antonucci, 1990; Block & Greenberg, 1985; Perlmutter & Hall, 1992; Schultz, 1991). Friendships may play a more significant role in women's lives than they do in men's (Block & Greenberg, 1985; Duck & Wright, 1993; Eichenbaum & Orbach, 1988).

Among ethnic minorities, research has shown that social networks influence the post-immigration experience, including physical and psychological well-being in the process of adjusting to a new environment (Denton, 1984; Kuo & Tsai, 1986; Meemeduma, 1992; Vega, Kolody, Valle, & Wier, 1991). The significance attributed to social networks is rooted in two assumptions: (a) instrumental, material, or informational resources, as well as emotional support, flow through social networks formed around individuals or families (Meemeduma, 1992; Oh, 1988), and (b) social network characteristics affect the flow of resources to the whole family as well as to the focal person (Hall & Wellman, 1985).

With the growing amount of empirical evidence that friendships and social networks are important contributors to women's development and well-being, it seems fitting to examine them among Asian American women. For immigrant women, the processes of immigration, cultural adaptation, and child rearing in a new culture are likely to require the support that friendships and social networks offer. Among Asian American women born and reared in the United States, friendships and social networks might still be needed during times of transition and stressful life events or in coping with acute or chronic stress induced by struggles with issues of ethnic identity, cultural conflicts, racism, gender discrimination at home and in the workplace, stereotyping, and cultural transmission to children (Denton, 1984; Schultz, 1991).

This chapter (a) examines Asian American women's friendships and social networks as depicted in selected historical and biographical literature, (b) reviews available research on these topics in the behavioral and social sciences, (c) delineates emerging themes, and (d) suggests a conceptual framework for future research. Following the available scholarly literature, the focus is on same-sex friendships and social networks of women who or whose ancestors came from China, Korea, and Japan and, to a lesser extent, India and the Philippines.

GLIMPSES FROM THE PAST

> . . . we, the exiled
> were forced to leave
> to make families our strangers
> and strangers our friends.
>   Brenda Park Sunno (1989, p. 80)

The overwhelming majority of Asians who first came to the United

States were men, but there were some women even in the largely bachelor societies of the early immigration period. Some were married women allowed into the United States to be with their husbands as helpmates and raise their children. Away from their kinship networks while trying to settle in a very different society, these women had to make new friends and form social networks that would orient them to the new ways and lend support during difficult times. It is worth noting that not every Asian woman who came to the United States had a husband. Some of the earliest women to immigrate to the United States from Asia came on their own, fleeing gender oppression and seeking independence (Okihiro, 1994). Others who came on their own were enticed to do so by men who exploited them for profit (Cheng, 1984). Relationships with other women must have played a vital role in the survival of the women who came alone. For example, some 3,000 Chinese women were reported to have been rescued from prostitution in San Francisco by a White American woman, Donaldina Cameron, with the help of supportive Chinese (Amott & Matthaei, 1991).

Surprisingly, biographies and historical accounts have had little to say about friendships and social networks. Friends are mentioned, but only in passing, woven into discourse about familial relationships, adaptation, and achievements of Asian American women. Learning about the friendships and social networks of Asian American women from biographical and historical accounts involved gleaning relevant bits of information about the social contexts and, to a much lesser extent, the patterns of interaction and formation, maintenance, and termination of these relational systems.

Contexts of Friendships and Social Networks

Existing biographical and historical accounts provided insight mainly into the opportunities available to Asian American women for meeting and becoming friends with other women. For adult women, these were immigration and settlement patterns, travel, neighborhoods, small groups, ethnic social clubs, and churches.

Chain immigration, a process of sequential immigration by members of a family or community (Yim, 1984) was characteristic of immigration from Asia. Given a choice, Asian immigrants often chose as their destination a locale where a relative or someone from their village, town, or prefecture in their country of origin had already settled. This relative or compatriot, usually a man, became the nucleus of the latest arrival's evolving social network. He and his wife, if he had one, introduced the new arrival to other members of the ethnic community.

For those women who traveled to the United States alone to join husbands who had preceded them or as picture brides who came to meet their new or soon-to-be husbands, travel presented opportunities for friendship formation. Drawn by similarities in their immigration experiences and expectations, some women became friends on board ship (Yu, 1989). In *Okaasan* (mother), Shibata (as cited in Nakano, 1990, pp. 73–95) described how her mother, en route from Japan to the United States to join her husband, made friends with some picture brides who compared photos of their future husbands; discussed their concerns; and sometimes joked, uneasily, about the future.

Once settled into their homes, women made friends with their neighbors. Often, however, the nearest neighbor was far away, evoking thoughts such as those expressed below:

> Neighbors are five miles away.
> Many days without seeing anyone.
> Today, too, without seeing anyone.
> The sun sets.
> Teiko Tomita (as cited in Nomura, 1987, p. 21)

Five miles may not seem to be such a great distance today in our densely populated cities and suburbs and with our fast modes of transportation, but in the sparsely populated farming communities of earlier times, such distances made visiting friends difficult and therefore infrequent. Some women were able to overcome these barriers through ingenuity and planning. For example, Shibata's mother, taught by her husband to hitch a horse and buggy so that she could go to town to shop, managed to combine visits to a friend with her shopping expeditions. On their way home from shopping, she and her two children would visit her friend, causing her husband to teasingly remark that her "shopping day became longer each time" (Shibata, as cited in Nakano, 1990, p. 81).

Small groups such as sewing circles also promoted friendships. In Hawaii, groups of four or five Filipino American wives met regularly in someone's home to sew and embroider while they also conversed (Espiritu, 1995).

As ethnic communities grew, opportunities for developing friendships increased through churches and ethnic social clubs, the primary avenues through which early immigrant women interacted with the world beyond their families. Christian churches in particular offered opportunities for social interactions with White Americans. Although most Asian American women tended to spend what little leisure time they had at home, sewing or making handicrafts (unlike their husbands, who preferred to spend their leisure time outside the home), they participated in church or ethnic social club activities that involved the whole family; they even saw it as their duty (Nakano, 1990). Most Christian missions and Buddhist churches in ethnic communities had women's groups whose purpose was to facilitate church activities. While engaging in social activities, fund-raising, visiting sick people, and even performing janitorial services, women formed friendships that often took lives of their own beyond the church-related activities.

Ethnic social clubs, particularly the associations formed by immigrants from the same locale in their countries of origin, also provided opportunities for socializing. Women, who typically were more isolated than other members of the family, willingly prepared the refreshments for these ethnic social gatherings that afforded them the rare opportunity to socialize, renew friendships, and make new acquaintances among the latest arrivals. Friendships formed at these gatherings led to collaborative efforts on behalf of the social club. Women working together played a major role in building permanent ethnic communities.

For the children of immigrants, schools, social clubs, and nonethnic social service organizations offered additional avenues for friendship formation. A Nisei woman recalled that she "made a lot of friends" in elementary school (Nakano, 1990, p. 110). A pioneer Korean American woman (Lee, 1990) who attended school with Mexican children enjoyed the tamales made by the mothers of these children. Positive attitudes instilled by these early friendships generalized to friendships with Mexican Americans and African Americans in later life.

In high school, the Nisei interacted with non-Japanese friends but socialized mainly among themselves, even at school functions such as high school dances and football games, so their closest friends tended to be other Nisei. In high schools with a large mix of ethnic groups, they made friends with members of some of these other groups. Recalling that her closest friends at school were of Jewish, Mexican, and Greek descent, a Nisei woman said that she felt comfortable with them rather than "different because of my race" (Nakano, 1990, p. 111), a feeling that presumably she experienced when with peers from other ethnic groups. This tendency to bond with peers who identified themselves as members of specific ethnic groups was also apparent among Filipinas. Describing growing up in the United States during the 1930s and 1940s, a daughter of Filipino immigrants said, "In high school, some of my friends were Greeks and Italians. They were White people but never talked about color" (Espiritu, 1995, p. 71). Even in the 1960s, the daughter of a Filipino in the U.S. Navy still perceived that in high school, "if you weren't White, you just didn't fit in" (Espiritu, 1995, p. 146). To her, only those Filipinos who showed themselves "to be more American than Filipino" (Espiritu, 1995, p. 146) could join the popular clique in high school. Acculturation or maybe even assimilation seemed to be the means to interracial friendship.

As the Nisei moved to life beyond high school, social clubs became the primary venue for establishing friendships. "Being popular," achieved through participation in social club activities, meant being popular in the Japanese American community, not in the White American community. As one Nisei put it, she did not mind being excluded from the social circle of her White American peers; "If you don't expect it, you don't care" (Nakano, 1990, p. 120). By the late 1930s, social activities were available through a broad network of organizations within the ethnic communities (Nakano, 1990). Youth organizations in churches, social clubs, the Young

Women's Christian Association, and athletic groups offered diversion and opportunities for friendship, communication, and support.

For Japanese American women, these opportunities disappeared with their internment in camps during World War II. But other opportunities for establishing friendships arose. In the laundry room, for example, a gathering point in the camps, women enjoyed socializing, exchanging gossip and information, and "forging lasting friendships over their washboards" (Nakano, 1990, p. 141). Women also formed literary and discussion groups. They banded together to serve as teachers and leaders for classes and youth groups formed to minimize the disruption of their children's education and development. Freed from many of their former household responsibilities by the conditions of their confinement, Japanese American women, particularly the Issei, actually had more leisure time than they enjoyed earlier and the freedom to choose how to spend it. Many chose to work or perform some service in the camp, but they and their friends also had "fun together, climbing mountains and collecting shells" (Nakano, 1990, p. 63).

Friendship Formation, Maintenance, and Termination

Descriptions of the processes of friendship formation, maintenance, and termination were not found in the literature but can be inferred from reports (e.g., Nakano, 1990) about social interactions that flourished and others that did not. For instance, social interactions with White American neighbors that resulted in some exchange of goods (e.g., trout and venison for vegetables grown by the immigrants) led to other similar interactions. Practical demonstrations (e.g., baking bread) by White American neighbors were also warmly received, but a didactic English lesson involving labeling of various objects was not. Interactions that appeared to be exchanges between peers were more conducive to friendship development than "teacher–pupil" interactions.

As noted earlier, friendships made by the Nisei with their White American classmates rarely extended to their social activities. This was also true for the Sansei, but to a lesser extent. Many reported having White American friends during their high school years and beyond. Acculturation and shifts in societal attitudes (e.g., university policies encouraging diversity) may account for this generational change. Support for this comes from a report (Ha, 1993) that college provided Korean American women opportunities for successful social integration through sororities, student government, and academic clubs.

Social Network Formation, Maintenance, and Termination

Information about the social networks of Issei and, particularly, Nisei women can be gleaned from accounts of their postinternment experiences.

It was networks of friends and relatives who assisted them, particularly in the relocation process. Replaying the earlier process of chain immigration, a single woman would get a job in a city, then her friends would follow and join her. One woman was so successful in making new friends that she wished more of her friends who remained at the internment camp "would take advantage of the many helpful hands offered to them" (Asanto as cited in Matsumoto, 1989, p. 124).

Social networks were maintained because they served such functions as facilitating job search. For example, California's Punjabi immigrant cannery workers commented, "You just talk to your friends and family about where they work, and you usually hear who is hiring" (Williams, 1989, p. 158). These women preferred to work within a close-knit social group "[be]cause that is where my friends are" (Williams, 1989, p. 158) and resisted being transferred to other units within the cannery. Filipino women in California also learned about job vacancies through their social networks, and friends often worked for the same company (Espiritu, 1995).

Some social networks became the bases of what has come to be called by some as the Asian American women's movement (Wei, 1993). Initially, these consisted mainly of middle-class Asian American women who gathered together for mutual support and political study in small informal groups or as members of large, formal organizations. Some, including students, were drawn together by their shared perceptions of sexism in the Asian American movement; they sought to foster sisterhood and to challenge the patriarchy of the movement (Wei, 1993). Others were brought together by their felt needs for self-discovery, self-recovery, and self-improvement (Nakano, 1990). Inevitably, the focus of these groups changed from self-study to educational programs that the groups sought to generalize to other women with the goal of ameliorating the negative conditions of Asian American women in general, including those from low-income groups. While preserving personal networks at the local level, these women's networks moved beyond the Asian American women's movement to become more formal national organizations seeking to improve the status of Asian American women throughout the country (Wei, 1993). This organizational evolution was an independent albeit parallel process to the mainstream women's liberation movement (Wei, 1993).

To summarize, biographical and historical accounts have indicated that the earliest Asian American women to immigrate to the United States were a diverse group, differing in age, marital status, social class, country of origin, and reasons for immigrating. Because of these and other factors, how they eventually lived their lives also differed, but friendships and social networks were constants in their lives.

Several themes emerged from this historical review. These included Asian American women's strong and lasting interest in developing friendships and networks; friendship through shared activities; the role of these relational systems in the development of women's sex role, ethnic, and personal identities; empowerment through friendships and social networks; and the importance of context in friendship and social network formation and maintenance.

CONTEMPORARY BEHAVIORAL AND SOCIAL SCIENCES RESEARCH

Friendships

In contemporary research, *friendships* are defined as dyadic peer relationships characterized by intimacy, closeness, emotional support, reciprocity, companionship, and nurturance (Duck & Wright, 1993; Larson et al., 1986; Schultz, 1991). Different levels of friendship have been identified, with the highest characterized by reciprocal interaction, mutuality, intimacy, and commitment (Reisman, 1981). To date, research on Asian American women's friendships is sparse. The available studies, undertaken primarily to understand interethnic or intercultural relations, have emphasized the determinants of friendship choice but have yielded some insights into the processes involved in friendships.

Friendship Formation and Maintenance

The few available studies on Asian American women's friendships have stemmed from theories of interpersonal attraction and have addressed the factors that draw one person to another or contribute to the attractiveness of an individual as a friend. In research on White American women, these factors have been found to include value and social class similarity, race, age, marital status, and ease of communication (Rose, 1995). It is logical to assume that ethnic similarity would also influence friendship formation among Asian Americans given the greater likelihood that individuals of the same ethnicity share similar values, attitudes, and experiences and have greater language compatibility. Recent studies have shown that ethnic similarity influences Asian American women's friendships, but its effect is moderated by place of birth and number of years in the United States.

Wang, Sedlacek, and Westbrook (1992) found that foreign-born Asian American students, including women, were more likely to have close friends from their own ethnic group than were Asian American students born in the United States. Consistent with this finding, Trice and Elliott, (1993) reported that Japanese students at a U.S. college preferred to spend their time studying, discussing personal problems, traveling, and attending social activities with other Japanese students than with U.S. students or other international students. Women were more likely than men to show this preference. A common cultural background among foreign-born Asian Americans may enable each partner in a friendship to more easily comprehend his or her own behavior and the behavior of the other, thereby reducing uncertainty and increasing predictability across social interactions (O'Conner, 1992). Furthermore, because friendships provide affirmation and support for one's identity, foreign-born Asian American women are more likely to receive these benefits from those who hold similar values and attitudes.

Proximity is believed to play an important role in friendship formation because individuals are more likely to become friends if they have more opportunities to interact and communicate with one another or initiate friendships (Berscheid & Walster, 1969). Research has shown that the ethnic composition of one's community plays a role in both intra- and interethnic friendships (Menne & Sinnett, 1971). Ting-Toomey (1981) reported that Chinese American college women and men who had attended a predominantly White American high school had predominantly White American friends, whereas those who had attended a predominantly Asian American high school had predominantly Asian American friends. Those who had resided in a White American neighborhood had mainly White American friends, whereas those from a predominantly Asian American neighborhood had mainly Asian American friends.

The relationship between ethnic identity and friendship formation is less clear. Ting-Toomey (1981) also examined the relationship between ethnic identity and close friendship patterns among Chinese American university students who, on the basis of their responses to an Ethnic Identity Questionnaire, were classified as having either a Chinese, American, or bicultural identity. Although a chi-square test of the relationship between ethnic identity and friendship network yielded a statistically significant finding, results from the cross-tabulations were not in the expected direction. Ethnic identity was not a reliable predictor of friendship choice. Based on this finding, Ting-Toomey (1981) suggested that although ethnic identity may be important at the beginning of a friendship, it may play a less important role than other friendship attraction variables once the friendship has been established. In support, she presented other data showing that Asian Americans in cross-ethnic friendships were not more likely than their peers with same-ethnic friends to perceive their friends as dissimilar or to report a lower degree of intimacy. However, these results should be considered with caution because most of the respondents were classified as having a bicultural identity; only 27% fell into the Chinese identity group and 10% within the American identity group. Further investigation of this phenomenon is required.

According to social exchange theory, friendship development or maintenance is dependent on the rewards one receives from a friendship.

The more one benefits from a relationship, and the less likely one is to find these rewards in other relationships, the more likely a friendship will continue and develop toward higher levels of closeness and intimacy (Lea & Duck, 1982). As in friendship formation, similarity between friends in values and attitudes is likely to make a relationship rewarding, whereas dissimilarity would make a friendship less rewarding or even threatening to the individuals' respective identities (Lea & Duck, 1982).

Among Asian American undergraduate students, perceived similarity has been found to be strongly correlated with frequency of communication and the degree of intimacy between friends (Ting-Toomey, 1981). Because sex differences were not examined in this study, it remains unclear whether this finding is more true for women than for men. That this might be the case is suggested by a study (Sudweeks, Gudykunst, Ting-Toomey, & Nishida, 1990) that yielded results consistent with Ting-Toomey's (1981). In this qualitative study of nine Japanese women in their mid-20s and their North American friends, those who identified their friendships as high in intimacy also reported lifestyle, attitude, and value similarities. Despite this finding, Sudweeks et al. (1990) concluded that, based on an analysis of themes and subthemes in the accounts of dyads representing three levels of intimacy, it was not necessarily cultural similarity that influenced the level of intimacy in friendships. Instead, what seemed to underlie the intimate relationships were the partners' shared understanding of the importance of communication and ability to accommodate the other individual as well as their awareness of the influence of differing cultural backgrounds.

The maintainance of friendships is also likely to depend on practices and behaviors that signify the importance of one person to another, such as sending cards and giving gifts on birthdays and sharing experiences. Some culturally based covert behaviors may help sustain the closeness associated with the development and stability of a friendship. For example, Asian American tendencies to emphasize harmony among individuals; avoid the expression of strong emotions, particularly negative ones; and place the needs and wishes of others before one's own (Uba, 1994) may sustain friendships by minimizing or even avoiding conflict between friends.

Friendship Termination

The topic of friendship termination or how and what causes friendships to lapse or end abruptly has rarely been studied. Friendships are thought to develop as individuals disclose information about themselves to one another; perception of dissimilarity in attitudes or values during the process of disclosure may impede further development of a budding friendship or end an established one (Lea & Duck, 1982). Some support for this hypothesis comes from a qualitative analysis of turning points, those events related to changes in relationships, of Japanese women. Sudweeks et al.

(1990) found that these events centered on individuals' commitment, responsiveness, and understanding. For example, events perceived by one partner as indicative of nonresponsiveness in the other (e.g., declining an invitation to a social activity), resulting in fewer interactions, were interpreted as an unwillingness to participate further in a relationship.

In summary, the primary goal in studies of Asian American women's friendships thus far has been to understand interethnic or intercultural relations. Research on the determinants of friendship choice among college students after 1965 yielded several themes: the importance of proximity, the many faces of perceived similarity, and the role of same- and cross-ethnic friendships in identity development. Thus far, research has failed to establish conclusively the role of ethnic identity in friendship formation.

Social Networks

A *social network* has been defined as "a cluster of persons, with the focal person at the center connected through affective and behavioral interdependence to others who are kin, friends, or associates" (Rands, 1988, p. 128). Of the four types of personal networks identified by Milardo (1992)—the network of significant others, exchange networks, interactive networks, and global networks—the first type has received the most attention from researchers.

The network of significant others, also called the personal network, includes people whose opinions of the respondent's personal life are important to him or her, such as immediate relatives or intimate friends (Milardo, 1988). Considered "representative of an individual's psychological network" (Milardo, 1992, p. 450), such networks are characterized as fairly stable once established, regardless of interaction frequency (Milardo, 1992). In delineating Asian American women's personal networks, researchers have used the most popular method, the social mapping technique (Blyth, 1982). According to Rands (1988), social mapping provides information on three major features of social networks: structure (size, density, and segmentation), composition (network member characteristics such as gender and marital status), and interaction patterns (frequency, duration, intensity, symmetry, and diversity of interchanges). All three features have been examined in Asian American women's social networks.

Women's Networks in Asia and the United States

From an ecological perspective, changes in individuals' roles or environmental settings necessarily bring about changes in their social relations (Blyth, 1982). Asian American women, whether they immigrated voluntarily or involuntarily, go through a series of disruptions in their networks within their country of origin (Denton, 1984; Meemeduma, 1992; Oh, 1988) while simultaneously facing the challenges of forming new networks in a different country.

A major challenge faced by women from Asia who have immigrated to the United States is adjusting to the new set of cultural norms regarding social networking. Traditionally, Asian women were family oriented, with few connections outside the household (Denton, 1984). Within the traditional extended family structure, multiple supports usually were available so that extrafamilial relations were not likely to be considered necessary or encouraged. When Asian women had to relate to extrafamilial people or groups, the process was likely to be mediated through interactions at the family level rather than at the individual level. This common phenomenon in traditional Asian societies for a woman to be put into a certain set of relations through birth or marriage implied that the likelihood of a woman's having a well-developed social network would depend on the goodness of fit between her and the relational network that was already framed long before she was introduced into it rather than on her personal networking skills. In traditonal Asia, social networks were a given rather than the products of a woman's own efforts.

In contrast, U.S. societal norms prescribe somewhat weaker family networks and place greater emphasis on developing extrafamilial or personal networks outside the home through individual efforts (Denton, 1984). Because the Asian cultural orientation toward network formation limits women's interpersonal experiences outside the home, many Asian women immigrants may be inadequately prepared to function within a society in which networks must be created mainly through an individual's efforts. In such an unfamiliar environment, developing new networks must seem a formidable challenge, particularly to those who have limited English proficiency or are deficient in the social, communication, and other (e.g., driving) skills required for continuous interactions with members of the majority society.

Women immigrants fortunate enough to have established their own personal networks as educational and job opportunities opened up to women in contemporary Asia face still another unique challenge. For them and for U.S.-born women of Asian ancestry raised in ethnic communities, the challenge is posed by cultural differences in norms governing social interactions and behaviors. Asians put more emphasis on formality in interpersonal relations (Sue, 1981). Their social relations and closeness are largely determined and structured by status in the family, gender, and other roles. Because they are used to such highly defined and patterned interactions in social relations, Asian Americans may not relate easily to those with different social norms and expectations (Ramisetty-Mikler, 1993).

Network Structure, Composition, and Interaction

Asian American women are a diverse group, differing in country of origin, reasons for immigration, American generational status, social class, and other factors. Yet they show many similarities in their network structure and composition. Significant differences in network size did not emerge in a study of the social networks of Chinese American, Japanese American, Korean American, and Filipino American women (Denton, 1984). Network composition also did not differ. All four groups of women had more women than men in their networks, and the vast majority of these women were not relatives but friends of the respondents. Ethnic group differences in network composition emerged only from a comparative study of seven ethnic groups' social support systems conducted by the Mental Health Promotion Branch of the California Department of Mental Health (1982) that analyzed the combined scores for men and women representing different ethnic groups. Because sex differences were not examined in this study and mean scores for each sex were not reported, it cannot be concluded that the observed ethnic group differences in network composition apply to women.

Ethnic group differences in women's relationships with members of their respective networks have not been found. Denton (1984) reported that all groups of Asian women in her study chose relatives for the first of five network members requested but gave a higher proportion of nonrelatives for their second through fifth choices. Furthermore, duration of the relationship between respondent and network members was similar among Chinese American, Filipino American, and Japanese American respondents. Moreover, across all four groups, attachment to network members decreased with increasing age.

Significant ethnic group differences emerged only for some interaction patterns (Denton, 1984). Unlike Chinese American, Filipino American, and Japanese American respondents, who reported having known their network members most of their lives, Korean American women reported that they had known their network members for only a short period. This difference might be a function of ethnic group differences in length of stay in the United States (i.e., Korean immigration to the United States being more recent than that of the other groups). Ethnic groups differed significantly in respondents' ratings of attachment to members of their respective networks (Denton, 1984). Chinese Americans were less attached to their network members than Korean Americans who, in turn, were less attached than Filipino Americans. Chinese Americans were less attached than Japanese Americans, but how the latter differed from Korean Americans or Filipino Americans was not reported.

Network Formation, Maintenance, and Termination

Studies of network formation have concentrated on the influential factors rather than the process. Factors include chain immigration, settlement in ethnic enclaves, cultural norms, and churches. Chain immigration (Yim, 1984) implied that by the time immigrants arrived to join their relatives or friends, some type of social network already had been established by those who preceded them (Kuo & Tsai, 1986). For women who did not work outside the home, chain immigration played a vital role in determining their intention to network and the nature of their networks (Kuo & Tsai, 1986).

Oh (1988) found that, for Korean immigrant couples, during the first phase of their settlement in the United States, their primary social networks centered on the church, the wife's relatives, co-alumni, close friends, or the husband's relatives, even if they did not settle in areas heavily populated by other Korean Americans. Almost half of the wives reported that establishing social networks was not an immediate need when they first arrived in the United States because their husbands had preceded them and developed some networks prior to their arrival. These women did not have to seek outside assistance or purely social interactions by themselves. Many of them reported more active involvement in their husbands' alumni associations, even when their own alumnae networks were available. Their own alumnae relations were found to be curtailed by the limited participation of their husbands (Oh, 1988). It remains to be seen whether this trend for Korean American wives' social networks to be almost automatically determined by their husbands' social networks is unique to this group or characteristic of immigrant wives in other Asian ethnic groups. A similar trend used to characterize the networks of middle-class White American wives.

Settlement pattern also plays an important role in immigrants' initial formation of social networks. Those who settle in ethnic enclaves or geographically segregated ethnic communities (e.g., Chinatown) are more likely to form networks composed mainly of relatives or those of the same ethnicity than those who settle in more ethnically diverse communities and have more opportunities to interact socially with a broader segment of society. Immigrant families who settle in suburban areas interact with their non-Asian neighbors at least through their children's activities or school and community events. Women in particular are likely to become involved in the community as they carry out their social responsibilities as wives and mothers.

Chain immigration and ethnic-enclave settlement ensure that cultural norms continue to influence the developing structure, process, and functions of the social network (Meemeduma, 1992). Cultural norms shape to a significant extent the patterns for communicating needs for networking and support, sending cues for needs, and recognizing others' cues for support. They also determine the manner of behavioral responses to indications of need for support and the meaning as well as value of relationships in general, thus determining preference for a certain type of relationship (Meemeduma, 1992). Religious and linguistic similarities, for example, were the major determinants of Asian Indian Americans' formation of informal networks of neighbors, friends, and coworkers (Balgopal, 1988).

Churches, especially those representing Protestant denominations, still play a vital role in the networking of contemporary Asian Americans, particularly immigrants. As they had done for the earliest immigrants from Asia to the United States, churches link their Asian American members to the larger society through their religious-based activities. The initial contacts of immigrant women from Sri Lanka with members of the majority society, for example, occurred mainly through introductory and welcoming programs sponsored by church groups (Meemeduma, 1992). Besides giving practical aid (e.g., assisting in job searches), churches help Asian Americans expand their existing social networks or form new ones by facilitating their participation in social and sports activities (Die & Seelbach, 1988; Min, 1995; Oh, 1988).

Social network maintenance and change among Asian Americans have received almost no attention from researchers. Maintenance patterns characterizing personal networks may bear some similarity to those found in kinship networks in which women play a central role in maintaining as well as shaping the network. Churches also contribute to network maintenance by providing opportunities for Asian Americans to continue interacting with one another through activities designed for the entire church congregation and by making their facilities available for the activities of ethnic associations.

Network formation and maintenance among Southeast Asian refugees may differ somewhat from those among voluntary immigrants because their old networks and support systems were dislocated by their unique experiences and U.S. government refugee settlement policies that resulted in refugees being scattered across the country (Haines, 1988; Lin, Masuda, & Tazuma, 1982; Pecora & Fraser, 1985). They have had to form more nonfamily networks and to search more extensively for family members to reconstruct kinship networks.

Social Network Functions

Recent studies of Asian American women's social networks have shown that these networks serve adaptive functions by providing a sense of security and belonging (Oh, 1988), reducing psychological distress (Kuo & Tsai, 1986; Mouanoutoua, Brown, Cappelletty, & Levine, 1991; Strober, 1994), decreasing problematic symptomatology (Davis, 1993), and, in general, enhancing mental health (Lin et al., 1982). They also have helped Asian Americans achieve economic self-sufficiency (Haines, 1988; Oh, 1988; Pecora & Fraser, 1985).

It cannot be assumed, however, that a social network can be equated with a supportive system (House, Umberson, & Landis, 1988; Vaux & Harrison, 1985). The general assumption (Berkman, 1985) that there is a consistent positive association between a network's structural aspects and its functioning ignores possible conflicts or stresses in network relations. A close-knit network or involvement in ethnic organizations may play a vital role for new arrivals by providing support, but in the long run it can work against immigrants' mobility, psychological well-being, and assimilation (Denton, 1984; Granovetter, 1973; Kuo & Tsai, 1986; Quisumbing, 1982; Yim, 1984). Asian American women in particular may generalize the traditional concept of a woman as a "kin-keeper" to their personal social networks and see themselves primarily as providers of support to the members, a role that can consume much time and effort and reduce their overall well-being (Belle, 1982; Denton, 1984). Meeting multiple support needs, especially in high-density networks, and conflicted or ambiguous relationships within the network may work against a person's well-being (Pierce, Sarason, & Sarason, 1990).

Emerging Themes

Friendships and Networks Across Space and Time

Biographical and historical accounts have indicated that the earliest Asian American women to come to the United States were a diverse group, differing with respect to age, marital status, social class, country of origin, and reasons for immigrating. Depending on these and other factors, how they eventually lived their lives also differed. One characteristic that they shared, however, was an abiding interest in friendship. They formed friendships and social networks, usually with members of their own ethnic group, and maintained these, often over great distances and infrequent meetings. That women went to great lengths to maintain their friendships demonstrates the value of these relationships as sources of support and buffers against loneliness and depression in a time when mainstream society was less friendly and there were so few others of their own ethnic group in proximity.

The importance of proximity in friendship formation among contemporary young Asian American women is highlighted by behavioral research in the post-1965 era showing that predominance of either Asian or White Americans in Asian American women's neighborhoods and high schools determined their friendship choices (e.g., Ting-Toomey, 1981).

Finding Common Ground: The Many Faces of Perceived Similarity

Ethnic similarity was the basis for friendship among many early immigrant Asian women. It also is a significant determinant of friendship
choice for contemporary foreign-born Asian American women. Women
born in Asia may be drawn together because they share a common culture
with its meanings and norms for friendship and also the problems of adapting to the norms of a new society, such as having to be more independent,
assertive, and able to overcome stereotypes.

For the children of immigrants, however, other determinants have
assumed importance in friendship formation, particularly in cross-ethnic
friendships. When the children or descendants of immigrants formed cross-
ethnic friendships, it was with peers who also acknowledged their own
ethnic or cultural origins (e.g., Greeks, Italians, Mexicans, and Jews). They
found common ground in valuing and sharing their respective ethnic customs and traditions. Cross-ethnic friendships also seemed to provide alli-
ances against perceived prejudice and discrimination. Without actually
speaking directly of prejudice or discrimination against them shown by
their peers, these children or descendants of Asian American immigrants
have hinted that peers from certain ethnic groups were more accepting of
them than others.

These findings suggest that beyond ethnic similarity, which may account for initial attraction, it is perceived similarity of attitudes, beliefs,
experiences, or values that consolidates and maintains friendships. Research has suggested that degree of friendship intimacy may depend on
awareness of the influence of differing cultural backgrounds, a shared understanding of the importance of communication, and the ability to accommodate to the other individual (Sudweeks et al., 1990). Broadening
the ethnic composition of Asian American women's friendships and social
networks requires getting past ethnic similarity to perceived similarity of
attitudes, beliefs, values, and so forth in others, a process promoted by
proximity and the opportunities for interaction that it provides.

Collectivist Orientation to Friendship

Little about the nature of friendships and how they were initiated,
sustained, or terminated has been discussed in biographical and historical
accounts. Verbal self-disclosure and intimacy, so heavily emphasized in the
literature on White American women's friendships, have not received the
same degree of prominence. Instead, what has been consistently emphasized
is the communication and interaction among friends centering on activities, usually undertaken on behalf of families, churches, and communities.
Bonds of friendship were forged and expressed through collaboration. Although Asian American immigrant women may have had personal concerns, it did not seem to be in their nature (or socialization) to speak of

these. Nonverbal behaviors may have conveyed what remained unspoken and were acknowledged in similar fashion. Reciprocal affection and comfort were expressed through working together in various activities toward a common goal.

Friendships, Social Networks, and Identity Development

Thus far, research has failed to conclusively establish the role of ethnic identity in friendship formation, but much evidence points to the possibility that friendships and social networks function to promote the development of sex role, ethnic, and personal identities. Among early Asian American immigrants, one salient function of these relational systems was the maintenance of a culturally defined sex role identity. Friends and social networks supported, enhanced, rewarded, and reinforced a woman's role as provider of cultural continuity through her child rearing practices and services to the ethnic community.

Friendships and social networks seem to promote the development of ethnic identity, be it monocultural or bicultural. Ethnic similarity as a determinant of friendship choice among the foreign born implies that for this group, same-ethnic friendships promote the maintenance of ethnic identity within a multicultural environment by providing a sense of connection to Asian heritage and strengthening Asian cultural norms, values, and traditions. Such friendships may also serve this function for the United States–born who are seeking to be reconnected to their roots and to reaffirm their ethnic identification. Research has indicated that social networks also function to maintain ethnic identification. Within a multicultural society, coethnic networks give Asian American women a sense of belonging and allow them to maintain their traditional way of life and social roles to a large extent, particularly if they reside in ethnic enclaves.

Ethnic identity achievement, however, is not the only developmental task facing women. For some in college, the more pressing tasks might be the development of autonomy and a personal identity. Some may try to accomplish these by moving away from same-ethnic friendships or at least seeking other similarities in same-ethnic friends. For those engaged in questioning their culturally defined roles and exploring alternatives, self-disclosure and intimacy may be more easily achieved with cross-ethnic friends who are perceived as similar in attributes other than ethnicity yet possessing cultural understanding. Asian American women's questioning of their culture and their exploration of others may be intensified by certain characteristics of American society, such as its emphasis on individualism, independence, and critical thinking. Meanwhile, the multicultural nature of society promotes exploration by making available alternative values, role definitions, and behavior norms. Within such an environment and with the support of friends and social networks, Asian American women can develop bicultural identities.

Biographical and historical sources also have suggested that friendships promoted personal growth. Through their friendships, women learned a new language; acquired new knowledge, skills, and attitudes; and reconstructed their personal identities. Likewise, empirical studies have indicated that social networks, depending on their composition, provide opportunities for personal growth. Within church-sponsored social networks and organizations, Asian American women try out new roles and responsibilities that prepare them for service in secular civic or professional organizations, and even in the public arena.

Empowerment

In the literature reviewed, personal growth through knowledge and skills acquisition facilitated by friends and social networks allowed women to reconstruct their personal identities and redefine their roles. It also empowered them. They felt emboldened to be more venturesome in ways ranging from driving a horse and buggy with only children for company to visit a friend living some distance away in a farming community to challenging sexism in the Asian American student movement and even to escaping the shackles of prostitution or, although not revealed by the review, perhaps domestic violence.

Context

Both historical and research reviews revealed that throughout the history of Asian Americans in the United States, certain social institutions —ethnic social organizations, churches, schools, social clubs, and service organizations—have played major roles in facilitating the formation and maintenance of friendships as well as social networks. In addition, they have served as a bridge between ethnic communities and the broader society. By creating learning opportunities for Asian American girls and women, they have enabled many to feel empowered enough to travel across that bridge. These facilitative effects may be partly due to the prosocial goals and stability of social institutions, factors to consider when trying to create environments conducive to women's development and well-being.

A VISION FOR THE FUTURE

Research on Asian American women's friendships and social networks is just beginning. Studies are few in number and vary so much in the topics addressed that the field lacks coherence. There does not appear to be any programmatic research. Conceptual issues, such as inconsistent operational definitions of the constructs of friendship and social network and methodological problems still must be resolved.

From Kinship Through Friendship to Social Networks

The theories from which the research has been derived (e.g., social psychological theories of interpersonal attraction) have proven to be of some heuristic value, but there seems to have been no serious attempt to modify them or to develop a more culturally syntonic theory. Such a theory should address the transformation of women's construction of relationships as they move beyond kinship relations to friendships and social networks, particularly personal and exchange networks, an inevitable progression given the degree of geographic mobility in the United States. In addition to describing and explaining the development of each of these relational systems, the theory should attempt to delineate the potential linkages among these three relational systems. The importance of these linkages has been shown in studies of other ethnic groups.

Research on attachment has indicated that internal working models of relationships between self and other, first acquired within the family, initially in the child's relationship with the primary caregiver and subsequently with other members (Bowlby, 1988; Hazan & Shaver, 1994a, 1994b), influence subsequent constructions of relationships. Similarly, expectations and perceptions of social support and the capacity to use available support are related to attachments formed early in life (Cable, Gantt, & Mallinckrodt, 1996). Conceivably, Asian Americans, especially first- and second-generation Asian Americans, bring to their friendships and social networks the expectations and interactional patterns initially acquired within a biological kinship system or surrogate kinship in the ethnic community.

All three relational systems are evolving systems, so studying them would be facilitated by a developmental perspective. Furthermore, all three are influenced by context, particularly culture, so a contextual perspective is also needed.

A Developmental–Contextual Framework

Previous research on Asian American women's friendships and social networks has lacked a developmental perspective. Stability and change over time in the course of a friendship have not been addressed. Nor has there been any attempt to examine whether the structure and dynamics of each of these two relational systems differ as a function of participants' age or developmental status.

A developmental–contextual framework in the study of friendships and social networks would address these theoretical issues. It would ensure that friendships and social networks would be viewed as dynamic systems whose meanings, structures, patterns of interaction, and functions may differ between individuals of different ages or between age periods, change in the same individual across the life span, over the course (i.e., initiation to termination) of a friendship or social network at a particular age period, or over generations.

Because this framework emphasizes organism–environment interaction, contexts such as culture should be assigned major explanatory roles in the development of friendships and social networks. Research should be grounded in cultural definitions and expectations of these relational systems, as well as in the norms for social interaction in general and interaction between friends or network members in particular. It should also be informed by research on kinship.

Much has been written about how differences between cultures along the individualism–collectivism dimension (Triandis, 1995) influence relationships such as that of parent and child, but these differences rarely have been taken into account in the study of Asian American women's friendships. Yet such differences are likely to influence the expectations and beliefs held about friendship, as well as the methods of communication and expressions of intimacy that occur between friends (Dion & Dion, 1993). Studies have shown that women from individualistic cultures are likely to have a need for expressive individualism, self-expression, and self-realization within intimate relationships and to expect reciprocal self-disclosure and the sharing of personal feelings and activities in their friendships. In contrast, because of cultural emphasis on harmony, individuals from a collectivist society may be more likely to diffuse levels of intimacy among friendships or to take into account the wishes of another as a basis for intimacy (Dion & Dion, 1993). Historical review suggests that collaborative activity may be a hallmark of friendship in a collectivistic society.

Finally, a developmental–contextual framework would be useful for examining stability or change in the structures, interactional patterns, and functions of friendships and social networks associated with acculturation, attitudinal changes in the host society, goals and stability of social institutions, and other factors.

REFERENCES

Adams, R. G., & Blieszner, R. (1989). *Perspectives on later life friendships*. Beverly Hills, CA: Sage.

Amott, T. L., & Matthaei, J. A. (1991). *Race, gender, and work*. Boston: South End Press.

Antonucci, T. C. (1990). Social supports and social relationships. In R. H. Binstock & L. K. George (Eds.), *Handbook of the psychology of aging* (3rd ed., pp. 205–226). New York: Van Nostrand Reinhold.

Balgopal, P. R. (1988). Social networks and Asian Indian families. In C. Jacobs &

D. D. Bowles (Eds.), *Ethnicity and race: Critical concepts in social work* (pp. 18–33). Silver Spring, MD: National Association of Social Workers.

Belle, D. (1982). The stress of caring: Women as providers of social support. In L. Goldberger & S. Bretznitz (Eds.), *Handbook of stress: Theoretical and clinical aspects* (pp. 496–505). New York: Free Press.

Berkman, L. F. (1985). The relationship of social networks and social support to morbidity and mortality. In S. Cohen & L. S. Syme (Eds.), *Social support and health* (pp. 241–262). Orlando, FL: Academic Press.

Berscheid, E., & Walster, E. H. (1969). *Interpersonal attraction.* Reading, MA: Addison Wesley.

Block, H., & Greenberg, D. (1985). *Women and friendship.* New York: Franklin Watts.

Blyth, D. (1982). Mapping the social world of adolescents: Issues, techniques, and problems. In F. C. Serafica (Ed.), *Social-cognitive development in context* (pp. 240–272). New York: Guilford Press.

Bowlby, J. (1988). *A secure base: Parent-child attachment and healthy human development.* New York: Basic Books.

Cable, M., Gantt, D. L., & Mallinckrodt, B. S. (1996). Attachment, social competency, and the capacity to use social support. In G. R. Pierce, B. R. Sarason, & I. G. Sarason (Eds.), *Handbook of social support and the family* (pp. 141–172). New York: Plenum Press.

California Department of Mental Health, Mental Health Promotion Branch. (1982). *In pursuit of wellness: Questions and answers?* San Francisco: California Department of Mental Health.

Cheng, L. (1984). Free, indentured, enslaved: Chinese prostitutes in nineteenth century America. In L. Cheng & E. Bonacich (Eds.), *Labor immigration under capitalism: Asian workers in the United States before World War II* (pp. 402–434). Berkeley and Los Angeles: University of California Press.

Davis, C. L. (1993). *A cross-cultural study on the role of social networks and acculturation in the physical and psychological functioning of Chinese students.* Unpublished doctoral dissertation, University of California, Los Angeles.

Denton, K. (1984). *Asian women's social networks and mental health.* Unpublished doctoral dissertation, University of Utah, Salt Lake City.

Die, A. H., & Seelbach, W. C. (1988). Problems, sources of assistance, and knowledge of services among elderly Vietnamese immigrants. *Gerontologist, 28,* 448–452.

Dion, K. K., & Dion, K. L. (1993). Individualistic and collectivistic perspectives on gender and the cultural context of love and intimacy. *Journal of Social Issues, 49,* 53–69.

Duck, S., & Wright, P. H. (1993). Reexamining gender differences in same gender friendships: A close look at two kinds of data. *Sex Roles, 28,* 709–727.

Eichenbaum, L., & Orbach, S. (1988). *Between women: Love, envy, and competition in women's friendships.* New York: Viking Press.

Erikson, E. H. (1963). *Childhood and society* (2nd ed.). New York: Norton.

Erikson, E. H. (1980). *Identity and the life cycle*. New York: Norton.

Espiritu, Y. L. (1995). *Filipino American lives*. Philadelphia: Temple University Press.

Granovetter, M. S. (1973). The strength of weak ties. *American Journal of Sociology*, 78, 1360–1380.

Ha, J. (1993). 1.5 and 2.0 generation of Korean women. In H. Kwon & S. Kim (Eds.), The emerging generations of Korean Americans (pp. 225–235). Seoul, Korea: Kyung Hee University Press.

Haines, D. W. (1988). Kinship in Vietnamese refugee resettlement: A review of the U.S. experience. *Journal of Comparative Family Studies*, 19, 1–16.

Hall, A., & Wellman, B. (1985). Social networks and social support. In S. Cohen & L. S. Syme (Eds.), *Social support and health* (pp. 23–41). Orlando, FL: Academic Press.

Hazan, C., & Shaver, P. R. (1994a). Attachment as an organizational framework for research on close relationships. *Psychological Inquiry*, 5, 1–22.

Hazen, C., & Shaver, P. R. (1994b). Deeper into attachment theory. *Psychological Inquiry*, 5, 68–79.

House, J. S., Umberson, D., & Landis, K. R. (1988). Structures and processes of social support. *Annual Review of Sociology*, 14, 293–318.

Kuo, W. H., & Tsai, Y. (1986). Social networking, hardiness, and immigrants' mental health. *Journal of Health and Social Behavior*, 27, 133–149.

Larson, R., Mannell, R., & Zuzanek, J. (1986). Daily well-being of older adults with friends and families. *Psychology and Aging*, 1, 117–126.

Lea, N., & Duck, S. (1982). A model for the role of similarity of values in friendship development. *British Journal of Social Psychology*, 21, 301–310.

Lee, M. P. (1990). *Quiet odyssey: A pioneer Korean woman in America*. Seattle: University of Washington Press.

Lin, K., Masuda, M., & Tazuma, L. (1982). Adaptational problems of Vietnamese refugees: III. Case studies in clinic and field: Adaptive and maladaptive. *Psychiatric Journal of the University of Ottawa*, 7, 173–183.

Matsumoto, V. (1989). Nisei women and resettlement during World War II. In Asian Women United of California (Eds.), *Making waves: An anthology of writings by and about Asian American women* (pp. 115–126). Boston: Beacon Press.

Meemeduma, P. (1992). Support networks of Sri Lankan women living in the United States. In S. M. Furuto, R. Biswas, D. K. Chung, & F. Ross-Sheriff (Eds.), *Social work practice with Asian Americans. Sage sourcebooks for the human services series. Vol. 20* (pp. 202–212). Newbury Park, CA: Sage.

Menne, J. M., & Sinnett, R. (1971). Proximity and social interaction in residence halls. *Journal of College Student Personnel*, 12, 26–31.

Milardo, R. M. (1988). Families and social networks: An overview of theory and methodology. In R. M. Milardo (Ed.), *Families and social networks* (pp. 13–47). Newbury Park, CA: Sage.

Milardo, R. M. (1992). Comparative methods for delineating social networks. *Journal of Social and Personal Relationships, 9,* 447–461.

Min, P. G. (1995). Korean Americans. In P. G. Min (Ed.), *Asian Americans: Contemporary trends and issues* (pp. 199–231). Thousand Oaks, CA: Sage.

Mouanoutoua, V. L., Brown, L. G., Cappelletty, C. G., & Levine, R. V. (1991). A Hmong adaptation of the Beck Depression Inventory. *Journal of Personality Assessment, 57,* 309–322.

Nakano, M. (1990). *Japanese American women: Three generations 1890–1990.* Berkeley, CA: Mina Press.

Nomura, G. M. (1987). Tsugiki, a grafting: A history of a Japanese pioneer woman in Washington state. *Women's Studies: An Interdisciplinary Journal, 14,* 15–37.

O'Conner, P. (1992). *Friendships between women: A critical review.* New York: Guilford Press.

Oh, S. (1988). *Korean immigrant families and their social networks.* Unpublished doctoral dissertation, State University of New York, Stony Brook.

Okihiro, G. Y. (1994). *Margins and mainstreams: Asians in American history and culture.* Seattle: University of Washington Press.

Pecora, P. J., & Fraser, M. W. (1985). The social support networks of Indochinese refugees. *Journal of Sociology and Social Welfare, 12,* 817–849.

Perlmutter, M., & Hall, E. (1992). *Adult development and aging.* New York: Wiley.

Pierce, G. R., Sarason, B. R., & Sarason, I. G. (1990). Integrating social support perspectives: Working models, personal relationships, and situational factors. In S. Duck (Ed.), *Personal relationships and social support* (pp. 173–189). London: Sage.

Quisumbing, M. S. (1982). *Life events, social support and personality: Their impact on Filipino psychological adjustment.* Unpublished doctoral dissertation, University of Chicago, Illinois.

Ramisetty-Mikler, S. (1993). Asian Indian immigrants in America and sociocultural issues in counseling. *Journal of Multicultural Counseling and Development, 21,* 36–49.

Rands, M. (1988). Changes in social networks following marital separation and divorce. In R. M. Milardo (Ed.), *Families and social networks* (pp. 127–145). Newbury Park, CA: Sage.

Reisman, J. M. (1981). Adult friendships. In S. Duck & R. Gilmour (Eds.), *Personal relationships. 2: Developing personal relationships* (pp. 205–230). New York: Academic Press.

Rose, S. (1995). Women's friendships. In J. C. Chrisler & A. H. Hemstreet (Eds.), *Variations on a theme: Diversity and the psychology of women* (pp. 79–105). Albany: State University of New York Press.

Schultz, K. (1991). Women's adult development: The importance of friendship. *The Journal of Independent Social Work, 5,* 19–30.

Strober, S. B. (1994). Social work interventions to alleviate Cambodian refugee psychological distress. *International Social Work, 37,* 23–35.

Sudweeks, S., Gudykunst, W. B., Ting-Toomey, S., & Nishida, T. (1990). Developmental themes in Japanese–North American interpersonal relationships. *International Journal of Intercultural Relations, 14,* 207–233.

Sue, D. W. (1981). *Counseling the culturally different.* New York: Wiley.

Sunno, B. P. (1989). We the exiled. In Asian Women United of California (Eds.), *Making waves: An anthology of writings by and about Asian American women* (pp. 79–81). Boston: Beacon Press.

Ting-Toomey, S. (1981). Ethnic identity and close friendship in Chinese-American college students. *International Journal of Intercultural Relations, 5,* 381–406.

Triandis, H. C. (1995). *Individualism and collectivism.* Boulder, CO: Westview Press.

Trice, A. D., & Elliott, J. (1993). Japanese students in America: College friendship patterns. *Journal of Instructional Psychology, 20,* 262–264.

Uba, L. (1994). *Asian Americans: Personality patterns, identity, and mental health.* New York: Guilford.

Vaux, A., & Harrison, D. (1985). Support network characteristics associated with support satisfaction and perceived support. *American Journal of Community Psychology, 13,* 245–268.

Vega, W. A., Kolody, B., Valle, R., & Wier, J. (1991). Social networks, social support, and their relationship to depression among immigrant Mexican women. *Human Organization, 50,* 154–162.

Wang, Y., Sedlacek, W. E., & Westbrook, F. D. (1992). Asian Americans and student organizations: Attitudes and participation. *Journal of College Student Development, 33,* 215–221.

Wei, W. (1993). *The Asian American movement.* Philadelphia: Temple University Press.

Williams, M. (1989). Ladies on the line: Punjabi cannery workers in Central California. In Asian Women United of California (Ed.), *Making waves: An anthology of writings by and about Asian American women* (pp. 148–158). Boston: Beacon Press.

Yanagisako, S. J. (1977). Women-centered kin networks in urban bilateral kinship. *American Ethnologist, 4,* 207–226.

Yanagisako, S. J. (1985). *Transforming the past.* Stanford, CA: Stanford University Press.

Yim, S. B. (1984). *Social networks among Korean immigrants in the United States.* Unpublished doctoral dissertation, University of California, Los Angeles.

Yu, C. Y. (1989). The world of our grandmothers. In Asian Women United of California (Ed.), *Making waves: An anthology of writings by and about Asian American women* (pp. 33–42). Boston: Beacon Press.

IV

PARADIGMS: FROM WHOSE LENS: PERSPECTIVES OF ASIAN AMERICAN WOMEN

As this book comes to its conclusion, crosscutting themes that lead toward a paradigm for Asian American women and understanding the relationships they form emerge. These themes are not exclusive to Asian American women, but they deserve emphasis in considering the lives of Asian American women. These themes should not be marginalized or trivialized by claims that they are "nothing new" or "we are one." Rather, the differences are subtle but important if theories and practice are to be inclusive.

What is the message? There is a need for new paradigms that are both feminist and multicultural. In addition to being women-centered, in looking at issues from a gender perspective, the goal also was to consider the ethnic perspective as well. In juxtaposing gender and ethnicity, the issues of adaptation and biculturalism become critical. It is the resilience of Asian American women amid sociopolitical change, and the interactive dualism of their experiences that makes them unique. It is clear that immigrant women and their children just do not forget the trauma, the losses, and the culture of their country of origin. Their memories, across generations and continents, have sustaining influences on adaptation, survival, and psychological development. It is clear that these experiences can be self-defining in influencing identities that remain (e.g., internment camps survivors, boat people, picture brides). Paradigms are needed that do not pathologize, but rather empower women as to how women can benefit from abuse experiences.

The two models offered in this section illustrate the different perspectives needed and the inclusion of variables not often used in the study, treatment, and understanding of Asian American women. As Fujino (chapter 10) demonstrates in her model of structural and individual factors, race influences choices and the nature of dating patterns. As Louie demonstrates in her model of interdependence (chapter 11), interpersonal relationships must be considered from a different viewpoint as well to understand their formation and maintenance among Asian American women.

In the final chapter, Chin calls attention to the dynamics of power and connections underlying feminist and diversity paradigms. How women form these bonds and how these bonds have been used to subjugate (i.e., domestic violence) needs definition from a more inclusive context.

This does not diminish the value of the perspectives of others and other groups. Instead, the goal is to add to these the perspective of the Asian American woman. Lest this be viewed as justification, preaching, or arrogance, it is the errors of commission (i.e., stereotypes perpetuating and defining the roles of Asian American women) and omission (i.e., inadequacy of data and research on Asian American women) that have driven the creation of this book. Precisely because there has been a failure to validate and value racial and ethnic differences, this book sought to have those voices heard. The suffering of our forebears, our individual identities, and the legacy we leave amid an ever-changing sociopolitical context need to be recorded and, more important, included in theory, practice, and policy.

10

STRUCTURAL AND INDIVIDUAL INFLUENCES AFFECTING RACIALIZED DATING RELATIONSHIPS

DIANE C. FUJINO

Forming intimate relationships is a significant developmental task facing young adults as well as increasing numbers of older adults. In the United States, many people cite individual preferences and personal tastes as reasons for choosing particular romantic partners. However, in the racially stratified United States, race matters in personal relationships. Race affects the characteristics individuals desire in romantic partners and the ways in which they view potential partners. Factors affecting partner choice include racial stereotypes, cultural standards of beauty (e.g., as reflected in the proliferation of cosmetic surgery), cultural values, racially influenced access to educational and occupational opportunities, and racial hierarchy attached to the social status of racial and ethnic groups within the United States and elsewhere.

I thank Jean Lau Chin for providing insightful advice on this chapter. I also extend my appreciation to Stanley Sue, Nolan Zane, David Takeuchi, and Nancy Henley for their guidance on the original study on which this chapter is based. Preparation for this chapter was supported by the National Research Center on Asian American Mental Health, National Institute of Mental Health Grant No. R01 MH44331.

How does race affect the dating patterns of young Asian American women? The basis for the discussion in this chapter are the results of a study that had two objectives: (a) to explore the racialized patterns of heterosexual dating among Chinese American and Japanese American women, and (b) to propose and test a model showing how structural and individual factors influence Asian American women's selection of intra- and interracial partners. Although they are important areas of inquiry, this chapter does not examine gay, lesbian, or bisexual relationships, nor does it focus on interactions within relationships (e.g., factors associated with relationship satisfaction).

HISTORICAL CONTEXT OF RACIALIZED MARRIAGE AND DATING RELATIONSHIPS

U.S. immigration policies, labor practices, and antimiscegenation laws played a significant role in shaping marital patterns among Asian Americans during three distinct historical periods: 1850s–1930s, 1940s–1965, and 1965–present.

Single Asian Men and Bachelor Societies: 1850s–1930s

The U.S. capitalist economy sought unattached Asian male workers who cost less than married men to maintain in terms of housing, food, and education for dependent children and whose labor was more flexible to meet short-term, seasonal demands (Bonacich, 1984; Espiritu, 1996; Sharma, 1984). Consequently, early Asian immigrants came largely as single men or unaccompanied married men from China beginning in the mid-19th century; from Japan in the late 19th century; and from Korea, the Philippines, and India in the early 20th century. As the harsh realities of unfulfilled economic dreams and lengthy stays in the U.S. set in, these Asian men began to seek marriage partners. However, U.S. policies sought to limit the immigration of Asian women and what they represented—children, families, and permanent residency. In 1875, Congress passed the Page Law (Chan, 1991b), which forbade the entry of Asian prostitutes. Because immigration officials and the U.S. public assumed that all Chinese women were prostitutes, the Page Law effectively resulted in the reduction of Chinese female immigration and the elimination of the primary source of wives for Chinese men in the United States (Chan, 1991b). In 1920, the Japanese Foreign Ministry succumbed to pressure from California's U.S. Democratic Senator James Phelan to cease issuing passports to Japanese and Korean picture brides. This decision left 24,000 Japanese American men in bachelorhood (Ichioka, 1988). Other exclusion laws left Filipino and Asian Indian men without the possibility of coethnic wives; this was significant because few Filipino or Indian women immigrated to the United States (Chan, 1991a; Okihiro, 1994; Sharma, 1984).

The formation of interracial relationships with White partners could have been an option for Asian men, but U.S. antimiscegenation laws forbade interracial marriages. The first antimiscegenation law banned marriage between White and Black people as early as the 17th century. When Asian immigration increased, several states established laws banning marriage between White people and Mongolians. California, where the majority of Asian immigrants lived, adopted such a law in 1880. These laws were not declared unconstitutional until 1948 in California and 1967 throughout the entire nation (Chan, 1991a; Spickard, 1989; Takaki, 1989). Despite the widespread antimiscegenation laws, some Asians did marry White Americans through a variety of mechanisms. First, because they were considered Malay and not Mongolian, many Filipinos were able to marry White people until 1933 when the California legislature, followed by other states, added Malay to the antimiscegenation codes (Chan, 1991a; Takaki, 1989). Seventy percent of Filipino men intermarried in Los Angeles County between 1924 and 1933, and about half of these marriages were to U.S.-born White women, mostly to U.S.-born "taxi-dancehall girls" (Panunzio, 1942). Second, a few Asian–White couples traveled to states that allowed interracial marriage. Third, even in states forbidding intermarriage, Asian–White marriages occurred, possibly through racial misidentification, given the somewhat arbitrary social construction of racial categories (Smedley, 1993; Spickard, 1992); through the falsification of records; or through inconsistent enforcement of the law. For example, one Chinese and seven Japanese obtained licenses to marry Whites in Los Angeles County between 1924 and 1933 when antimiscegenation laws were in effect (Panunzio, 1942). However, antimiscegenation laws generally were successful in thwarting the formation of Asian–White unions.

One solution to the scarcity of Asian women was for heterosexual Asian men to marry Latina American, African American, or other Asian American women. For example, 80% of Asian Indian men married Mexican American women in California before 1946 (Jensen, 1988). Filipino men regularly married African American and Mexican American women. Chinese men tended to marry Japanese American women (a greater proportion of Japanese than Chinese, Filipino, or Asian Indian women immigrated), followed in number by marriages to African American women (Panunzio, 1942). Given the imbalance between men and women, it is not surprising that more Asian men than Asian women intermarried (Panunzio, 1942).

Rise in Asian Women's Immigration and Family Formation: 1940s–1965

The period following World War II signified a shift in gender-related immigration policies. For the first time, from the late 1940s to 1965, women predominated Asian immigration, thus allowing family formation on a larger scale than previously (Chan, 1991a). Moreover, Asian women began outmarrying at higher rates than Asian men. Asian women married U.S. servicemen in Asia during the post World War II American occupation of Japan and later during the Korean and Vietnam wars. The 1945 War Brides Act, which was amended in 1947 to include the wives of Asian American veterans, allowed spouses of U.S. citizens to immigrate. In addition, the 1952 McCarran–Walter Act enabled spouses of U.S. citizens to immigrate outside the extremely restrictive quota system as nonquota immigrants. Chinese war brides mainly married intraethnically to coethnics, whereas Japanese, Korean, and Filipino women primarily married interracially to non-Asian U.S. servicemen (Chan, 1991a).

Sharp Increase in Asian Immigration and Intermarriage: 1965–Present

The passage of the 1965 Immigration and Nationality Act, which eliminated the national origins quota system and inadvertently opened the doors to Asian immigration (Chan, 1991a), marked another shift in Asian immigration and marriage patterns. The significant rise in the Asian American population after passage of the 1965 act, along with the banning of antimiscegenation laws by the U.S. Supreme Court in 1967 and the liberalization of national attitudes toward race relations, contributed to the increase in outmarriage rates. The fact that Asian Americans outmarry at relatively high rates has been shown by the convergence of results from several studies using various methods of data collection and geographic areas (Fugita & O'Brien, 1991; Kitano, Fujino, & Takahashi, 1998; Lee & Yamanaka, 1990). A note on outmarriage terminology: *Intraethnic* refers to coethnic unions (e.g., Chinese–Chinese); *interethnic* refers to unions with a partner from a different ethnic, but same racial, group (e.g., Chinese–Filipino); and *interracial* refers to unions between racially different partners (e.g., Chinese–White). *Outmarriage* and *intermarriage* refer to marriages outside an individual's specific grouping and can be interethnic or interracial.[1] According to 1990 U.S. census data, 40.4% of Asian and Pacific

---

[1]Omi and Winant's (1994) definitions of race and ethnicity and conventional social science definitions for outmarriage terminology are used in this chapter. Omi and Winant define *race* as social and political constructions enabling racism. Cambodians, Koreans, and Filipinos are considered part of the "Asian" racial umbrella. As an illustration, consider that Vincent Chin, a young Chinese man, was beaten to death by two White autoworkers in Detroit in 1982 at the height of Japan bashing in the American auto industry. He was killed because he was

Islander American wives and 31.2% of husbands were intermarried nationwide (Shinagawa & Pang, 1996). In California, where 39% of Asian and Pacific Islander Americans lived, 36% of wives and 28.9% of husbands were intermarried (Shinagawa & Pang, 1996). According to marriage licenses in Los Angeles County in 1989, 39% of Asian Americans had married outside their ethnic group (Kitano, Fujino, & Takahashi, 1998).

Five patterns characterize Asian American intermarriage. First, the majority of Asian Americans marry intraethnically. Even though U.S. policies no longer prevent interracial marriage to White people, and partners from other ethnic groups are numerically more available than coethnics, most Asian Americans choose to marry coethnics. Second, using generational or immigration status as a marker for acculturation, the marriage literature has consistently found that acculturation is directly related to outmarriage rates; the third generation outmarries more than the second generation, which in turn outmarries more than the immigrant generation (Fugita & O'Brien, 1991; Kitano et al., 1998; Lee & Yamanaka, 1990; Shinagawa & Pang, 1996).

Third, Asian Americans are outmarrying at increasingly high rates (Kitano et al., 1998), with a particular upsurge in pan-Asian marriages. Although the decade from 1970 to 1980 was characterized by a rise in interracial marriages, a dramatic rise in interethnic marriages among Asian American women and men marked the decade from 1980 to 1990. Nationally in 1980, 4.0% of Asian and Pacific Islander Americans were married interethnically and 21.4% interracially, including 19.5% to White Americans (Lee & Yamanaka, 1990). By 1990, 16.2% of Asian and Pacific Islander American wives were married interethnically and 24.2% interracially, including 20.8% to White Americans, and 18.9% of husbands were married interethnically and 12.3% interracially, including 9.9% to White Americans (Shinagawa & Pang, 1996). In California in 1980, 5.8% of Asian Americans were married interethnically and 29.8% interracially (Shinagawa & Pang, 1988). By 1990, 16.4% of Asian and Pacific Islander American wives were married interethnically and 19.6% interracially, including 16.2% to White Americans, and 18.4% of Asian and Pacific Islander American husbands were married interethnically and 10.5% interracially, including 7.7% to White Americans (Shinagawa & Pang, 1996).

Fourth, numerous studies have shown that Asian American women currently outmarry at higher rates than Asian American men, and they have been doing so since the late 1940s (Barnett, 1963; Kitano et al., 1998; Lee & Yamanaka, 1990; Shinagawa & Pang, 1996; Sung, 1990). This gen-

---

Asian, not because he was Chinese. In contrast, *ethnicity* refers to the grouping of people who share a common culture, history, language, and customs; the Chinese are an ethnic group that is separate from the Japanese. Outmarriage terminology flows from these definitions.

der difference holds for each Asian ethnic group and for Asian Americans collectively. Based on marriage license data in Los Angeles from 1975 to 1989, Asian American women uniformly accounted for the majority (54%–80%) of Asian American outmarriages (Kitano et al., 1998). Fifth, when outmarrying, Asian American women most often marry White men, whereas Asian American men usually marry women from other Asian groups (Kitano et al., 1998; Lee & Yamanaka, 1990; Shinagawa & Pang, 1988, 1996; Sung, 1990).

RACIALIZED DATING PATTERNS

In contrast to the copious literature addressing intermarriage, there is a paucity of material on Asian American interracial dating (see Fujino, 1997). The few existing studies have suggested that outdating is not as gender-based as intermarriage. Using the same data presented in this chapter, Fujino (1997) found that women and men outdated at similar rates. But like intermarriage, when outdating, Asian American women most often dated White men, and Asian American men most often dated women from other Asian groups. The findings also suggested that Asian Americans, like other groups, were more likely to date than to marry outside their own ethnic group. Johnson and Ogasawara (1988), however, found that in Hawaii, Asian American men were more likely to outdate than their female counterparts. This finding contradicts the outmarriage rates in Hawaii where, from 1980 to 1989, Asian American women outmarried more frequently than their male counterparts (Kitano et al., 1998). Clearly, more research is needed to determine the relationship of gender in interracial dating.

STRUCTURAL AND INDIVIDUAL INFLUENCES ON RACIALIZED DATING CHOICES

Historically, structural influences such as immigration policies, labor practices, and antimiscegenation laws constrained Asian American marriage patterns. Today, with the liberalization of racialized laws, the choice of dating and marriage partners appears to be, more than ever, the result of individual choices and preferences. However, structural influences continue to affect Asian Americans' choices of intimate partners. More precisely, although racial ideology has changed, race continues to matter. Following the social movements of the 1960s and 1970s, which challenged U.S. constructions of race and racial superiority, it is no longer acceptable to express blatantly racist views and legislation (e.g., segregation laws; Omi & Winant, 1994). Instead, racism has become more covert, operating through more subtle mechanisms such as legislative attacks on immigrant rights and affirmative action and through media representations. These

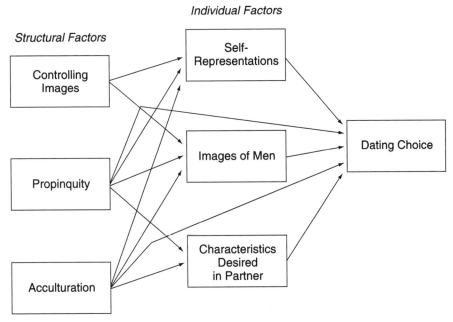

Individual Factors

Structural Factors

Controlling
Images

Propinquity

Acculturation

Self-
Representations

Images of Men

Characteristics
Desired
in Partner

Dating Choice

Figure 10.1. Model illustrating structural and individual factors affecting
racialized dating choices.

more subtle forms of racialized policies and images continue to influence
ideas and attitudes about race in the United States as well as individuals'
choices of dating partners.

The study reported in this chapter had two objectives. The first goal
was to understand the racialized patterns of dating among young Asian
American women. As with intermarriage, I expected to see evidence that
Asian American women would most often date intraracially, that is, Asian
American men. However, when dating interracially, I expected that they
would mostly date White men and that dating African American and Latino American men would be infrequent, especially among immigrant
women. The second goal was to present a model to illustrate how structural
and individual influences—as affected by race—shape dating choices (see
Figure 10.1). Structural influences affect dating choices in two ways. First,
structural influences (controlling images, acculturation, and propinquity)
exert a direct effect on dating. I anticipated that acculturation would be
related to increased interracial dating; that is, that U.S.-born women would
date interracially more than immigrant women. Propinquity would also be
related to increased interracial dating; those women growing up in predominantly Asian communities would mostly date Asian American men and
those growing up in predominantly White communities would mostly date
White men. Second, structural influences indirectly affect dating choices
through their effect on individual influences. Structural influences such as

propinquity affect the characteristics desired in partners, which in turn affect dating choices. Finally, individual influences (self-representations, images of Asian American and White men, and characteristics desired in partners) directly affect choices of dating partners.

Structural Influences

Controlling Images

One powerful social institution shaping racialized views in both overt and covert ways is the media. In particular, the media shape individuals' consciousness by indoctrinating the ideology, including the racial hegemony, of the dominant group (Jhally, 1989). In the absence of antimiscegenation laws and gender-based immigration policies, the social construction and racialization of media representations play an important role in shaping individual preferences and behaviors. The stereotypic images of Asian American women have been dichotomized along the virgin–whore dimension. The Asian American woman is viewed as either the submissive "lotus blossom" or the conniving "dragon lady." As the lotus blossom, the Asian woman is endowed with excessive femininity; she is the Confucian ideal wife who obediently serves her husband's every desire, from feeding him to giving erotic massages to satisfying his sexual passions. She is the objectified other who exists to fulfill the (White) man's fantasies. Whenever she asserts her humanity, she is transformed into the manipulative, evil, castrating dragon lady (Espiritu, 1996; Soe, 1992; Spickard, 1989; Tajima, 1989).

The association of early Asian American women with prostitution, the immigration of Asian war brides following multiple U.S. wars in Asia, the prevalence of U.S. military-based prostitution and sex tourism (vacation packages designed to maximize sexual encounters with Asian women) in Asia, the emergence of the mail-order bride industry, and the representations of Asian women in the media contribute to, and are partially a function of, the social construction of the submissive, ultrafeminine, and sexually exotic lotus blossom image of the Asian woman. In turn, this social construction of the lotus blossom image affects how people view Asian American women. The personal ads in U.S. newspapers and the mail-order bride catalogs illustrate the demand for Asian women by American men who are looking for this traditional, subservient wife (Glodava & Onizuka, 1994; Villapando, 1989). In fact, a scandal involving a man impersonating women through personal ads was discovered a few years ago. After experimenting with portrayals of African, Latina, and White women, the impersonator discovered that his representations of Asian women generated the largest number of responses from men and the most money. His impersonations of three variations of Asian women—the lotus blossom, the dragon lady–whore, and the high-powered executive—drew correspondence from more than 120,000 men who sent more than $200,000 over a 12-year period (Chin, 1997).

These images limit Asian American women's social, economic, and political experiences because they constrain how others view them in relationships, in school, and on the job. These images also bind Asian women's self-representations. But these are not the only function of these images. Patricia Hill Collins (1990) called these representations controlling images because they are created and perpetuated by dominant social institutions to make the racial- and gender-based treatment of women and people of color appear natural and normative. In doing so, these controlling images serve to justify the existence of racism, sexism, classism, and heterosexism. These images also affect Asian American women's intimate relationships.

Propinquity

Propinquity, or the physical distance between groups, functions to expand or limit racialized dating opportunities through the availability of partners from various ethnic backgrounds. In addition to the obvious thesis that geographic closeness and availability increase the chances of meeting, studies have indicated that propinquity is related to attraction. People tend to like others with whom they have repeated interactions and close proximity. The mere exposure effect asserts that individuals presented with neutral stimuli begin to like the objects more with repeated exposure (Saegert, Swap & Zajonc, 1973). Festinger, Schachter, and Back (1950) found that residents of a large apartment building who lived on the same floor were more likely to be friends with one another than residents living on different floors. Blau (1977) proposed the sociological theory of relative group size, which corresponds with the psychological concept of propinquity. Empirical studies have found that relative group size is inversely related to outmarriage rate (Blau, Blum, & Schwartz, 1982; Fugita & O'Brien, 1991). When Asians comprise a small percentage of the overall population, they are more likely to outmarry.

Acculturation

Acculturation, or the process of integrating into the dominant society without necessarily losing aspects of one's ethnic culture, is another structural influence that affects racialized dating choices. Immigration or generational status, which have been used as markers of acculturation, have been found to be directly related to outmarriage rates (Fugita & O'Brien, 1991; Lee & Yamanaka, 1990; Sung, 1990). Kitano et al. (1998) found that among each of the five Asian American groups studied (Chinese, Filipino, Japanese, Korean, and Vietnamese), the third generation or later outmarried more than the second generation, which in turn outmarried more than the immigrant group (or first generation). Shinagawa and Pang (1996) found that among the 16 Asian and Pacific Islander groups analyzed using 1990 U.S. census data, U.S.-born Asian women and men outmarried at much higher rates than their foreign-born counterparts. There were only three groups that deviated from this pattern. Among Hmong men, Laotian women, and Japanese women, immigrants outmarried more than did their U.S.-born counterparts. The vast majority of immigrant Hmong men and Laotian women married interethnically to other Asians. Most of the immigrant Japanese women married White men, which may be explained by the presence of U.S. servicemen in Japan during World War II and U.S. military occupation of Japan following the war and the subsequent immigration of Japanese war brides.

Individual Influences

The study reported in this chapter examined the effects of three individual-level factors (self-representations, images of Asian American and White men, and characteristics desired in partners) on racialized dating choices. I believed that Asian American women's self-representations would differ by their racialized dating patterns. I also anticipated that Asian American women's images of Asian American and White men would differ by racialized dating patterns. I expected that Asian American women who held positive images of Asian American men would be more likely to date intraracially and that those with negative images of Asian American men would likely date interracially. Finally, I anticipated that the characteristics Asian American women valued in partners would predict racialized dating when they matched images of Asian American and White men; for example, those Asian American women who valued caring qualities in partners and viewed Asian American men as more caring than White men would most likely date intraracially.

STUDY METHODS

Study Participants

Participants were 163 Asian American female undergraduate students (94 Chinese and 69 Japanese) who had never been married and identified themselves as heterosexual and monoracial. The participants, whose average age was 19.9 years, had had an average of 3.5 boyfriends. About 55% of the Chinese and 25% of the Japanese women were immigrants. They generally came from families of above-average socioeconomic status. The Nam–Powers (Miller, 1991) socioeconomic status (SES) scores (0–100), which are derived from median education, median income, and occupation for women and men in the civilian labor force in 1980, yielded a mean SES score of 78 for fathers and 51 for mothers. On average, participants' fathers had graduated from college and mothers had attended some college. Participants grew up in communities with vastly different racial groupings, but the mean racial composition was 41.8% White, 34.9% Asian, and 21.2% African or Latino. In addition, 88 Chinese American men, 57 Japanese American men, and 92 White men were surveyed to examine their views about Asian American women.

Measures Used

The data for this study came from a 50-minute questionnaire completed for a larger study on Asian American interracial dating (Fujino, 1992). In addition to providing demographic information such as ethnicity and birthplace, participants reported the number of significant relationships (operationally defined as an exclusive, girlfriend–boyfriend relationship that lasted at least 2 months) they had with Chinese American, Japanese American, other Asian Americans, African American, Latino, and White partners. They also completed the Attitude Toward Women Scale (AWS) to assess their degree of liberal attitudes toward the rights and roles of women (Spence, Helmreich, & Stapp, 1973). The AWS consists of 25 items that are rated on a 4-point Likert-type scale from *disagree strongly* to *agree strongly*. The AWS short form has been found to have high internal-consistency reliability ($\alpha > .80$ for various populations) and high validity (Beere, 1990). In a review of measures, Beere (1990) stated that the AWS, used in 371 published studies, was the most commonly used measure of attitudes toward women.

The Attributional Relationship Scale developed for this study was used to measure the following: (a) characteristics desired in romantic partners, (b) characteristics the participant perceived herself to possess, and (c) characteristics imputed to members of the opposite gender. Items were selected from past studies of qualities desired in potential mates (Buss & Barnes, 1986) and of personality characteristics (Wiggins, 1979) emphasizing race and gender themes and power relations. The 30 items cover areas such as attractiveness, sexual expectations, personality characteristics, and socioeconomic status.

For the characteristics desired in romantic partners, labeled *valued attributes*, participants indicated the importance of each of the 30 items on a 7-point Likert-type scale. For the self-perceived characteristics, identified as *self-attributes*, participants rated the extent to which they believed themselves to possess each of the 30 attributes on a 5-point Likert-type scale. For the characteristics imputed to members of the opposite gender, labeled *imputed attributes*, the same 30 items were presented to examine participants' perceptions of members of the opposite gender by ethnic group. The instructions to female participants were as follows: "Imagine that there are 100 Chinese American men in the room. How many of these 100 men do you think possess each of the following characteristics?" Participants indicated from 0 to 100 the number of individuals they perceived to possess each attribute. The same procedure was used to assess the attributes imputed to White men and Japanese American men. Because it was fairly obvious that participants were being asked to compare ethnic groups, the three ethnic groups were listed on the same page in the following order: Chinese American, White American, and Japanese American. Although it would have been interesting to examine the views of African American and Latino American men and men from other Asian groups, time constraints limited the number of groups that could be examined. The decision to study Chinese American, Japanese American, and White men was made because these are the groups that Chinese American and Japanese American women most often date. Male particpants rated Chinese American and Japanese American women in a similar manner.

Principal-components factor analysis with varimax rotation was used to determine that the 30 interpersonal characteristics of the Attributional Relationship Scale could be explained by three underlying factors. The first factor, labeled Attractiveness, consists of 11 attributes: sexually exciting, physically affectionate, physically attractive, outgoing/sociable, romantic, good sense of humor, exotic, equal sex roles, strong personality, easygoing, and cute. The second factor, Power, consists of 8 attributes (masculine, high-status occupation potential, high income potential, ambitious, college graduate potential, dominant, independent, and feminine), including a negative eigenvalue for feminine that was reverse coded in further analyses. The third factor, Caring, consists of 9 attributes: considerate, polite, reliable, humble, obedient, sensitive to my feelings, nurturing, domestic, and traditional sex roles. The two attributes, quiet and shares feelings did not consistently load on a single factor and were excluded. (See Fujino, 1997, for more information about the factor analysis procedures and psychometric properties.)

STUDY RESULTS

Rates and Patterns of Dating

The study's first goal was to examine the patterns of intra- and interracial dating among Asian American women. Table 10.1 shows the percentage of Asian American women, by ethnicity and immigration status, who have dated men from various racial backgrounds. It is important to note that Asian American women most often date intraracially, that is, Asian American men. This is especially true for immigrant women, about

TABLE 10.1
Percentage of Asian American Women in Various Relationship Types by Ethnicity and Immigration Status

Ethnicity/immigration status	Relationship type[a]							
	Asian only ($n = 51$)	Asian + White ($n = 41$)	White only ($n = 18$)	Asian + A/L ($n = 6$)	Asian + White + A/L ($n = 17$)	White + A/L ($n = 5$)	A/L only ($n = 0$)
U.S.-born Chinese ($n = 34$)	32.4	29.4	17.6	5.9	8.8	5.9	0.0
Immigrant Chinese ($n = 42$)	54.8	21.4	11.9	2.4	9.5	0.0	0.0
U.S.-born Japanese ($n = 47$)	21.3	38.3	12.8	2.1	19.1	6.4	0.0
Immigrant Japanese ($n = 15$)	46.7	26.7	6.7	13.3	6.7	0.0	0.0
Total Asian women[b] ($n = 138$)	37.0	29.7	13.0	4.3	12.3	3.6	0.0

Note. A/L = African American or Latino American.
[a]Seven mutually exclusive relationship types are presented: (a) dating Asian American men exclusively; (b) dating both Asian American and White men, but not dating others; (c) dating White men exclusively; (d) dating Asian American men and other men of color, but not dating White men; (e) dating Asian American, White, and African American or Latino American men; (f) dating White and African American or Latino American men, but not dating Asian American men; and (g) dating African American or Latino American men but not dating Asian American or White men.
[b]Collapsed across ethnicity and immigration status.

half of whom have dated only Asian American men. The second most frequent relationship type among Asian American women is dating both Asian American and White men to the exclusion of other men of color. After this, immigrant and U.S.-born Chinese American women date White men exclusively, and Japanese immigrant women date men of color exclusively. Interestingly, U.S.-born Japanese American women are an exception to this pattern, dating Asian American and White men more often than Asian American men exclusively. Dating African American and Latino American men, in any combination, is less common. In fact, not a single Asian American woman in the study had dated African American or Latino American men exclusively. However, across the four groups that dated African American or Latino American men in any combination, 27.6% of U.S.-born Japanese American women had dated at least one African American or Latino American man, as had 20.6% of U.S.-born Chinese American women, 20.0% of immigrant Japanese women, and 11.9% of immigrant Chinese women.

Structural and Individual Influences Affecting Racialized Dating Choices

The study's second goal was to examine how structural influences (controlling images, acculturation, and propinquity) and individual influences (self-representations, images of Asian American and White men, and characteristics desired in partners) affect the choice of an intimate partner. Note that in subsequent analyses, the last four relationship types presented in Table 10.1 are combined given the small numbers in each category.

Images of Asian American Women

The study explored how Asian American women's self-representations differed by their dating patterns. In addition, the study assessed the images of Asian American women held by Asian American and White men. The majority of Asian American women were seen as kind, other focused, and caring (e.g., polite, considerate, sensitive, reliable, and nurturing) as well as being a college graduate by all four women's groups as well as by both men's groups (see Table 10.2). Among the women participants, those dating both Asian American and White men held the most distinctive self-representations. They were the only group who saw themselves as having a strong personality and being outgoing/sociable. In contrast, Asian women who had dated Asian American men exclusively had the fewest number of characteristics, and every characteristic listed was shared with at least two of the other women's groups.

I anticipated that Asian American and White men would hold images of Asian American women that differed from each other as well as from

TABLE 10.2
Characteristics Imputed to Asian American Women by Themselves and by Men

Characteristics imputed to Asian American women					
By Asian American Women[a]				By men[b]	
By those dating Asian American men only	By those dating Asian American and White men	By those dating White men only	By those dating African American or Latino American men	By Asian American men	By White men
college graduate potential	college graduate potential	college graduate potential	reliable	feminine	polite
polite	considerate	reliable	college graduate potential	polite	feminine
considerate	reliable	polite	considerate	domestic	nurturing
sensivite to feelings	romantic	nurturing	polite	reliable	domestic
reliable	nurturing	considerate	sensitive to feelings	nurturing	reliable
domestic	polite	romantic	good sense of humor	considerate	humble
nurturing	sensitive to feelings	sensitive to feelings	nurturing	college graduate potential	considerate
romantic	shares feelings	domestic	ambitious	humble	introverted/quiet
independent	ambitious	good sense of humor	easygoing	sensitive to feelings	sensitive to feelings
feminine	physically affectionate	physically affectionate	high-status occupation potential		traditional sex roles
	domestic	shares feelings	high income potential		college graduate potential
	high-status occupation potential	independent	equal sex roles		obedient
	good sense of humor	feminine	independent		
	strong personality	high income potential			
	high income potential	ambitious			
	equal sex roles	high-status occupation potential			
	outgoing/sociable	easygoing			
	independent	equal sex roles			
	feminine				

[a]Characteristics that 60% or more of respondents viewed themselves as possessing *pretty much* (4) or *a lot* (5) on a 5-point Likert-type scale. Characteristics are listed in descending order; respondents viewed themselves as possessing the first characteristic more than the last.

[b]Male respondents viewed 60% or more of Asian American women as possessing the listed characteristics. Characteristics are listed in descending order; respondents viewed Asian American women as possessing the first characteristic more than the last.

the self-representations held by Asian American women. White men had a distinctive view of Asian American women. Unlike Asian American men, White men viewed the majority of Asian American women as intro-verted/quiet and obedient and observing traditional sex roles. The view of the White men contrasted sharply with the self-representations of Asian American women. Asian American women saw themselves as being in-dependent (all four groups) and having equal sex roles (three groups); none of the women's groups saw themselves as introverted/quiet and obedient and observing traditional sex roles.

Images of Asian American and White Men

The characteristics that Asian American women imputed to Asian American men differed little by the women's relationship type (see Table 10.3). The only notable differences were that those dating White men exclusively viewed Asian American men as quiet, whereas those dating African American or Latino American men viewed Asian American men as independent and considerate. Racialized dating patterns also had little effect on how Asian American women viewed White men. The only no-table differences were that Asian women dating Asian American men ex-clusively saw most White men as sharing their feelings, whereas those dat-ing African American or Latino American men viewed most White men as having high-status occupation potential and high income potential and as being physically affectionate and considerate.

Regardless of relationship type, Asian American women imputed strikingly different characteristics to Asian American and White men. Across all four relationship types, Asian American women viewed the ma-jority of Asian American men as having high socioeconomic status (college graduate potential, high income potential, high-status occupation poten-tial, and ambitious) as well as being polite and reliable and observing tra-ditional sex roles. In contrast, these women attributed to the majority of White men the characteristics of independent, outgoing/sociable, easygo-ing, masculine, ambitious, and having a good sense of humor. In fact, the only characteristics consistently imputed to the majority of Asian Ameri-can men and the majority of White men were ambitious, dominant, and college graduate potential.

Characteristics Desired in Romantic Partners

Asian American women differed in the characteristics they valued in romantic partners by relationship type. Although a number of character-istics were shared by all four groups (reliable, sensitive to my feelings, considerate, polite, shares feelings, good sense of humor, college graduate potential, and romantic), Table 10.4 shows that the qualities desired by Asian American women dating White men exclusively differed substan-

196   *DIANE C. FUJINO*

TABLE 10.3

Characteristics Asian American Women Imputed to Asian American and White Men by Relationship Type

Characteristics imputed to Asian American men

By those dating Asian American men only	By those dating Asian American and White men	By those dating White men only	By those dating African American or Latino American men
college graduate potential ambitious high income potential traditional sex roles high-status occupation potential polite dominant reliable	college graduate potential high income potential ambitious traditional sex roles reliable high-status occupation potential polite dominant nurturing	college graduate potential polite ambitious reliable traditional sex roles high income potential high-status occupation potential introverted/quiet nurturing	college graduate potential ambitious high income potential high-status occupation potential polite reliable traditional sex roles independent considerate nurturing dominant

Characteristics imputed to White men

By those dating Asian American men only	By those dating Asian American and White men	By those dating White men only	By those dating African American or Latino American men
independent outgoing/sociable easygoing shares feelings strong personality romantic masculine ambitious good sense of humor dominant	outgoing/sociable independent easygoing masculine good sense of humor ambitious college graduate potential dominant strong personality romantic	outgoing/sociable independent ambitious easygoing romantic good sense of humor college graduate potential masculine	outgoing/sociable independent ambitious dominant easygoing masculine high-status occupation potential high income potential college graduate potential good sense of humor strong personality physically affectionate considerate

Note. These are the characteristics Asian American women respondents viewed 60% or more of each men's group to possess. Characteristics are listed in descending order; respondents viewed more men to possess the first characteristic than the last.

TABLE 10.4
Characteristics Asian American Women Value in Romantic Partners by Relationship Type

	Valued characteristics		
Date Asian American men only	Date Asian American and White men	Date White men only	Date African American or Latino American men
reliable	sensitive to my feelings	reliable	reliable
sensitive to my feelings	reliable	considerate	good sense of humor
considerate	good sense of humor	sensitive to my feelings	sensitive to my feelings
polite	considerate	shares feelings	considerate
shares feelings	shares feelings	good sense of humor	polite
good sense of humor	polite	romantic	ambitious
college graduate potential	romantic	polite	shares feelings
independent	ambitious	outgoing/sociable	independent
romantic	college graduate potential	easygoing	romantic
	physically affectionate	domestic	outgoing/sociable
	outgoing/sociable	masculine	college graduate potential
	easygoing	sexually exciting	physically affectionate
		college graduate potential	
		independent	

Note. Asian American women rated each of these characteristics, on average, *moderately desirable* (6) or *desirable* (7) on a 7-point Likert-type scale.

tially from the other three groups. This group is the only one for whom having a partner who is masculine, sexually exciting, and willing to do domestic tasks are important.

Acculturation and Propinquity and Attractiveness, Power, and Caring

The study next examined whether acculturation, propinquity, and other factors would differ by relationship type. As shown in Table 10.5, no differences in age, parental occupation, or parental education were found by relationship type, suggesting that socioeconomic status has little effect on racialized dating choices. However, acculturation does have an effect. The majority of Asian American women who date Asian American men exclusively were immigrants, whereas most of the women involved in the other relationship types were born in the United States. Also, Asian American women dating Asian American men exclusively held the most conservative views toward women's rights and roles. As expected, the racial composition of hometown and high school communities was positively related to the ethnicity of partners: Those Asian American women dating Asian American men exclusively had the highest proportion of Asians in their hometown or high school community; those dating White men exclusively or both Asian American and White men had a significantly higher proportion of White people in their communities compared with the only group of women who did not date White men, that is, those dating Asian American men exclusively; and those dating African American or Latino American men had the highest proportion of African Americans or Latino Americans in their hometown or high school communities. Also noteworthy is that Asian American women who date both Asian American and White men and those who date African American or Latino American men do not date Asian American men less. In addition to dating Asian American men at rates similar to those women who date Asian American men exclusively, these Asian American women also date non-Asian men.

Clustering the 30 characteristics by underlying factors (Attractiveness, Power, and Caring) provides an alternate way of examining differences in relationship types in terms of Asian American women's self-representations, images of Asian American and White men, and characteristics desired in partners (see Table 10.5). First, with respect to their self-representations, Asian American women dating Asian American men exclusively reported viewing themselves as less attractive than those dating White men exclusively or dating both Asian American and White men. The former group also saw themselves as less powerful than those women dating African American or Latino American men. No differences were found in terms of caring. Second, Asian American women did not differ by relationship type in their images of Asian American or White

TABLE 10.5
Information About Female Study Participants by Relationship Type

	Relationship type			
	Date Asian men only	Date Asian American and White men	Date White men only	Date African American or Latino American men
Age	20.1_a	19.9_a	19.7_a	19.7_a
Parental occupation	76.3_a	74.7_a	89.9_a	78.4_a
Parental education	5.8_a	6.1_a	6.5_a	6.1_a
Immigration status	58.8_a	31.7_b	$33.3_{a,b}$	28.6_b
Propinquity				
% Asian	44.7_a	31.2_b	24.3_b	28.5_b
% White	34.7_b	52.3_a	55.2_a	$38.6_{a,b}$
% African or Latino	19.1_b	14.7_b	$18.2_{a,b}$	30.2_a
Attitudes Toward Women Scale score	54.1_b	59.9_a	60.6_a	61.8_a
Total number of partners[1]	2.3_b	5.6_a	3.3_b	5.9_a
Chinese American partners	1.2	1.5	0	0.9
Japanese American partners	0.7	0.9	0	1.0
Other Asian American partners	0.3	0.7	0	1.0
White partners	0	2.4	3.0	1.5
African American partners	0	0	0	0.3
Latino American partners	0	0	0	1.0
Self-representations				
Attractiveness	3.2_b	3.6_a	3.6_a	$3.5_{a,b}$
Power	3.2_b	$3.4_{a,b}$	$3.4_{a,b}$	3.5_a
Caring	3.8_a	3.8_a	3.7_a	3.8_a
Images of Asian American men				
Attractiveness	40.0_a	35.1_a	32.4_a	40.8_a
Power	67.2_a	67.3_a	65.2_a	69.1_a
Caring	55.1_a	54.9_a	58.1_a	56.9_a
Images of White men				
Attractiveness	58.0_a	57.1_a	56.4_a	56.7_a
Power	64.1_a	63.9_a	64.7_a	66.5_a
Caring	46.1_a	45.8_a	49.2_a	47.9_a
Valued attributes				
Attractiveness	5.4_b	5.8_a	5.8_a	5.8_a
Power	5.6_a	5.7_a	5.7_a	5.5_a
Caring	5.9_a	5.7_a	5.7_a	5.7_a

Note. Subscripts refer to significance levels for pairwise comparisons between the four relationship type groups. The same letter indicates nonsignificant difference; different letter indicates significant difference. Tukey honestly significant difference procedure for pairwise comparison, $p < .05$, was used to reduce the possibility of Type I errors. Comparisons were not made for the number of partners from specific ethnic groups because these figures are largely a function of how each relationship type group is defined; that is, by definition, those dating Asian American men only have not dated White, African American, or Latino American men.
[1]Participants decided whether their partners fit into one of the above six categories; if not, they were given the option of selecting "other." The total number of partners includes men from the "other" category.

men as attractive, powerful, and caring. However, Asian American women's images of Asian American men differed considerably from their images of White men. Within each relationship type, Asian American women viewed Asian American men as substantially less attractive and somewhat more caring than White men. Asian American and White men were viewed as equally powerful. Third, there were differences in how much attractiveness was valued in partners by relationship type: Those women dating Asian American men exclusively valued attractiveness significantly less than did the other three groups. Across relationship types, Asian American women valued partners' power and caring equally.

Model Predicting Racialized Dating Choices

Simultaneous multiple regression analyses were performed to determine which variables predict various relationship types after controlling for the effects of other factors (see Table 10.6). Because the numbers in

TABLE 10.6
Standardized Beta Weights for Variables Predicting Dating by
Type of Relationship

	Type of relationship	
Variable	Rate of dating Asian American men	Rate of dating White men
Immigration status[a]	.02	−.03
Propinquity		
% Asian	1.33*	−.48
% White	1.10	−.17
% African or Latino	.79	−.22
Liberal attitude toward women	−.01	.02
Total number of partners	.03	−.05
Self-representations		
Attractiveness	−.05	.10
Power	−.11	.07
Caring	−.02	.08
Images of Asian American men		
Attractiveness	.34**	−.46***
Power	−.08	.03
Caring	−.16	.17
Images of White men		
Attractiveness	−.12	.13
Power	.12	−.09
Caring	−.12	.18
Valued attributes		
Attractiveness	−.23*	.14
Power	.17	−.15
Caring	.28**	−.19*

[a]Baseline = U.S. born.
*$p < .05$. **$p < .01$. ***$p < .001$.

each of the four relationship types were too small to be useful in a regression analysis, models that predict dating Asian American men and, separately, dating White men were developed. The first regression model in Table 10.6 shows that the following variables predicted the rate of Asian American women's dating Asian American men: being raised in a community with a higher percentage of Asians, viewing Asian American men as more attractive, placing less value on the attractiveness of one's partner, and valuing caring qualities in one's partner. In contrast, the second regression model in Table 10.6 shows that viewing Asian American men as less attractive and placing a lower value on caring qualities of one's partner predicted the rate of Asian American women's dating White men.

DISCUSSION

Patterns of Intraracial and Interracial Dating

It is important to recognize that Asian American women most often date within their race, and most frequently coethnics (Fujino, 1997; Kitano et al., 1998; Lee & Yamanaka, 1990; Shinagawa & Pang, 1996). In the study discussed in this chapter, the vast majority of Asian American women have dated at least one Asian American man, including 93.4% of immigrant Japanese Americans, 88.1% of immigrant Chinese Americans, 80.8% of U.S.-born Japanese Americans, and 76.5% of U.S.-born Chinese Americans. As with marriage, intraracial dating continues to occur most frequently even though U.S. policies no longer prevent interracial relationships and partners from other ethnic groups are numerically more available than Asian American men. Certain structural influences affect Asian American women's racialized dating choices. For example, those living in predominantly Asian communities are more likely to date Asian American men. Simultaneously, Asian American women frequently choose to date Asian American men based on their own personal preferences and desires.

However, interracial relationships are also on the increase, and Asian American women are dating non-Asian men, particularly White men, at relatively high rates. In the study discussed in this chapter, the majority of U.S.-born Asian American women have dated at least one White boyfriend (76.6% of Japanese American women and 61.7% of Chinese American), and about 40% of immigrant Chinese American and Japanese American women had had at least one White boyfriend. In contrast, it was less common for Asian American women to have ever had a Latino American boyfriend (20.3% of Japanese American women and 10.6% of Chinese American), and an African American boyfriend was even rarer (7.2% of Japanese American women and 2.1% of Chinese American women). As noted earlier, Asian American women who date interracially do not date fewer Asian American men. In fact, these women date Asian American men at a rate similar to those women dating Asian American men exclusively. The former group simply has had more boyfriends.

Model of Factors Influencing Racialized Dating Choices

Most people in the Unites States discuss their dating choices in terms of individual preferences and fail to recognize the effect of structural influences. This is not surprising, given that U.S. society is guided by the ideology of individualism and freedom of choice. The effects of the media and other social institutions often remain invisible in people's everyday lives. However, structural influences (controlling images, acculturation, and propinquity), in addition to individual influences (self-representations, images of Asian American and White men, and characteristics desired in partners), affect Asian American women's selection of racialized dating partners (see Figure 10.1). Structural influences affect dating in both direct and indirect ways through their effects on individual influences. The findings of the study discussed in this chapter provided partial support for this proposed model.

Controlling Images

The results of this study indicated that controlling images have come to determine how men view Asian American women. As shown in Table 10.2, White men hold the most stereotypic images of the Asian American woman as the quiet, submissive, other-focused lotus blossom (Espiritu, 1996; Soe, 1992; Tajima, 1989). Only White men impute the characteristics of introverted/quiet, obedient, and traditional in sex roles to the majority of Asian American women. Asian American men also view Asian American women in somewhat stereotypic ways. In contrast, Asian American women's self-representations, which include being independent and equal in gender roles, differ sharply from the lotus blossom image.

Controlling images also can account for why Asian American women hold substantially different views of Asian American and White men (see Table 10.3). White men were viewed by study participants as being independent, outgoing/sociable, easygoing, masculine, ambitious, having a good sense of humor and strong personality, romantic, dominant, and having college-graduate potential. In contrast, Asian men were seen as having high socioeconomic status (college graduate potential, high income potential, high-status occupation potential) and as being polite, reliable, traditional in sex roles, dominant, and nurturing. These findings suggest that controlling images have influenced Asian American women's views of Asian American men. In juxtaposition to the previous representations of Asian men as hypermasculine "Yellow Peril" threats to U.S. national security and sexual threats to White women, images of Asian American men have now been transformed into asexual, passive, "model minorities" since the 1960s (Chua & Fujino, 1999; Espiritu, 1996).

In what ways do these controlling images affect the formation of racialized dating relationships? Overall, I was surprised to not find a strong relationship between Asian American women's images of Asian American and White men and their racialized dating choices (see Table 10.3). I had anticipated that Asian American women who dated Asian American men would hold more positive, less stereotypic images of Asian American men compared with women who dated only non-Asian men. But this study's findings suggest that the images of men exerted only a moderate effect on women's racialized dating choices even though Asian American women's views of Asian American men and White men diverged sharply. Nonetheless, there are two important findings. First, images of Asian American men approximate patriarchal patterns of masculine heterosexual roles (through economic power and male authority), whereas images of White men approximate U.S. standards for masculine roles (through masculinity, dominance, and romance). Thus, one would suspect that the gender role identity of women would predict their racialized dating choices. The results of this study indicate that Asian American women who date Asian American men exclusively did have the most conservative attitudes toward women's rights (see Table 10.5), but these effects were eliminated after controlling for other variables (see Table 10.6). Second, as expected, the more Asian American women viewed Asian American men as attractive, the more likely they were to date Asian American men. Conversely, the less Asian American women viewed Asian American men as attractive, the more likely they were to date White men (see Table 10.6). Note that Asian American women's views of White men's attractiveness did not predict their dating choices. It is possible that as the racialized other, media images of Asian American men are more salient and exert a greater effect on dating choices than do images of mainstream White American men.

Propinquity

Propinquity was found to directly affect dating choices. Those Asian American women dating Asian American men exclusively had the highest proportion of Asian Americans in their hometown and high school communities. Those dating White men exclusively or both Asian American and White men had a significantly higher proportion of White Americans in their community compared with the only group that did not date White men, that is, those dating Asian American men exclusively. Those dating African American or Latino American men had the highest proportion of African Americans or Latino Americans in their communities (see Table

10.5). After controlling for the effects of other variables, propinquity continued to predict dating (see Table 10.6).

Propinquity appears to indirectly affect dating choices through its impact on individual influences. The racial composition of their communities affects the characteristics that Asian American women value in their partners. Those growing up around more Asian Americans tend to place less value on attractiveness ($r = -.24$, $p < .01$) and caring ($r = -.16$, $p < .05$), whereas those growing up around more White Americans tend to place more value on these two qualities. In other words, what individuals desire in romantic partners is not merely reflective of personal choices; the cultural environment in which individuals are socialized also shapes their values.

Acculturation

Although the intermarriage literature consistently shows that acculturation is related to the presence of interracial unions, the study discussed in this chapter found that acculturation exhibited mixed direct effects on interracial dating. As shown in Tables 10.1 and 10.5, immigrant Asian American women participated in less interracial dating than those born in the United States. But, after controlling for the effects of other variables, immigration status did not significantly predict Asian American women's racialized dating choices (see Table 10.6). This contrasts sharply with the marriage literature, which has consistently found immigration or generational status to be related to outmarriage. It is possible that methodological differences between this study and marriage studies contributed to the discrepancy in findings. The intermarriage studies examined differences in immigration status in outmarriage rates, which include interethnic (e.g., Chinese–Japanese) and interracial (e.g., Chinese–White) unions. This study only assessed differences in interracial rates. In addition, the smaller sample size ($N = 163$) compared with the studies on intermarriage (e.g., Kitano et al., 1998, had a sample of 6,281 participants) may explain the lack of statistically significant differences by immigration status found in rates of interracial dating.

Despite the mixed findings on the effects of acculturation, Table 10.1 shows that on college campuses in large, multiracial metropolitan areas, substantial numbers of Asian American immigrant women (45% of Chinese American women and 53% of Japanese American women) are participating in interracial dating. The experience of living away from the demand for intraethnic relationships imposed by parents or the ethnic community may enable college students to explore dating partners from various ethnic backgrounds. Perhaps being socialized in American society, for example, through controlling images and hometown friends, for at least a few years has an impact on whom one chooses to date. Finally, it is possible that Asian American immigrant college students date people from other ethnic backgrounds but then tend to marry coethnics (Fujino, 1997). Whatever the reasons, it does appear that immigration status has an impact on interracial dating, but to a lesser degree than it does on outmarriage.

In addition, acculturation exhibited indirect effects on racialized dating choices. Specifically, the more acculturated an Asian American woman was, the more she valued attractiveness ($r = .16$, $p < .05$) and the less she valued power ($r = -.19$, $p < .05$) in dating partners. Thus, the characteristics desired in dating partners appear to be shaped by acculturation as well as by propinquity.

Individual Influences

The model proposes that individual influences (self-representations, images of Asian American and White men, and characteristics desired in partners) directly affect dating choices. Asian American women's self-representations had a moderate effect on racialized dating choices. Asian American women who dated Asian American men exclusively tended to see themselves as less attractive and less powerful compared with other groups (see Table 10.5), but these effects did not hold after controlling for the effects of other factors (see Table 10.6). It is important to note that self-perceptions are not necessarily reflective of objective reality; in other words, to assume that those dating intraracially are less attractive would be erroneous. It is also a mistake to assume that lower self-ratings are indicative of lower self-esteem. Rather, it is plausible that these women are more self-effacing or they rate themselves lower on attractiveness because they place less value on attractiveness. Also, there is only a small difference in magnitude in self-representation ratings among the four groups of women (see Table 10.5).

The regression model found that Asian American women's images of Asian American men as well as characteristics valued in partners affected dating choices (see Table 10.6). Viewing Asian American men as more attractive predicted dating Asian American men, as did placing less value on attractiveness in partners and more on caring. In contrast, viewing Asian American men as less attractive and placing less value on caring in partners predicted dating White men. However, note that it is the match between attributes valued in partners and Asian American women's views of Asian American and White men that most strongly influenced racialized dating choices. For example, Asian American women exclusively dating Asian men value characteristics in partners (reliable, polite, college graduate potential) that match their images of Asian American men (see Tables 10.3 and 10.4). Those Asian American women exclusively dating White men value characteristics (romantic, outgoing/sociable, easygoing, masculine) that match their images of White men.

CONCLUSION

The study described in this chaper showed the extent to which Asian American women participate in dating relationships with men of various racial backgrounds. Despite the popular attention given to interracial dating, Asian American women most often date Asian American men. But the attention is also justified. In increasing numbers over the past few decades, especially since the 1970s, young Chinese American and Japanese American women have ventured into interracial dating, particularly with White men, but also with Latino American men, although far less often with African American men. The study indicated that dating, whether in inter- or intraracial relationships, is not simply a matter of personal choices. Certainly, individual tastes and preferences play a role in the selection of a romantic partner. However, to stop here would be myopic. Structural influences also affect dating choices. This is particularly true of choices about race because U.S. society, in all its social institutions, operates in a highly racialized fashion. Controlling images of Asian American women and men, who are often characterized as the ultrafeminized other and sometimes as the hypermasculinized threat, influence Asian American women's self-representations and their views of Asian American and White men. The racial composition of one's neighborhood also matters, both in terms of with whom one is accustomed to interacting and, more important, the values one brings to a relationship. Let us be aware of the ways in which race and gender operate within a highly race- and gender-stratified society like the U.S. to influence the most intimate areas of our lives.

REFERENCES

1945 War Brides Act, 79 P.L. 271; 79 Cong. Ch. 591; 59 Stat 659. (8 U.S.C. §§232–236—Act Dec. 28, 1945, Ch. 591, §§ 1–5, 59 Stat. 659 is omitted from the United States Code as having expired three years after Dec. 28, 1945).

1952 McCarran-Walter Act, 82 P.L. 414; 82 Cong. Ch. 477; 66 Stat. 163.

Barnett, L. D. (1963). Interracial marriage in California. *Marriage and Family Living, 25,* 424–427.

Beere, C. A. (1990). *Gender roles: A handbook of tests and measures.* New York: Greenwood Press.

Blau, P. M. (1977). *Inequality and heterogeneity.* New York: Free Press.

Blau, P. M., Blum, T. C., & Schwartz, J. E. (1982). Heterogeneity and intermarriage. *American Sociological Review, 47,* 45–62.

Bonacich, E. (1984). Asian labor in the development of California and Hawaii. In L. Cheng & E. Bonacich (Eds.), *Labor immigration under capitalism: Asian workers in the United States before World War II.* Berkeley: University of California Press.

Buss, D. M., & Barnes, M. (1986). Preferences in human mate selection. *Journal of Personality and Social Psychology, 50,* 559–570.

Chan, S. (1991a). *Asian Americans: An interpretive history.* Boston: Twayne Publishers.

Chan, S. (1991b). The exclusion of Chinese women. In S. Chan (Ed.), *Entry denied: Exclusion and the Chinese community in America, 1882–1943.* Philadelphia: Temple University Press.

Chin, S.-Y. (1997). *Gazing through APA femininity to American masculinities.* Paper presented at Crosstalk: Asian and Pacific American Sensuality and Sexuality Conference, Northridge, CA.

Chua, P., & Fujino, D. C. (1999). Negotiating new Asian American masculinities: Attitudes and gender expectations. *Journal of Men's Studies, 7,* 391–413.

Collins, P. H. (1990). *Black feminist thought: Knowledge, consciousness, and the politics of empowerment.* New York: Routledge.

Espiritu, Y. L. (1996). *Asian American women and men.* Newbury Park, CA: Sage.

Festinger, L., Schachter, S., & Back, K. (1950). *Social pressures in informal groups: A study of a housing community.* New York: Harper & Row.

Fujino, D. C. (1992). *Extending exchange theory: Effects of ethnicity and gender on Asian American heterosexual relationships.* Unpublished doctoral dissertation, University of California, Los Angeles.

Fujino, D. C. (1997). The rates, patterns, and reasons for forming heterosexual interracial dating relationships among Asian Americans. *Journal of Social and Personal Relationships, 14*(6), 809–828.

Fugita, S., & O'Brien, D. (1991). *Japanese American ethnicity: The persistence of community.* Seattle: University of Washington Press.

Glodava, M., & Onizuka, R. (1994). *Mail-order brides: Women for sale.* Collins, CO: Alaken.

Ichioka, Y. (1988). *The Issei: The world of the first generation Japanese immigrants, 1884–1924.* New York: Free Press.

Immigration and Nationality Act of 1965, P.L. 89–236, §§ 8, 24, 79 Stat. 916, 922.

Jensen, J. M. (1988). *Passage from India: Asian Indian immigrants in North America.* New Haven, CT: Yale University Press.

Jhally, S. (1989). The political economy of culture. In I. Angus & S. Jhally (Eds.), *Cultural politics in contemporary America.* New York: Routledge.

Johnson, R. C., & Ogasawara, G. M. (1988). Within- and across-group dating in Hawaii. *Social Biology, 35,* 103–109.

Kitano, H. H. L., Fujino, D. C., & Takahashi, J. S. (1998). Interracial marriage: Where are the Asian Americans and where are they going? In L. Lee & N. Zane (Eds.), *Handbook of Asian American psychology* (pp. 233–260). Newbury Park, CA: Sage.

Lee, S. M., & Yamanaka, K. (1990). Patterns of Asian American intermarriage and marital assimilation. *Journal of Comparative Family Studies, 21,* 287–305.

Miller, D. C. (1991). *Handbook of research design and social measurement* (5th ed.). Newbury Park, CA: Sage.

Okihiro, G. Y. (1994). *Margins and mainstreams: Asians in American history and culture.* Seattle: University of Washington Press.

Omi, M., & Winant, H. (1994). *Racial formation in the United States: From the 1960s to the 1980s.* New York: Routledge.

Panunzio, C. (1942). Intermarriage in Los Angeles, 1924–33. *American Journal of Sociology, 47,* 690–701.

Saegert, S. C., Swap, W., & Zajonc, R. B. (1973). Exposure, context, and interpersonal attraction. *Journal of Personality and Social Psychology, 25,* 234–242.

Sharma, M. (1984). Labor migration and class formation among the Filipinos in Hawaii, 1906–1946. In L. Cheng & E. Bonacich (Eds.), *Labor immigration under capitalism: Asian workers in the United States before World War II.* Berkeley: University of California Press.

Shinagawa, L. H., & Pang, G. Y. (1988). Intraethnic, interethnic, and interracial marriages among Asian Americans in California, 1980. *Berkeley Journal of Sociology, 33,* 95–114.

Shinagawa, L. H., & Pang, G. Y. (1996). Asian American panethnicity and intermarriage. *Amerasia Journal, 22,* 127–152.

Smedley, A. (1993). *Race in North America: Origin and evolution of a worldview.* Boulder, CO: Westview Press.

Soe, V., Director (1992). *Picturing Oriental Girls* [Video tape]. San Francisco, CA: Distributed by National Asian American Telecommunications Association.

Spence, J. T., Helmreich, R. L., & Stapp, J. (1973). A short version of the Attitude Toward Women Scale (AWS). *Bulletin of the Psychonomic Society, 2,* 219–220.

Spickard, P. (1989). *Mixed blood: Intermarriage and ethnic identity in twentieth-century America.* Madison: University of Wisconsin Press.

Spickard, P. (1992). Illogic of American race categories. In M. Root (Ed.), *Racially mixed people in America.* Newbury Park, CA: Sage.

Sung, B. L. (1990). *Chinese American intermarriage.* New York: Center for Migration Studies.

Tajima, R. E. (1989). Lotus blossoms don't bleed: Images of Asian women. In Asian Women United of California (Ed.), *Making waves: An anthology of writings by and about Asian American women.* Boston: Beacon Press.

Takaki, R. (1989). *Strangers from a different shore: A history of Asian Americans.* Boston: Little, Brown.

Villapando, V. (1989). The business of selling mail-order brides. In Asian Women United of California (Ed.), *Making waves: An anthology of writings by and about Asian American women.* Boston: Beacon Press.

Wiggins, J. S. (1979). A psychological taxonomy of trait-descriptive terms: The interpersonal domain. *Journal of Personality and Social Psychology, 37,* 395–412.

11

INTERPERSONAL RELATIONSHIPS: INDEPENDENCE VERSUS INTERDEPENDENCE

S. CATHY LOUIE

In recent years, the population of Asian and Pacific Islander Americans has increased dramatically. More than 2.3 million Asian and Pacific Islander immigrants and refugees arrived in the United States between 1981 and 1988 (U.S. Bureau of Census, 1990). In 1995, the Asian and Pacific Islander population in the United States reached 10 million, and it is estimated that this figure will reach 17 million by 2010 (U.S. Bureau of Census, 1995). Asian women, particularly Chinese women, increased most rapidly in numbers after 1965 when U.S. immigration policies were revised to favor family reunification. In fact, Chinese women of various ethnic backgrounds constitute more than half of the current number of Chinese immigrants in the United States. It is evident that when addressing issues regarding Asian American women the effect of acculturation on these more recent immigrants should be considered.

As an ethnic minority becomes increasingly exposed to the values and standards of the dominant host culture, there is progressive inculcation of these norms. Although there is nothing inherently wrong with acculturation and assimilation, Jones and Nisbett (1972) argued that when it is forced by a powerful group on a less powerful one, it imposes a restriction of choice; hence, the processes of acculturation and assimilation are no longer subject to the values of natural order. In other words, the adoption of the values of the dominant group may not serve the well-being of the individual. Furthermore, it is believed that, for ethnic minority immigrants, being rooted in one's own cultural values enhances the process of adaptation.

SENSE OF SELF: INDEPENDENT VERSUS INTERDEPENDENT

One major cultural difference that most Asians in the United States experience is the tension between collectivism, a central theme for many Asian cultures, and individualism, a central theme for Western European and North American cultures (Cocking & Greenfield, 1994; Fieldman & Rosenthal, 1990; Rhee, Uleman, Lee, & Roman, 1995; Tata & Leong, 1994; Triandis, 1996). This cultural difference has been linked to individual differences in how one construes the self, that is, self-construals (Markus & Kitayama, 1991; Singelis, 1994). *Self-construals*, in this context, refer to an individual's sense of self in terms of beliefs about the relationship between oneself and others, especially the degree to which one sees oneself as separate from or connected with others. A sense of oneself as being separate from others is referred to as *independent*, whereas a sense of oneself as being connected to others is referred to as *interdependent*.

Individualistic and collectivistic cultures stress and value independence and interdependence differently. An increasing amount of empirical research has demonstrated that people in different cultures have strikingly different concepts of the self. In the individualistic culture of North America, for example, the self is defined primarily by one's internal attributes that are believed to be invariant over time and context (Markus & Kitayama, 1991; J. G. Miller, 1988; Newman, 1993). Geertz (1974/1984) summarized this image of the independent self as "a bounded, unique, more or less integrated motivational and cognitive universe" (p. 48). In other words, the self is a dynamic center of awareness of one's emotions, judgments, actions, and motivations that are organized into a distinctive whole and set in contrast both against other such wholes and against its social and natural backgrounds. The behavior of such an independent self is oriented and made meaningful primarily by reference to one's own thoughts, feelings, actions, and goals rather than by reference to those of others. This view of the self is referred to as the *independent self-construal* (Markus & Kitayama, 1991). In contrast, many collectivist cultures, such as Asian cultures, stress the fundamental connectedness of human beings to each other and to the environment (De Vos, 1985; Hofstede, 1980; Hsu, 1985; Markus & Kitayama, 1991; J. G. Miller, 1988; Schweder & Bourne, 1984).

One sees oneself as a part of an encompassing social relationship and one's behavior as being determined, contingent on, and, to a large extent, organized by what one perceives to be the thoughts, feelings, actions, and goals of others. Hsu (1985) summarized this sense of self as arising from consensual validation between the self and others. This view of the self is referred to as the *interdependent self-construal* (Markus & Kitayama, 1991).

The most significant difference between the independent and interdependent self-construals is in the role that is assigned to the other in self-definition. Others and the surrounding social context are important in both construals. However, for the interdependent self-construal, others are partially included within the boundaries of the self because relations with others are the defining features of the self. For the independent self-construal, others are less integrated into one's self-identity; others are important for social comparison, for reflective appraisal, and for their role as the target of one's actions, yet at any given moment, the self is assumed to be a complete whole, an autonomous entity, that is separate from others.

This distinction in the view of the self as independent versus interdependent has been graphically depicted by Markus and Kitayama (1991). In Figure 11.1, the self is represented by the large oval. The circles around the oval represent other significant people in one's life, such as mother, father, siblings, friends, and coworkers. The Xs in the oval and the circles represent attributes of the individual that influence the thoughts, feelings, actions, and motivations of the self. In Figure 11.1A, all the circles representing others are outside the boundary of the oval, emphasizing the distinctness of the self—a motivational, emotional, and cognitive universe on its own—the independent self-construal. In Figure 11.1B, the self is represented by an oval formed by a dotted line, and others are represented by the circles along the boundary that overlap with portions of the oval. The Xs are personal attributes as described for Figure 11.1A. This representation conveys the idea that a person is in part defined by social relationships. The dotted line of the oval boundary illustrates the fluid nature of the individual, with some of its attributes (represented by the Xs in the overlapping areas) realized through consensual validating processes between the self and others, that is, the interdependent self-construal.

THE DUAL SELF

Triandis (1989), in his study of the Self and social behavior in differing cultural contexts, conceptualized the self as a mediating variable between culture and individual behavior. He identified three aspects of the self: (a) the private self-cognitions of innate traits and feeling states, (b) the public self-cognitions of the generalized other's view and feelings toward the self, and (c) the collective self-cognitions of one's role and re-

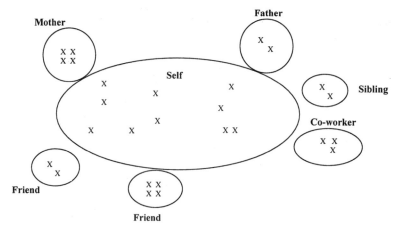

A. Independent View of Self

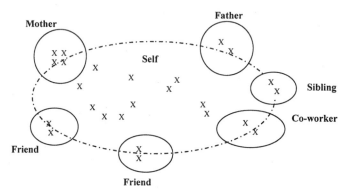

B. Interdependent View of Self

Figure 11.1. Conceptual representations of independent and interdependent self-construals. From "Culture and the Self: Implications for cognition, emotion, and motivation," by H. Markus and S. Kitayama, 1991, *Psychological Review, 98*, pp. 224–253. Copyright 1991 by the American Psychological Association. Reprinted with permission of the author.

sponsibility in the collective group. The tendency for an individual to act primarily based on the private self is associated with the independent self-construal; the tendency for an individual to act primarily based on the public and the collective self is associated with the interdependent self-construal. The premise is that these tendencies are developed as a function of cultural norms and individual differences.

The concept of a dual self is that both the independent and interdependent dimensions of the self tend to coexist in each person. Each dimension may be developed to differing degrees depending on the individual's cultural and personal experiences. Graphically, the dual self may be represented by a modified version of Markus and Kitayama's interde-

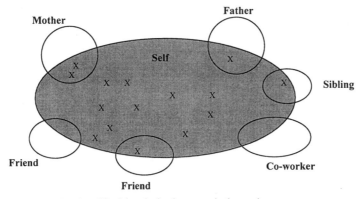

A. A self with relatively more independence

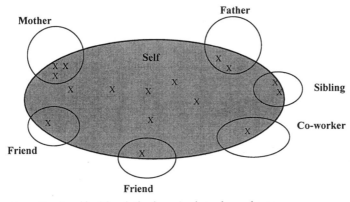

B. A self with relatively more interdependence

Figure 11.2. Independence and interdependence from the perspective of the dual-self paradigm.

pendence model (Figure 11.1B), with the dotted boundary line of the oval replaced by a solid line. This modification denotes the self as having a firm rather than fluid boundary. With this depiction (Figure 11.2), the independent dimension of the self corresponds to the nonoverlapping areas of the oval, whereas the interdependent dimension of the self corresponds to the areas of the oval that overlap with the circles representing other selves. The attributes that define the self are represented by Xs. These self-attributes are either realized through a process of autonomous self-actualization (the Xs in the nonoverlapping areas) or through a process of mutual validation (the Xs in the overlapping areas). Thus, for a person with more developed independence, the Xs are more densely scattered in the nonoverlapping areas relative to the overlapping areas (Figure 11.2A) and vice versa for a person with more developed interdependence (Figure 11.2B). This conceptualization views the two dimensions as neither dichotomous nor mutually exclusive. Rather, it views the two dimensions as having the potential for development given the proper environmental support. In general, Asian cultures foster the development of interdependence, whereas Western cultures foster the development of independence.

The implication of the dual self is that development of one's sense of self is an evolving process. This implication is particularly relevant for recent Asian American immigrants who face drastic cultural, social, and personal changes. Research on self-construals and empathy in Asian Americans (Louie, 1997) showed that the concept of a dual self is more adequate in understanding the human experiences in a multicultural context than a unidimensional approach. With a sample of 118 participants in an urban university (70 White American students and 48 recent Asian American immigrant students), I found evidence supporting the notion of a dual self. On the basis of self-report, all participants appeared to possess both independent and interdependent dimensions of the self, with each dimension developed to a different degree. As a group, the Asian American students had a more developed interdependent dimension compared with their White counterparts, whereas the level of independence was equivalent between the two groups.

THE RELATIONAL SELF: A FEMINIST PERSPECTIVE

In the feminist literature, a woman's identity often is defined in the context of relationships. Both J. B. Miller (1986) and Gilligan (1982) have addressed women's sense of self as being very much organized around the ability to make and maintain affiliations and relationships. The threat of losing an affiliation may be experienced as a loss of self. How does this feminist view of self differ from the culturally defined interdependent self? The distinction may be understood in the context of the difference between a collective versus a relational orientation of interdependence. A collective orientation places emphasis on one's place in the collective and the associated responsibility and care; a relational orientation places emphasis on one's emotional experience in the process of making connections with others. Kashima et al. (1995) conducted a study to test this distinction. They found that the collective orientation was clearly related to culture in that Asians, regardless of gender, were more collective than European Americans, whereas relational orientation was more related to gender in that women, regardless of cultural background, were more relational than men. My own study on self-construals and empathy in Asian Americans (Louie, 1997) showed that although there was no difference in interdependence between the men and women in the Asian group, Asian women had a lower tendency, relative to their male counterparts, to endorse attributes characterizing the independent self. Furthermore, the Asian American women in the study were the only ones among the four ethnicity-by-gender groups in the study (i.e., Asian women, Asian men, White women, and White men) to display a group profile with relatively more developed interdependence than independence. The other three groups produced group profiles of the opposite composition, with relatively more developed independence than interdependence. It appears that these Asian American women's sense of self is structurally different from others in the society. One interpretation of this phenomenon is that Asian American women's sense of self in terms of interdependence is both cultural (collective orientation) and feminist (relational orientation) in nature. Thus, compared with others, Asian American women's sense of self is relatively more firmly rooted in interdependence. The conceptualization of this unique self-structure may serve as a tool to understand the psychosocial aspects of certain common experiences of Asian American women. The experiences shared by Asian American women workers in the Chinatown garment industry, a significant socioeconomic platform from which many Asian immigrant women and their families have made the transition to adapt to the United States, are the focus of the following discussion.

THE CHINATOWN GARMENT INDUSTRY

In major U.S. cities such as New York, San Francisco, and Boston, Chinatown's garment industry flourished in the mid-1970s when there was a large influx of Chinese immigrant women and a decline in the manufacturing industry. This combination of available inexpensive female labor and a ready market made the Chinatown garment industry a significant economic anchor for the Chinese American community and the major employer for new Chinese immigrant women. Zhou (1992) provided a thorough and comprehensive treatment on this subject from a socioeconomic perspective in her 1992 book, *Chinatown: The Socioeconomic Potential of an Urban Enclave.* Zhou contended that because of the seasonal nature of the work, the low pay, and the segregated environment of Chinatown, these garment factory jobs were almost exclusively held by Asian immigrant women. In general an Asian immigrant women's family is always the priority; the family—the husband and the children—come first. In this respect, a woman's role is first of all that of mother and wife. The Chinatown garment industry, although low paying, tended to have more flexible working hours and demanded no English skills, thus allowing the Chinese immigrant woman to fulfill her primary responsibilities and to contribute financially to support the family or to push the family toward social mobility.

However, most of the time, her work outside of the home was still unappreciated and devalued. These women have traditionally been viewed as being exploited for cheap labor, not only because of the initial disadvantages associated with immigration but also because of deep-rooted male dominance in both Chinese Western cultures. Zhou (1992) pointed out that despite the women's crucial role in sustaining the family and the Chinatown community, they continue to be perceived as subordinate in the social system, and their economic contribution is considered secondary to that of the men. This misperception is perpetuated primarily through the women's positions being contained in the ethnic social networks that are built into the structure of social and cultural values. Even so, Zhou (1992) found that the women do not view themselves as victims of immigration stress and gender inequality. Rather, they accept their struggle to achieve the American dream. They set their priorities on status attainment for their families and are willing to sacrifice to achieve their family goal. In this respect, Zhou (1992) concluded that the Chinatown garment industry provided them with a viable economic path for adaptation.

From these socioeconomic perspectives, the experience of these Asian American women can be understood as sacrifice and exploitation for the good of the family and the community. Although this certainly appears true, one has to wonder which psychological processes are involved in such experiences. As mentioned earlier, these women do not consider themselves to be victims. To the contrary, it seems to indicate a sense of empowerment.

Through my clinical practice in a community health center in the heart of Boston's Chinatown, I came into contact with many Chinese American women from the local garment industry. Many of their stories supported this notion of empowerment. One woman's story is particularly rich and illustrative of the empowerment process, not just in the socioeconomic sense, but also in a personal and psychological sense. The following is an account of her story. To respect her privacy, her name and certain details have been changed.

LING: A STORY OF EMPOWERMENT

Ling was 23 years old in Hong Kong in the mid-1960s when she was introduced to her future husband, a first generation Chinese American. While in Hong Kong, she obtained a junior college education and worked at a clerical job in which she was not particularly interested. Being unmarried, she lived with her parents and four siblings and the extended family that spanned three generations. Because of her age, she was under pressure from her family as well as society to be married. She described herself as a girl who was dependent, timid, and obedient. She accepted her father's arrangement for her marriage to the young man from the United States and moved across the ocean to join his family in a segregated Chinese community in Boston. Soon after her arrival, she found herself closely monitored by her in-laws, who were concerned that she might run away while their son (her husband), an only child, was finishing college in the South. Her in-laws' concern was fairly common in the segregated Chinese community at the time, given that eligible young Chinese women were still scarce as a result of historically strict immigration laws. Consequently, Ling was prevented from learning English and establishing connections in the community. When her husband returned after finishing his college education, the young couple continued to reside with his parents, following the Chinese tradition. The parents were the heads of the household and controlled the family finances and general operations. Even though Ling was in the United States, she was subjected to treatment by her in-laws that was characteristic of the oppressive culture of the rural agricultural region of China from which the in-laws came years ago. Dependent and without a solid sense of self, Ling relied on her husband to rescue her. However, Ling's husband was constrained by his belief in the traditional Chinese doctrine of filial piety and harmony and was unable to support and protect her. Under these conditions, she gave birth to four children (three sons and one daughter) within 6 years while working in the family laundry business. She succumbed to her in-laws' control and relinquished her responsibility as mother to her three sons whom the grandparents demanded to care for themselves. Meanwhile, they (the grandparents) devalued Ling's daughter. Unable to fend off his parents' power, Ling's husband became increasingly detached emotionally from the family. It was not until the late 1970s, when the family laundry business folded, that Ling got the opportunity to work outside of the home in a Chinatown garment factory to help support the family.

In the factory, she related to the other women workers, many of whom had similar experiences. The existing workers taught her how to sew and she in turn helped newcomers. They covered for each other's mistakes, chipped in when one fell behind, and competed with one another for better performance and higher productivity. They took their meals together and commiserated with each other about their hardships. Deep empathy developed among them. They watched each other's younger children when they were sick or when school was out. Later, Ling, like many other women in the factory, brought her daughter in to work alongside her during after-school hours when she was a preadolescent. Ling once told me that it was better for her daughter to be treated in the factory as a capable girl who is helpful to her mother than being left at home to be treated by her grandmother as someone less valuable than her brothers. I can't help but think that Ling felt competent in the factory herself and wanted the same for her daughter. During the same period, Ling applied for her mother to immigrate from Hong Kong as she (Ling's mother) was having severe marital problems with Ling's father. Ling was able to convince her mother that she would be able to bring her into the factory to work a less-demanding job that she could handle. Ling arranged for her mother to join the sewing group as a thread cutter, a position traditionally held by older women, shortly after her arrival in the United States. In this collectivist environment, Ling enjoyed a closeness with her daughter and her mother as they worked together. Both her daughter and her mother came to regard her as the one on whom to depend.

It struck me as ironic that a socioeconomically oppressive sweatshop, such as a garment factory, served as a nurturing haven for building self-esteem and a sense of competency for Ling. However, considering this phenomenon from a cultural perspective in the context of the development of Ling's sense of self, it became clear that the relationships among the women in the factory strengthened Ling's sense of self as an interdependent person in a culturally congruent as well as emotionally satisfying manner. In other words, her relationships with the women in the factory were mutually enabling and validating. These relationships served as the fundamental building blocks for Ling's self-esteem.

Consistent with the cultural conception of interdependence, Ling chose to stay with her husband and his family even after she achieved a position in which she was neither financially nor emotionally dependent on that family system. She decided to stay to honor her commitment and to claim her position within the family. Expanding on a strong relationship with her daughter and her mother, she developed a sense of compassion toward her husband and her father, who were emotionally cut off from the family system. She reached out to them in a way that they could respond to. She invited her husband to take some trips with her to visit their grown children, and at times she included her parents in some of these trips. These gestures gradually allowed the men in her life to reconnect with the family. She broke the cycle of oppression of women in the family by encouraging and supporting her daughter to fulfill her educational and career aspiration. As the previous generation passed away, Ling and her husband attained the status of heads of their own household. The children are grown and married. Ling's daughter is now a confident young professional woman who looks up to her mother for her strong sense of self. Ling continues to maintain a close connection with her garment industry "gee-mui" (sisters), who often have social gatherings that include Ling, her daughter, and her mother.

CONCLUSION

Interpersonal relationships are dynamic manifestations of a person's sense of self and of others. The paradigm of the dual self, in terms of independence and interdependence, has been presented to be used as a lens through which to view relationships among Asian American women. Asian American women's experiences in the garment industry traditionally have been examined from a socioeconomic perspective. From this perspective, these women's experiences were considered to be oppressive and exploitative. Ling's story, however, when viewed from the perspective of psychological development of the self based on the paradigm of the dual self, illustrates that her relationships with other women facing similar oppression and immigration stress fostered her development of a strong sense of self as an interdependent woman. Her sense of interdependence generated a sense of agency that enabled her to reconnect the men into the family and to end the pattern of oppression for the next generation of women. Ling's story is truly a process of empowerment through interpersonal relationships that are rooted in interdependence.

REFERENCES

Cocking, R. R., & Greenfield, P. M. (1994). Diversity and development of Asian Americans: Research gaps in minority child development. *Journal of Applied Developmental Psychology, 15*, 301–303.

De Vos, G. (1985). Dimensions of the self in Japanese culture. In A. Marsella, G. DeVos, & F. L. K. Hsu (Eds.), *Culture and self* (pp. 149–184). London: Tavistock.

Fieldman, S. S., & Rosenthal, D. A. (1990). The acculturation of autonomy expectations in Chinese high schoolers residing in two western nations. *International Journal of Psychology, 25*, 259–281.

Geertz, C. (1984). From the native's point of view: On the nature of anthropological understanding. In R. A. Shweder & R. A. LeVine (Eds.), *Culture theory: Essays on mind, self and emotion* (pp. 123–136). Cambridge, England: Cambridge University Press. (Original work published 1974)

Gilligan, C. (1982). *In a different voice: Psychological theory and women's development.* Cambridge, MA: Harvard University Press.

Hofstede, G. (1980). *Culture's consequences.* Newbury Park, CA: Sage.

Hsu, F. L. K. (1985). The self in cross-cultural perspective. In A. J. Marsella, G. D. Vos, & F. L. K. Hsu (Eds.), *Culture and self: Asian and western perspectives* (pp. 24–55). New York: Tavistock.

Jones, E. E., & Nisbett, R. (1972). The actor and the observer: Divergent perceptions of causality. In E. E. Jones, D. E. Kanouse, H. H. Kelly, R. E. Nisbett, S. Valins, & B. Weiner (Eds.), *Attribution: Perceiving the causes of behavior* (pp. 79–94). Morristown, NJ: General Learning Press.

Kashima, Y., Yamaguchi, S., Kim, U., Choi, S., Gelfand, M. J., & Yuki, M. (1995). Culture, gender, and self: A perspective from individualism-collectivism research. *Journal of Personality and Social Psychology, 69 (5)*, 925–937.

Louie, S. C. (1997). *Self-construals and empathy in Asian Americans.* Unpublished doctoral dissertation, University of Massachusetts, Boston.

Markus, H., & Kitayama, S. (1991). Culture and the self. Implications for cognition, emotion, and motivation. *Psychological Review, 98,* 224–253.

Miller, J. B. (1986). *Toward a new psychology of women* (2nd ed.). Boston: Beacon Press.

Miller, J. G. (1988). *Bridging the content-structure dichotomy: Culture and the self.* Beverly Hills, CA: Sage.

Newman, L. S. (1993). How individualists interpret behavior: Idiocentrism and spontaneous trait inference. *Social Cognition, 11,* 243–269.

Rhee, E., Uleman, J. S., Lee, H. K., & Roman, R. J. (1995). Spontaneous self-descriptions and ethnic identities in individualistic and collectivistic cultures. *Journal of Personality and Social Psychology, 69(1),* 142–152.

Schweder, R. A., & Bourne, E. J. (1984). Does the concept of person vary cross-culturally? In R. A. Shweder & R. A. Levine (Eds.), *Culture theory: Essays on mind, self, and emotion* (pp. 158–199). Cambridge, England: Cambridge University Press.

Singelis, T. M. (1994). The measurement of independent and interdependent self-construals. *Personality and Social Psychology Bulletin, 20,* 580–591.

Tata, S. P., & Leong, F. T. L. (1994). Individualism-collectivism, social network orientation, and acculturation as predictors of attitudes toward seeking professional psychological help among Chinese Americans. *Journal of Counseling Psychology, 41,* 280–287.

Triandis, H. C. (1989). The self and social behavior in differing cultural contexts. *Psychological Review, 96,* 506–520.

Triandis, H. C. (1996). The psychological measurement of cultural syndromes. *American Psychologist, 51,* 407–415.

U.S. Bureau of Census. (1990). *Statistical yearbooks of the immigration and naturalization service (1981–1988).* Washington, DC: U.S. Government Printing Office.

U.S. Bureau of Census. (1995). *Census data* (P25-1111). Washington, DC: U.S. Government Printing Office.

Zhou, M. (1992). *Chinatown: The socioeconomic potential of an urban enclave.* Philadelphia: Temple University Press.

12

PARADIGMS FOR ASIAN AMERICAN WOMEN: POWER AND CONNECTIONS

JEAN LAU CHIN

This book views the differences among Asian American women in the formation of relationships from an Asian American lens, or the different perspectives through which to view the world and psychological phenomena. These differences are both qualitative and quantitative. Although commonality exists among the various ethnic groups and between Asian and Western cultures, differences in emphasis and content are both significant and meaningful. In this concluding chapter, I present crosscutting themes to assist in developing a feminist process that is both inclusive and valuing of ethnic differences and the experiences of Asian American women to guide policy, theory, and practice. The formation of relationships is the basis for the connections that individuals make, and they inherently influence the power dynamics in people's lives. The inadequacy of existing models by both omission and commission illustrates the need to seek paradigm shifts that include the voices of Asian American women and that are consistent with a feminist process. The strengths of Asian American women are to be celebrated.

DIVERSITY OF VOICES

The diversity of the voices of Asian American women has been underscored throughout this volume as needing to be heard. Although much of the existing literature has focused on Chinese and Japanese groups, the inclusion and discussion of issues of other Asian ethnic groups in this book is a significant contribution. Although historical accounts of immigration and cultural values are undoubtedly important, the focus and emphasis of this book are the psychosocial and psychological strengths associated with adaptation and coping. Although there are biases within this book, they should not diminish the importance in balancing Asian American views against the biases of non-Asian perspectives of Asian issues. Central to this volume are the principles of diversity (Greene & Sanchez-Hucles, 1997, p. 185), that is, an openness to and valuing of differences and cultivation, appreciation, and nurturance of different perspectives. However, these principles should not be too quickly embraced without appreciation for their subtleties of form and function. For example, although McDonald's hamburgers are known worldwide as the same, their differences in different countries has been noted. They are modified and adapted to the tastes, preferences, and practices of local populations. As diversity is embraced by the larger society, caution must be taken to prevent homogenization. From the lives of early Chinese and Japanese immigrants to the more recent arrivals of Vietnamese refugees, there are both commonalities and differences. They should be listened to and heard. From the pioneering voice of Reiko Homma True in the introduction to this book across the voices of Asian American students to the hopeful voice of Alice F. Chang in the afteword following this chapter, this volume presents both the individual and collective voices of Asian American women and describes how these women connected to meet their needs through others and, in that process, transcended the racism, oppression, and trauma that they encountered in their lives.

SOCIOPOLITICAL CONTEXTS: DEVELOPMENTAL PERSPECTIVES

War and poverty continue to significantly affect the lives and coping strategies of Asian Americans. They are the most important reasons for immigration to and refugee resettlement in the United States. They result in disruptive and traumatic consequences for individuals, families, and communities. Consequently, sociopolitical contexts taking into account developmental perspectives need to be integrated into understanding the psyche of and adaptation strategies among Asian Americans.

However, psychology and studies of human behavior all too often view their focus on the individuals, thus ignoring the sociopolitical contexts that bring together individuals, families, and communities through history, shared memories, experiences, and affect. These group psyches and group memories often drive the unique characteristics of ethnic groups and form the basis of interpersonal relationships, social interactions, and communities.

Moreover, these sociopolitical contexts are evolving rather than static. In attempting to grapple with ethnic differences, researchers and the psychological literature often attempt to capture these contexts in specific, static time frames. Consequently, Asians are depicted as they were, without appreciation for and integration of the developmental evolution of behavior, practices, beliefs, and so forth over time of Asian cultures and individuals and of Asian Americans in the United States. These images are captured by Liang Tien (chapter 3), Divya Kakaiya (chapter 8), and Diane C. Fujino (chapter 10) in their respective chapters. The philosophical and religious underpinnings of Hinduism, Confucianism, Taoism, and Buddhism are important in the psyche and lifestyles of Asian Americans; the diversity and evolution of these systems is reflected in the practices, beliefs, and values of individuals, families, groups, and communities.

OPPRESSION: RACE AND THEN GENDER

The sociopolitical contexts discussed in this book speak to the prominence of race over gender in the lives of Asian Americans. The shared experiences of suffering and oppression are common to most Asian American groups. Although differences in individual and group experiences exist, the common memory among different ethnic groups and the shared outrage toward historical events serve both as bonds within ethnic groups and as the source of distance from others. How much military terrorism has there been in which sexual aggression was used against Asian women as a weapon of war, both within the countries of origin and by the United States. The rape of Nanking, China (Chang, 1998), a phrase now used metaphorically, it refers to the rape of women, massacre of people, and destruction of property during World War II. It has been replicated in many Asian countries during war and under various military regimes. This has happened with Korean, Chinese, Japanese, and Cambodian women to symbolize the power and control of the military forces and, often, to accomplish ethnic cleansing. This occurred recently with Indonesian women during their civil strife. This stands alongside the use of Asian women as both willing and unwilling prostitutes, the former as an unwelcome choice against poverty for many. Although the United States prides itself on its humanitarian policies, the effects of stereotypes and racism perpetuate controlling images as described by Fujino. The exercise and misuse of power continue to be played out during war and economic downturns. The passion and commitment described by Kem Louie of Asian American women as social advocates (chapter 2) can be understood in the context of oppression described by Tien.

DIFFERENCE AS STRENGTH: RESILIENCY

Much in the literature has discussed the concept of risk-factor approaches to prevention, disease, and intervention. Although offering a certain usefulness, these approaches often are at odds with the adaptive striving and survival motivations found among ethnic minority groups. Emphasizing resiliency factors is often important to counter the disempowering aspects of socioeconomic factors, environment, adversity, and racism. Additionally, risk-factor approaches often are at odds with cultural and ethnic values. Emphasizing difference generally has been construed as weakness and deficit and as insignificant for ethnic minority groups within the mainstream culture. Consequently, an approach to difference as strength to be celebrated and valued is more important to promoting growth and development than are risk-factor approaches. Adaptation should be considered from the perspective of resiliency and strength, that is, the ability of Asian American women to adapt and cope during the World War II internment of Japanese Americans as described by Donna K. Nagata (chapter 4), with domestic violence as discussed by Carolee GiaoUyen Tran and Kunya Des Jardins (chapter 5), and the effects of Hinduism and Muslim rule as described by Divya Kakaiya (chapter 8).

A psychology of difference is proposed to address the troublesome concepts and assumptive frameworks that reflect a Eurocentric view yet often are presumed to be universal (Chin, 1993). When differences in cultural experiences and worldviews are construed as resistance or deviance, diverse voices are invalidated. The contrast in worldviews, so marked between Asian and Western perspectives, can contribute to an understanding of how differences should be used to achieve culturally competent models for understanding relationships. Several illustrations are offered. Although the psychological literature is replete with examples of the fact that Asian cultures subscribe to the Confucian view of filial piety that supports a hierarchical ordering of society and familial relationships, it has ignored and oversimplified the ways in which Taoism permeates many Asian cultures with a more egalitarian approach.

BICULTURALISM: DUAL SELVES ARE OK

Although Asians have immigrated to the United States since the 1850s, Asian Americans are still perceived as immigrants and newcomers.

Race and physical differences largely account for these perceptions as older generations are lumped together with new immigrants and refugees and as available choices, expectations, and behaviors directed at Asian Americans continue to be limited because of racial stereotypes and images. Consequently, the issue of acculturation is a poor concept for capturing the differential process for Asian Americans adapting to life in the United States. Despite the generations of immigrants coming to the United States, culture and affiliation among Asian American groups has been retained, and Asian American communities have continued to exist, both physically and psychologically; thus, it is important and relevant to address the issue of biculturalism. As discussed in the introduction to part 3, the concept of interactive dualism is proposed to describe the evolutionary and historical perspectives, the oppression of socioeconomic and sociopolitical contexts, and the diversity of experiences and cultural groups that come together, interact, and influence one another within the lives of Asian American women. The tendency of these forces to interact and yet remain separate causes inherent tension and reflects the inability to eliminate and amalgamate differences. Consequently, individuals, ethnic groups, and communities establish lifestyles and develop coping and adaptation strategies that are bicultural in nature.

Within a bicultural framework, these contexts are not static, but result in heightened awareness, intensity, and ambiguity of identity that cannot and should not be construed as ambivalence, pathology, or confusion over sense of self. These struggles are identified by Fujino and Kakaiya in their chapters. As described by Christine M. Chao (chapter 6), these contexts also include ancestral memories and connections that are contained in physical ancestor altars or carried within one's heart.

These struggles should be viewed as developmental phenomena and bicultural identity as a developmental process that does not always integrate the various parts of the self or the duality of cultures that may be dissonant with one another. Consequently, biculturalism is the result of an interactive dualism whereby individuals form relationships in divergent or parallel directions, at times splitting off one set of experiences, connections, and coping strategies from another. When viewed from a Western or monocultural perspective, these behaviors and strategies may appear irrational, inappropriate, maladaptive, or pathological. When viewed from a bicultural perspective, however, they are rational, appropriate, adaptive, and healthy. In other words, dual selves are OK.

TOWARD A PARADIGM FOR ASIAN AMERICAN WOMEN

From whose lens; this is where the dialogue began. To understand the formation of relationships among Asian American women, it is necessary to look at the power and connectedness inherent in those relationships. Throughout the chapters of this book, these themes were pervasive across contexts, ethnic groups, and coping strategies. It has been the misuse and abuse of power that has had adverse effects on the adaptation of Asian American women. It has been through the reactions and responses of Asian American women to the racism and oppression that they formed the structures and bases of many of their relationships. The connectedness experienced in these processes maintained and sustained these relationships. The situations and means of formation of these relationships were both unique and diverse; the processes and structures that evolved became the foundations for coping and resiliency and promoted a positive sense of self and bicultural identity for many Asian American women.

The models available are limited because few integrate race and culture as active components. To understand Asian American women and the relationships they form, the idea that race and culture matter must be accepted. And, in this regard, power and connectedness underlie the nature of these relationships.

Power

Fujino addresses the importance of race and structural factors influencing the selection of dating partners. Controlling images, acculturation (or biculturalism), and propinquity (i.e., physical distance between groups) are three such factors that are used in proposing a model for looking at how race influences dating relationships. This is an important paradigm shift because it emphasizes the importance of contextual factors in partner choice.

To develop models that are relevant and appropriate for understanding relationships among Asian American women there need to be paradigm shifts that empower both the individuals and the groups being considered. A model that empowers would consider at least the following factors:

- *Contexts*: What are the sociopolitical contexts or the memories and experiences that are passed down through the group psyche or group unconscious? What wars were fought? How do these influence the images of and held by Asian Americans and their behavior choices?
- *Story*: Who writes the history? Who validates what is passed down? For example, the Hawaiian culture's *talk story* is used for interpersonal sharing of stories. It is an important and valid method for the transmission of culture and values by the elders.
- *Cultural competence*: How to develop not only sensitivity but also the skills needed to address cultural issues? What are the

assumptions, biases, and frameworks used to define and be defined?

- *Lens:* The perspective through which historical events and psychological phenomena are viewed. Significance and meaning are altered by the experiences of the individual.

Connectedness

S. Cathy Louie (chapter 11) discusses the importance of interdependence as a distinguishing value within Asian cultures compared with Western cultures. She redefines the relational self and how it influences interpersonal relationships, using as a paradigm interdependence for the development of a sense of self and biculturalism (i.e., dual self). This represents an important paradigm shift, given that existing models emphasize an integrated sense of self and consider dependency as deficient and developmentally immature.

When speaking of connectedness among Asian American women, biculturalism and their bicultural experiences must also be considered. The formation of relationships is influenced not only by conscious choice, but also by forced expectations and sociocultural and sociopolitical context and circumstances. Consequently, individual psychological development of a sense of self, decisions about self-identity, and the developmental process involved in these tasks are influenced by race and culture. Asian Americans bring with them particular expectations while pursuing career goals, interpersonal relationships, and so forth. For example, an Asian American taking public office or another prominent role often is expected to do so for his or her own ethnic group and race; this can be viewed as an expectation to represent his or her ethnic group or as a perceived bias that invalidates his or her credibility. White Americans do not have these same expectations for other White people; in fact, those who do so often are accused of being racist.

Thus, there is an unequal burden associated with race and culture that influences the nature of relationships among Asian American women. Ultimately, it is power and connectedness that define these relationships across all contexts, whether romantic, familial, social, work-related, or recreational. Models to define these relationships must include paradigm shifts that empower and validate. The inequities of power must be transformed toward a more benevolent authority that both affirms and empowers. The connectedness that promotes adaptation, strength, and resiliency also needs affirmation and validation, not fear or suspicion. An empowerment paradigm would affirm a feminist position in which gender and culture intersect, would include interactive dualism as a factor in the definition of self (i.e., biculturalism), and would value differences and diversity as reflective of strength and resiliency.

REFERENCES

Chang, I. (1998). The rape of Nanking: The forgotten holocaust of World War II. New York: Viking Press.

Chin, J. L. (1993). Toward a psychology of difference: Psychotherapy for a culturally diverse population. In J. L. Chin, V. De La Cancela, & Y. M. Jenkins, *Diversity in Psychotherapy: The politics of race, ethnicity, and gender* (pp. 69–92). Westport, CT: Praeger.

Greene, B., & Sanchez-Hucles, J. (1997). Diversity: Advancing an inclusive feminist psychology. In J. Worell & N. Johnson (Eds.), *Shaping the future of feminist psychology* (pp. 173–202). Washington, DC: American Psychological Association.

AFTERWORD:
PUBLIC POLICY AND PRACTICE CHALLENGES REMAIN

ALICE F. CHANG

As a multidefined individual (Chinese American, scientist–practitioner, survivor–advocate), I suppose I should not be surprised to find myself of two minds regarding *Relationships Among Asian American Women.* Clearly, this book begins to fill an important void in the psychological literature on Asian American women. For that reason I find it exhilarating. On the other hand, because this volume has such a singular place in the psychological literature, it illustrates just how vast the void remains. I find it disheartening to be so concretely reminded that Asian American women, among other diverse populations, remain so marginalized within psychology in 2000.

When it finds an appropriately wide audience, *Relationships Among Asian American Women* can assist clinicians in treating Asian American women and can improve the quality of services available to them. In identifying strategies for adaptive relationships within a variety of contexts, in describing the potential impact of bicultural identity on Asian American women, and in positing a paradigm for Asian American women and their relationships from their own perspectives and experiences, the contributors to this book describe important variables at the intersection of ethnicity and gender. Kem Louie's exploration of "Asian American Women and Social Advocacy" (chapter 2) and Jean Lau Chin's delineation of cross-cutting themes in chapter 12, "Paradigms for Relationships Among Asian American Women: Power and Connections," also point the way to the next steps that must be taken to systematize and institutionalize these perspectives within professional psychology through the proper training of psychologists.

As Christine C. Iijima Hall observed in her G. Stanley Hall lecture at the 103rd Annual Convention of the American Psychological Association (APA) in August 1995, "A mental health provider who is unfamiliar with diverse populations may make erroneous assumptions that lead to misdiagnosis and mistreatment" (p. 644). This should not come as news to any ethical practitioner. And yet, given the dearth of previous literature, I have to wonder how practitioners working with Asian American women became familiar with the unique or universal aspects of these women's experiences. It is my hope that psychologists will stretch beyond the comfortable bounds of their own experience of the dominant culture in the United States to avail themselves of this book. It exhausts me to think that the challenge of incorporating appropriate information about Asian American women into their treatment will rest primarily with contributors to this volume and others perceived as directly affected and not be taken up broadly across the discipline.

Years before her G. Stanley Hall address, Chris Hall was among the members of the Task Force on Delivery of Services to Ethnic Minority Populations, which prepared the APA's *Guidelines for Providers of Psychological Services to Ethnic, Linguistic, and Culturally Diverse Populations*, approved by the APA Council of Representatives in 1990 and published in the *American Psychologist* in 1993. Although some literature relevant to the concerns and experiences of Asian populations was cited in the references supporting the guidelines (Nishio & Bilmes, 1987; Root, 1985; Sue & Sue, 1987), this book should provide invaluable assistance to those seeking to authentically incorporate the principles of the guidelines into their provision of services to Asian American women. Every chapter in this book is relevant to psychologists attempting to fulfill the aspiration expressed in the second ("Psychologists are cognizant of relevant research and practice issues related to the populations being served," p. 46) and third ("Psychologists recognize ethnicity and culture as significant parameters in understanding psychological process," p. 46) guidelines.

Carolee GiaoUyen Tran and Kunya Des Jardins's "Domestic Violence in Vietnamese Refugee and Korean Immigrant Communities" (chapter 5), Chin's "Mother–Daughter Relationships: Asian American Perspectives" (chapter 7), Divya Kakaiya's "Identity Development and Conflicts Among Indian Immigrant Women" (chapter 8), and Diane C. Fujino's "Structural and Individual Influences Affecting Racialized Dating Relationships" (chapter 10) illuminate particular populations and contexts addressed in the fourth guideline ("Psychologists respect the roles of family members and community structures, hierarchies, values and beliefs within the client's culture," p. 46). Felicisima C. Serifica, Alice Weng, and Hyoun K. Kim's "Friendships and Social Networks Among Asian American Women" (chapter 9) and S. Cathy Louie's "Interpersonal Relationships: Independence Versus Interdependence" offer broader perspectives and directly address distinctions of Asian American women from the dominant culture.

Guideline 5 ("Psychologists respect clients' religious and/or spiritual beliefs and values, including attributions and taboos, since they affect world view, psychosocial functioning, and expressions of distress," p. 46) is powerfully explicated in Christine M. Chao's "Ancestors and Ancestor Altars: Connecting Relationships" (chapter 6).

Micro- and macroperspectives on Guideline 7 ("Psychologists consider the impact of adverse social, environmental, and political factors in assessing problems and designing interventions," p. 47) emerge from Liang Tien's "U.S. Attitudes Toward Women of Asian Ancestry: Legislative and Media Perspectives" (chapter 3) and Donna K. Nagata's "World War II Internment and the Relationships of Nisei Women" (chapter 4).

Since Guthrie's landmark criticism of the exclusion of ethnic minority participants from psychological research, *Even the Rat Was White*, much has been written about the negative effects of failing to incorporate appropriate understanding of ethnicity and other cultural factors in the treatment of members of diverse populations (Guthrie, 1996/1998). More recently, however, appeals to the profession have been based in self-interest. Demographic statistics and projections have been cited to convince psychologists that they must be prepared to work effectively with diverse populations or risk obsolescence. Despite the absence of evidence that either argument has had much tangible impact, I hope that *Relationships Among Asian American Women* will reach a wide enough audience to have a real effect.

A book of this quality and significance ultimately presents several challenges. The challenge to the contributors and others already committed to providing appropriate services to diverse populations is to continue the efforts so well described in Kem Louie's, "Asian American Women and Social Advocacy" (chapter 2). We must not let ourselves be exhausted by the effort already expended or discouraged by the distance left to cover. The challenge to organized psychology is to make use of resources like this volume to effect the changes in attitude, training, research, and treatment that will make the discipline relevant to and effective with the diverse populations of the United States.

That U.S. society has not always been welcoming Asian American women is illustrated in Nagata's "World War II Internment and the Relationships of Nisei Women" (chapter 4). News coverage of the ostensible role of Asian American contributors to the 1996 U.S. presidential campaign illustrates how powerfully suspicion and sterotypes still dominate portrayals of Asian Americans in the media and, by extension, in large portions of the consciousness of the general public. It is chilling to see how little progress seems to have been made in 50 years.

A recently released study of Asian American families conducted by the Greater Chicago Chapter of the Organization of Chinese Americans (Tam, Lee, & Chin, 1998) revealed a telling aspect of Asian Americans' own view of their role in the national political process. Sixty-nine percent of the parents surveyed and 74% of their children did not believe that it would be possible for a person of Asian descent to become president of the United States during the parents' lifetime. Both Asian Americans and U.S. society as a whole have much to lose if Asian Americans continue to feel marginalized from national public life and disenfranchised from the political process.

Chin's "Paradigms for Relationships Among Asian American Women: Power and Connections" (chapter 12) explores the crosscutting themes that emerge from the rest of this volume and points the way to paradigm shifts that can incorporate the values and experiences of Asian American women in the development of public policy as well as the constructive evolution of the professional practice of psychology. Although some Asian American women may benefit directly from changes in public policy that might mitigate stressors around immigration and linguistic barriers, U.S. society as a whole can benefit from a true incorporation of aspects of the interdependent perspective that characterize the relationships explored throughout this book.

REFERENCES

American Psychological Association. (1993). Guidelines for providers of psychological services to ethnic, linguistic, and culturally diverse populations. *American Psychologist, 48,* 45–48.

Guthrie, R. V. (1998). *Even the rat was white: A historical view of psychology.* Needham Heights, MA: Allyn & Bacon. (first published 1976).

Hall, C. C. I. (1997). Cultural malpractice: The growing obsolescence of psychology with the changing U.S. population. *American Psychologist, 52,* 642–651.

Nishio, K., & Bilmes, M. (1987). Psychotherapy with Southeast Asian American clients. *Professional Psychology: Research and Practice, 18,* 342–346.

Root, M. P. P. (1985) Guidelines for facilitating therapy with Asian American clients. *Psychotherapy, 22,* 349–356.

Sue, D., & Sue, S. (1987). Cultural factors in the clinical assessment of Asian Americans. *Journal of Consulting and Clinical Psychology, 55,* 479–487.

Tam, F., Lee, J., & Chin, C. (1998). *Inter-generational Asian American attitudes toward family values, interracial dating and marriage.* Chicago: Organization of Chinese Americans—Chicago Chapter.

ADDITIONAL READING

Espiritu, Y. L. (1996). *Asian American women and men.* Thousand Oaks, CA: Sage.

Gudykunski, W. B., & Tsukasa, N. (1994). *Bridging Japanese/North American Differences.* Thousand Oaks, CA: Sage.

Lee, E. (Ed.). (1998). *Working with Asian Americans: A guide for clinicians.* New York: Guilford Press.

Leong, T. L., & Whitfield, J. R. (Eds.). (1992). *Asians in the United States: Abstracts of the psychological and behavioral literature, 1967–1991.* Washington, DC: American Psychological Association.

Min, P. G. (Ed.). (1995). *Asian Americans: Contemporary trends and issues.* Thousand Oaks, CA: Sage.

Zane, N. W. S., Takeuchi, D. T., & Young, K. N. J. (Eds.). (1993). *Confronting critical health issues of Asian and Pacific Islander Americans.* Thousand Oaks, CA: Sage.

AUTHOR INDEX

237

Delmar, R., 68, 69
Denton, K., 152, 162, 163, 166, *172*
Deutsch, H., 5, *11*
DeVos, G., 8, *11*, 212, *221*
Die, A. H., 165, *172*
Dion, K. K., 171, *172*
Dion, K. L., 171, *172*
Donovan, M. E., 6, *12*
Drachsler, J., 53, 69
Du, N., *94*
Duck, S., 151, 152, 158, 160, *172, 173*

Eat a Bowl of Tea, 37, 46
Eichenbaum, L., 152, *172*
Elliott, J., 158, *175*
Erikson, E. H., 151, *172, 173*
Espin, O., 27, 28

Espiritu, Y. L., 8, *11*, 51, 58, 59, 69, 154,
　　155, 157, *173*, 182, 188, 203,
　　204, *208*
Everett, J., 135, *149*
Exec. Order No. 9066, 110, *117*

Far Pavilions, 29, 46
Faust, S., *94*
Festinger, L., 189, *208*
Fieldman, S. S., 212, *221*
50 APP U.S.C.A., 66, 69
Fine, M., 68, 69
Forbes-Martin, S., 73, *94*
Forrest, V., 79, *95*
Forward, S., 5, *11*
Fraser, M. W., 165, 166, *174*
Freeman, J., 73, *94*
Fugita, S., 185, 189, *208*
Fujino, D. C., 185, 186, 191, 192, 202,
　　204, 206, *208*
Fujitomi, I., 8, *11*

Ganesan, S., 76, *93*
Gantt, D. L., 170, *172*
Gawelek, M., 27, 28
Geertz, C., 212, *221*
Gelfand, M. J., *221*
Gelles, R., 71, *95, 96*
G.I. Fiancées Act of 1946, 36, 46
Gilligan, C., 5, *11*, 216, *221*

Glenn, E. N., 31, *46*, 50, 52, 69
Glodava, M., 188, *208*
Gold, A., 137, *149*
Goldstein, D., 76, *94*
Granovetter, M. S., 166, *173*
Gray, J., 6, *11*
Greenberg, D., 152, *172*
Greene, B., 10, *11*, 27, 28, 224, *230*
Greenfield, P. M., 212, *221*
Gudykunst, W. B., 160, *175*
Guthrie, R. V., 233, *234*

Haines, D. W., 165, 166, *173*
Hall, A., 152, *173*
Hall, C. C. I., 232, *234*
Hall, E., 152, *174*
Harrison, D., 166, *175*
Hauff, E., 76, *94*
Hazan, C., 170, *173*
Helmreich, R. L., 191, *209*
Hinton, W. L., 73, 74, *94*
Ho, C., 72, 74, 80, *94*
Hofstede, G., 212, *221*
Hong, K. M., 102, *117*
Horney, K., 5, *11*
Hosokawa, B., 52, 69
House, J. S., 166, *173*
Houston, J., 66, *70*
Houston, J. W., 104, *117*
Hsu, F. L. K., 8, *11*, 212, 213, *221*
Hurh, W. M., 73, 74, *94*

Ichioka, Y., 183, *208*
Ida, D., 111, *117*
Ida, D. J., 113
Immigration Act of 1917, 31, 46
Immigration Act of 1943, 33, 34, 46
Immigration Act of August 9, 1946, 37,
　　46
Immigration Act of 1982, 40, 46
Immigration and Nationality Act of
　　1952, 38, 46
Immigration and Nationality Act of
　　1965, 74, *94*, 184, *208*
Immigration and Nationality Act
　　Amendments of 1965, 39, 46
Immigration Reform and Control Act of
　　1986, 41, 46
India Currents, 135, *149*

Ja, D., 8, *12*, 77, 78, 95
Jamieson, N., 77, 78, 79, *94*
Jenkins, Y., 6, *11*
Jensen, J. M., 183, *208*
Jhally, S., 188, *208*
Johnson, N. G., 5, 8, *12*
Johnson, P., 75, *93*
Johnson, R. C., 186, *208*
Jones, A., 71, *94*
Jones, E. E., 211, *221*
Joshi, R., 136, 137, *149*
Jung, C., 112, *117*

Kahn, A. S., 6, *12*
Kakaiya, D., 142, *149*
Kaplan, H., 71, *94*
Kashima, Y., 216, *221*
Kassam, S., 142, *149*
Kibria, N., 75, 76, 77, 78, 79, 80, *94*
Kikumura, A., 79, *95*
Kim, A., 39, 44, *46*
Kim, B., 79, *95*
Kim, E., 44, *46*
Kim, H.- C., 34, 41, *46*
Kim, K. C., 73, 74, *94*
Kim, T. H., 75, 80, 91, *95*
Kim, U., 74, *93*, *221*
Kitagawa, D., 52, 57, *69*
Kitano, H., 79, *95*
Kitano, H. H. L., 52, 57, 60, 69, 185, 186, 189, 202, 205, *208*
Kitayama, S., 212, 213, 214, *221*
Kolody, B., 152, *175*
Kuo, W. H., 152, 164, 165, 166, *173*

Lalonds, R. N., 14, *23*
Lam, D. J., 115
Landis, K. R., 166, *173*
Larson, R., 151, 158, *173*
Lavelle, J., 73, *95*
Lea, N., 160, *173*
Lee, G., 103, *117*
Lee, H. K., 212, *222*
Lee, J., 234, *235*
Lee, M. P., 155, *173*
Lee, S. M., 185, 186, 189, 202, *209*
Leong, F. T. L., 212, *222*
Letko, C., 75, *95*
Levine, R. V., 165, *174*

Liddle, J., 136, 137, *149*
Lie, R., 115
Lin, K., 165, 166, *173*
Lin, S. C., 110, *117*
Lockhart, L. L., 92, *95*
Loo, C. M., 50, *64*
Louie, S. C., 216, *221*
Lu, F., *94*
Lui, M., 10, *11*

Mallinckrodt, B. S. 170, *172*
Malone, J., 92, *95*
Mannell, R., 151, *173*
Markus, H., 212, 213, 214, *222*
Masuda, M., 165, *173*
Matsumoto, V., 52, 57, 58, 59, 60, 61, *64*, 157, *173*
Matthaei, J. A., 153, *171*
McCarran-Walter Act, 39, *46*
Meemeduma, P., 152, 162, 164, 165, *173*
Menne, J. M., 159, *173*
Milardo, R. M., 161, *173*, *174*
Miller, D. C., 190, *209*
Miller, J. B., 5, *12*, 216, *222*
Miller, J. G., 212, *222*
Min, P. G., 165, *174*
Minault, G., 138, *149*
Minde, T., 74, *93*
Min, J. S., 114
Miranda, J., *94*
Mok, D., 74, *93*
Mollica, R. F., 73, *95*
Morishima, J. K., 8, *12*, 57, *69*
Mouanoutoua, V. L., 165, *174*

Nagata, D. K., 64, 66, 67, 68, *69*
Nakanishi, D. T., 66, *69*
Nakano, M., 49, 50, 51, 52, 56, 57, 58, 59, 61, 62, 63, 64, 65, 66, 68, 69, 154, 155, 156, 157, *174*
National Origins Act of 1924, 31, *46*
New York Times, 1943, 33, *46*
New York Times, 1945, 35, *46*
Newman, L. S., 212, *222*
1945 War Brides Act, 184,, *207*
1952 McCarran-Walter Act, 184, *207*
Nisbett, R., 211, *221*
Nisei Research Project, 51, 53, *69*
Nishida, T., 160, *175*

SUBJECT INDEX

Acculturation. *See also* Biculturalism
  biculturalism, 99, 226
  and dating choices, 199–201, 205–206
  Indian immigrant women, 139–140
  Korean immigrants, 74–76
  and outmarriage rates, 189–190
  Vietnamese refugees, 74–76
Adolescent daughters, Indian immigrants, 141–144
Advocacy. *See* Social advocacy
African American men, interracial dating, 193–202, 207
Ahimsa, 138–139
Alcohol abuse, and domestic violence, 77, 85
Alien Wife Bill, 32, 37–38
Amerasian Homecoming Act, 42–43
Amerasian Immigration Act (1982), 41–42
Amerasians
  exclusionary immigration policies, 40–43
    and children, 42
  origin of term, 40
Ancestor altars, 101–117
  in Asian American life, 112–116
  connectedness experience in, 112–113
  family conflicts, 108–109
  individual expression in, 101–102
  and Japanese-American internment, 110–111
  and ritual, 112
  psychological dilemmas, 106–107
  transformative role of, 107–112
Ancestor veneration, 101–117
  Asian Americans, 112–116
  and biculturalism, 104–105
  clinical implications, 103–104
  cultural clashes, 107–110
  escape clause, 104–105
  negative dynamics, 106
  psychological role, 102–107
  "rites" controversy, 109–110

Ancestor worship, 102, 109
Anger, Indian women, 147
Antimiscegenation laws
  banning of, 184
  history, 53, 183
Arranged marriages
  Indian immigrant families, 145–146
  in Korean/Vietnamese culture, 79–80
  modernized version, 146
  Nisei women, 53
Asian American women's movement, 157
Asian American Women's Task Force, 7
Asian-White marriages. *See* Interracial marriages
Assimilation, Indian immigrant women, 140–141
Attitude Toward Women Scale, 191
Attractiveness, and dating choices, 199–201, 204
Attributional Relationship Scale, 191

Bachelor societies, 7, 182–183
Battered women. *See* Domestic violence
Battered women's shelters, 88
Biculturalism
  acculturation comparison, 99, 227
  and developmental processes, 131–132
  and filial piety escape clause, 104–105
  college-age Indian women, 144–145
  concept of, 99–100
  connectedness considerations, 229
  overview, 227–228
  male-female dualism, 136
  picture brides, 31
  social advocacy, 14
  voices, 3, 9
  War brides, 35
"Boat people," 73
Buddhism
  ancestor status in, 105–106, 109
  gender roles in, 79
Butsudan, 113–114

Caste system
  hierarchical world view, 135–136
  and women's movement implications,
    136
Chain immigration
  and friendship formation, 153, 157
  and social network formation, 164
Child custody rights, 86
Chin, Jean Lau, 13–14
Chin, Vincent, 41
China Boy (Lee), 103
Chinatown (Zhou), 217
Chinatown garment industry, 217–220
Chinese American men, and antimisce-
    genation laws, 182–183
Chinese American women
  cultural values, 121
  developmental process, 131–132
  interracial dating patterns, study, 192–
    207
  The Joy Luck Club themes, 123–131
  social networks, 163
Chinese Exclusion Act of 1882, 31, 33–
    34
Chinese war brides
  exclusionary immigration policies, 34,
    36–37
  post-World War II period, 37
Ching Ming, 103
Churches
  and friendship formation, 154
  and social networks, 164–165
Civil Liberties Act of 1988, 66
Client-therapist relationship, Indian
    women, 148
Collectivist orientation
  in Asian American women, 216–217
  case example, 218–221
  connectedness emphasis, 212–213
  friendship influence, 171
  individualism tension, 212
  interpersonal relationships effect of,
    211–222
  relational orientation distinction, 216
  self-construals in, 212–213
Commission on Wartime Relocation and
    Internment of Civilians, 50
Confidentiality, Indian women clients,
    148
Confucian-based values
  and ancestor worship, 103, 109

and biculturalism, 104–105
  domestic violence link, 77–80
  filial piety escape clause, 104–105
  and gender roles, 78–79
  maternal sacrifice ideal, 122
Connectedness
  ancestor veneration function, 112–113
  Asian women's responsibility, 120–121
  cultural context, 120, 212–213
  individualism tension, 212
  and interpersonal relationships, 211–
    222
  as paradigm, 229
  self-construals link, 212–213
Coping behavior. *See* Resilience
Cross-ethnic friendships, 167–168
Cross-racial marriage. *See* Interracial
    marriage
Cultural values. *See also* Collectivist
    orientation
  domestic violence influence, 77–80,
    86–88
  interpersonal relationships effect of,
    211–222
  Nisei women, 51–53
Custody rights, 86

Dasgupta, Sayantani, 143
Dasgupta, Shamita Das, 143
Dating relationships, 181–209
  and acculturation, 189–190, 199–201,
    205–206
  college-age Indian women, 144
  historical context, 182–186
  individual influences, 190–207
  media images effect on, 188–189,
    203–204
  predictive model, 201–202
  and propinquity, 189, 199–201, 204–
    205
  racialized patterns, 186–207
  structural factors, 186–207
  study of, 192–207
Days of the Dead, 116
Dependency, Asian perspective, 131
Depression, Indian women, 147–148
Dharma, 147
Dias do los Muertos, 116
Difference, 226
Disclosure

rates of, 185
Intergenerational conflict, Indian immigrants, 123, 130, 140–141, 146
Intermarriage. *See also* Interracial marriage
  definition, 184
  rates of, 185
Internal Security Act of 1950. Title II, 66
Internal working models, and friendships, 170
Internalized mother/father, 104
Internet marriage bureaus, Indian women, 145–146
Internment camps. *See* Japanese-American internment
Interpersonal relationships. *See also* Friendships
  case example, 218–221
  collectivist orientation in, 216–217
  independence versus dependence in, 211–222
Interracial dating
  and acculturation, 205–206
  individual influences, 190, 194–201
  patterns of, 186–207
  structural influences, 194–201, 205–206
  study of, 192–207
Interracial marriage
  and acculturation, 190
  antimiscegenation laws, 182–183
  Asian American attitudes toward, 44
  definition, 184
  and erotic Oriental stereotype, 44
  historical context, 182–186
  Indian immigrants, 141
  Nisei women, pre-World War II period, 53
  rates of, 185–186
Intimacy level
  and cultural similarity, friendships, 160
  in individualistic societies, 171
Intraracial dating patterns, 202–203
Issei
  enemy alien label, 54
  friendship formation, 156
  internment redressing bill inadequacies, 67
  social networks, 156–157

and World War II internment, 51–52, 54, 58, 61, 63, 67, 156

Japanese American Citizens League, 65
Japanese American families
  pre-World War II period, 51–52
  as stress buffer, 8, 68
  World War II internment impact, 54, 57–59, 61–64
    buffering effect, 68
Japanese-American internment, 49–70
  and ancestor altars, 110–111
  CWRIC investigation of, 50
  family relations effect of, 57–59, 61–62, 68
  friendship opportunities, 156
  Nisei women relationships, 49–70
  peer and community relations impact, 52–53, 55, 59–60, 62–65
  redressing injustice movement, 66–67
  and resilience, 53, 55–56, 63, 65–66
  reunions, 65
  Sansei generation effects of, 64
Japanese American men, antimiscegenation laws effect, 182
Japanese American women. *See also* Nisei women
  friendships 155–156
  interracial dating patterns, study, 192–207
  social networks, 163
  World War II internment impact, 49–70
Japanese war brides
  exclusionary immigration policies, 37–38
  and Soldier Brides Act, 38
Jati, 135–136
"Jivan" newspaper sections, 146
Job training, domestic violence prevention, 90
The Joy Luck Club (Tan), 7, 129–131
  mother-daughter relationships in, 129–131
  mother-son relationships in, 121
  psychological analysis, 123–129

Karma, 139–140, 147
Kazoku no tame ni, 51

ABOUT THE EDITOR

Dr. Jean Lau Chin is a second-generation Chinese American and a psychologist with 30 years of clinical and administrative experience. As president of CEO Services, she provides clinical, educational, and organizational development services with a private practice in Quincy, Massachusetts, holds an appointment as assistant professor at Tufts University School of Medicine. Dr. Chin received her EdD in psychology from Columbia University in 1974. She has held administrative positions as director of the eastern region of the Massachusetts Behavioral Health Partnership, as executive director of South Cove Community Health Center, and a codirector of Thom Child Guidance Clinic. She has served on many national, state, and federal boards and committees on policy and advocacy related to community health, mental health, women, and ethic minority issues, including the Massachusetts Board of Registration in Psychology, the American Psychological Association, the Massachusetts Department of Public Health, the Minority Health Advisory Board, and the National Asian Pacific American Families Against Substance Abuse. Dr. Chin received the Leading Women 2000 award from the Patriot's Trail Girl Scouts, the Outstanding Executive Director award from the Massachusetts League of Community Health Centers, and the Women Who Care award from Women in Philanthropy. Her professional work includes over 100 presentations and publications on diversity, cultural competence, psychotherapy, and women's issues. Recent publications include *Community Health Psychology: Empowerment for Diverse Communities*, a book: coauthored by De La Cancela, Chin, and Jenkins (1998); "Feminist Curriculum," a chapter, in Worell and Johnson's *Feminist Visions: New Direction in Research, Training, and Practice* (1997); "Mental Health Services and Treatment," a chapter in Zane and Lee's *Asian American Handbook of Psychology Research* (1998); and *Cultural Competence and Health Care*, Public Health Reports (2000).